Sociocultural Theory in Second Language Education

MIX
Paper from
responsible sources
FSC
www.fsc.org FSC® C018575

MM Textbooks

Advisory Board:

Professor Colin Baker, *University of Wales, Bangor, UK*

Professor Viv Edwards, *University of Reading, Reading, UK*

Professor Ofelia García, *Columbia University, New York, USA*

Dr Aneta Pavlenko, *Temple University, Philadelphia, USA*

Professor David Singleton, *Trinity College, Dublin, Ireland*

Professor Terrence G. Wiley, *Arizona State University, Tempe, USA*

MM Textbooks bring the subjects covered in our successful range of academic monographs to a student audience. The books in this series explore education and all aspects of language learning and use, as well as other topics of interest to students of these subjects. Written by experts in the field, the books are supervised by a team of world-leading scholars and evaluated by instructors before publication. Each text is student-focused, with suggestions for further reading and study questions leading to a deeper understanding of the subject.

Full details of all the books in this series and of all our other publications can be found on http://www.multilingual-matters.com, or by writing to Multilingual Matters, St Nicholas House, 31-34 High Street, Bristol BS1 2AW, UK.

MM Textbooks

Sociocultural Theory in Second Language Education
An Introduction Through Narratives

Merrill Swain, Penny Kinnear and Linda Steinman

MULTILINGUAL MATTERS
Bristol • Buffalo • Toronto

Library of Congress Cataloging in Publication Data
A catalog record for this book is available from the Library of Congress

Swain, Merrill.
Sociocultural Theory in Second Language Education: An Introduction Through Narratives/
Merrill Swain, Penny Kinnear and Linda Steinman.
MM Textbooks: 7
Includes bibliographical references and index.
1. English language--Study and teaching--Foreign speakers--Social aspects. 2. Second language
acquisition--Social aspects. 3. Language and culture. I. Kinnear, Penny. II. Steinman, Linda. III. Title.
PE1128.A2S923 2010
418.0071–dc22 2010041287

British Library Cataloguing in Publication Data
A catalogue entry for this book is available from the British Library.

ISBN-13: 978-1-84769-330-3 (hbk)
ISBN-13: 978-1-84769-329-7 (pbk)

Multilingual Matters
UK: St Nicholas House, 31-34 High Street, Bristol BS1 2AW, UK.
USA: UTP, 2250 Military Road, Tonawanda, NY 14150, USA.
Canada: UTP, 5201 Dufferin Street, North York, Ontario M3H 5T8, Canada.

The policy of Multilingual Matters/Channel View Publications is to use papers that are natural,
renewable and recyclable products, made from wood grown in sustainable forests. In the
manufacturing process of our books, and to further support our policy, preference is given to printers
that have FSC and PEFC Chain of Custody certification. The FSC and/or PEFC logos will appear on
those books where full certification has been granted to the printer concerned.

Typeset by Saxon Graphics Ltd
Printed and bound in Great Britain by the MPG Books Group

Contents

Acknowledgments

The following individuals have helped us in one or several ways during the writing of this textbook: reading and providing feedback on chapters; translating terms; providing information about contexts relevant to our narratives; and encouraging us in our work. We express our appreciation to: Artem Babayants, Khaled Barkaoui, Lindsay Brooks, Rick Donato, Jean-Paul Duquette, Sophie Gavel, Ying Gong, Yas Imai, David Ishii, Ibtissem Knouzi, Sharon Lapkin, Iryna Lenchuk, Marti Munk, Colette Peters, Hyunjung Shin, Neomy Storch, Maria Trovela and Deryn Verity.

Our very special thanks go to Colin Baker who kept us going with his feedback, and to Jim Lantolf who shared his considerable scholarship in SCT while reading many of our chapters.

Some of the materials used in this book were tried out in various courses, and we are grateful to the students for their participation: ENG ED 8655 (Temple University Japan, 2008); WRI 395 (University of Toronto Mississauga), CTL3806; 2008, 2010 (Ontario Institute for Studies in Education/University of Toronto 2008); APLNG 596K (Pennsylvania State University Summer Institute, 2009).

Finally, we wish to thank Grace, Jody, Mona, Sandra, Sarah, Sophie, Rachel, Thaya, and Yang. Most of these names are pseudonyms but behind these pseudonyms breathe real people who were generous in sharing their personal stories with us.

Vygotsky's story in brief

A man with a passion for remaking the world

Lev Semenovich Vygotsky was born in 1896 and died of tuberculosis in 1934 at the age of 37. Although his life was short, it was remarkably full and prolific.

The second child of eight in a middle-class Russian-Jewish family, he was educated by a tutor at home, in a public gymnasium, in a private Jewish school, at the University of Moscow (medicine and law) and at Shaniavsky People's University where his passions included philosophy, history, psychology and literature.

Vygotsky married at age 28 and had two daughters. Gita became an educational psychologist and Aysa, a specialist in biophysics. (Gita is a major narrator of the film listed in the references at the end of this page.)

Vygotsky's impressive range of interests included theatre, literature, philosophy, psychology, linguistics and neurology. He had careers as a literary and theatre critic, teacher, developmental psychologist and researcher. Vygotsky spoke Russian, English, German, Hebrew and French. He also studied Latin, Greek and Esperanto.

The political climate of Vygotsky's youth influenced his work. WWI led to chaos and deprivation in Russian society, and eventually the Russian Revolution. An outcome of the Russian Revolution was that 'Whole new realms of inquiry were opened, and opportunities for younger scholars, were greater than had previously been imaginable' (Wertsch, 1985, p. 7).

However, the political climate after Vygotsky's death resulted in efforts to destroy his writings. Stalin ruled, and there was political repression and persecution of revolutionaries.

After Stalin died, Vygotsky's work was again published, thanks to his colleague Luria. English translations became available in the West in the 1960s.

Here are some of the resources that chronicle the life and work of Lev Vygotsky.

Wertsch, J.V. (1985). *Vygotsky and the social formation of mind* (pp. 1–16). Cambridge, MA: Harvard University Press.

Gajdamaschko, N. (1999). Lev Semenovich Vygotsky. In M.A. Runco & S.R. Pritker (Eds), *The encyclopedia of creativity* (pp. 601–697). San Diego, CA: Academic Press.

van der Veer, R. (2007). Vygotsky in Context: 1900–1935. In H. Daniels, M. Cole & J.V. Wertsch (Eds).*The Cambridge companion to Vygotsky* (pp. 21–49). Cambridge: Cambridge University Press.

Lev Vygotsky Documentary. Film produced by Valerie Lowe (2008). http://www.vygotskydocumentary.com/

The Vygotsky online archive: http://www.marxists.org/archive/vygotsky/.

Introduction

Sociocultural Theory in Second Language Education: An Introduction Through Narratives

This textbook is designed to introduce you to the concepts of sociocultural theory (SCT). You may not be familiar with SCT but you certainly are familiar with stories. This textbook is, in some respects, a story book. You will read stories narrated by people who learn and teach second languages, people who research second language learning and teaching, and people who have their language learning assessed. Each story will then be interpreted through the lens of SCT. That is, you will discover how each story illustrates one or more SCT concepts. What may seem daunting (SCT) will become clearer as you meet the various characters and contexts in the chapters of this textbook. We feel confident that by the time you have finished reading the chapters, you will be ready to interpret the last two stories with others or on your own.

'I don't know anything about sociocultural theory. What would you recommend I read?' Each of the authors of this textbook has been asked this question many times as we have talked about or used the terminology and concepts of SCT. Each of us has paused, considered various available book chapters, books, and journal articles only to sigh and wish for a solid, accessible *introductory text* that addresses sociocultural theory and second language learning and teaching for teachers and researchers. These questions gave shape to this project. **We** would write the introductory textbook we wanted to use. Furthermore, we would use narratives of second language learning, teaching, testing and research to illuminate the concepts that are integral to an understanding of SCT. Narratives and SCT are natural partners as we will demonstrate later in this introduction.

There is a range of SCT-related courses and collaborations in the field of applied linguistics. A brief internet search of 'sociocultural theory and university courses' revealed courses offered in Canada, the USA, Australia, Japan, Norway and elsewhere at both graduate and undergraduate levels. It is interesting to note that SCT courses appear in departments of Literacy, English, Second Language Education, Linguistics, Applied Linguistics, Anthropology and Psychology. Of note, is the increasing number of colloquia, research lectures and presentations grounded in SCT at diverse conferences. There is an active study group 'SCOLAR' (sociocultural orientation to language acquisition research) in Toronto, as well as an SCT research-oriented working group that has been holding annual meetings for over 15 years. Furthermore, a valuable tool, the searchable online SCT/SLA bibliography, has been set up by Pennsylvania State University: http://language.la.psu.edu/SCTBIB/.

We see an enormous growth potential as the field of second language acquisition (SLA) continues to explore the difference between the social as an influence on learning and the social as the source of learning itself. This growing interest in SCT confirms the need for an accessible introductory textbook. The audience for this textbook includes students, teachers and researchers who are new to SCT; those who are familiar with the concepts but are looking for examples/referents; those who are familiar with cognitive/individual theories of SLA and want to explore other ways of knowing; and those with data who are looking for a theory that helps them to understand their data. In the chapters of this introductory textbook, we will direct you to the work of others who have addressed SCT at more advanced levels.

Sociocultural theory is simultaneously new and old. It is a theory about how humans think through the creation and use of mediating tools. It is a theory that has been extended to a wide number of domains including second language learning and teaching.

Because context is integral in sociocultural theory, we begin with a brief overview of Lev Vygotsky, the 'father' of SCT and the times in which he lived, thought and wrote. (See *Vygotsky's story in brief* on the preceding page.) A literary critic, psychologist and educator, Vygotsky wrote that the source of learning and development is found in social interaction rather than solely in the mind of an individual. The West, however, heard little of Vygotsky's work until it was translated into English in the 1960s. Scholars across many disciplines continue to draw on and develop ideas from Vygotsky's short but prolific intellectual life. Those working in psychology, anthropology, sociology, education, and second language learning and teaching have found relevance in what is perhaps the most basic concept of Vygotsky's work: the individual cannot be studied or understood in isolation but only as part of a history, of a culture and of a society. The theories of the time involved separation of thought and emotion. Vygotsky rejected this Cartesian dualism and other dualisms and argued for interrelatedness, for contextualization, and for non-atomistic examination of people and activities. 'Snapshot'-style analyses cannot result in the types of understanding that studying people over time can.

The authors of this textbook are educators and researchers in second language learning and teaching. We do not argue that SCT supersedes all other theories that can be used to explicate second language acquisition. We *do* intend to show how SCT enriches the understanding of SLA and second language education in important ways.

Like so many fields, SLA has taken a social turn (Block, 2003). Our textbook explores language learning and teaching through the metaphor of 'meaning-making' rather than 'information-processing' (Bruner, 1990). We introduce readers to key concepts of SCT as they arise in narrative contexts. The concepts, embedded in these narratives, do 'make meaning' of language learning and teaching, and of the concepts themselves. Why narratives? Which concepts? We will discuss the rationale behind our narrative approach first.

The narrative turn

Recent turns have been not only social, but also narrative. Narrative turns have taken place across such diverse disciplines as economics, anthropology, psychotherapy, psychiatry, health sciences, business, law, divinity, education and applied linguistics. Papers from all of these fields (and others) were presented at the 2008 biannual conference of Narrative

Matters (http://w3.stu.ca/stu/sites/cirn/conference.aspx). Even science has been characterized as connected closely to narrative. Lyotard (1984) equated scientists to storytellers who follow master narratives of their own. Postmodernism favors personal stories; it waves aside the claims of master narratives and proposes that we have only our own local stories and we construct our own realities which change from moment to moment. The authors of this textbook are cautious in this regard and believe that while the local is important, our cultural and historical past are very much present in the present. That is, stories of the past, with their embedded cultural, social and historical events, both affect and effect stories of the present and future (Bakhtin, 1981; Cole, 1995; Vygotsky, 1978; Wertsch, 1998).

Our task in this book is not to make a theoretical case or even an interpretive one for the value of narratives. If you are not already convinced that we *are* our stories, that we organize our minds through stories (Bruner, 1990), that the world is made up not only of atoms but also of stories, then you can find eloquent and provocative statements about the primacy of story among humans in the books on narrative that we list in the reference section at the end. Using current and popular terminology, stories have the quality of 'stickiness' that lasts after discrete bits of information are forgotten (Heath & Heath, 2007). Here is how one advocate of learning through stories expressed their value to her:

> I think I am an example of why Jesus talked in parables because without story, I can't learn a damned thing. Give me philosophy, psychology, spirituality and mortality—just give it to me with somebody's voice behind it and I'll re-tell it to you in 50 years.... (Schalm, 2009)

Narrative and education

Narrative inquiry and narrative analysis have vigorous roles in education generally. Storying the experience of teaching, particularly novice teaching, and of learning has become an accepted method of research. Learners and teachers maintain reflective journals and participate in interviews and in focus group discussions. As well, published narratives authored by those who have crossed languages and cultures are rich sources of data for applied linguistics. Some examples of narrative research from education in general and second language education in particular are listed in the box below. It is intriguing to note the titles themselves as they illustrate how educators have viewed narrative. Here are some titles:

Bailey, K. & Nunan, D. (1996). *Voices from the language classroom*. Cambridge: Cambridge University Press.

Bell, J. (2002). Narrative inquiry: More than just telling stories. *TESOL Quarterly, 36*(2), 207–213.

Benson, P. & Nunan, D. (2004). *Learner stories: Difference and diversity in language learning*. Cambridge: Cambridge University Press.

Campbell, E. (2008). Teaching and learning through lived experience. *Curriculum Inquiry, 38*(1), 1–5.

Carter, K. (1993). The place of story in teaching and teacher education. *Educational Researcher, (22)*1, 5–12.

Casey, K. (1996). The new narrative research in education. *Review of Research in Education,* 21, 211–253.

Colter, C., Michael, C. & Poynor, L. (2007). Storytelling as pedagogy: An unexpected outcome of narrative inquiry. *Curriculum Inquiry, 37*(2), 103–122.

Pavlenko, A. (1998). Second language learning by adults: Testimonies of bilingual writers. *Issues in Applied Linguistics, 9*(1), 3–19.

Nunan, D. & Choi, J. (Eds) (2010). *Language and culture: Reflective narratives and the emergence of identity.* New York: Routledge.

Narratives serve SCT concepts

Stories and SCT are natural partners (Taniguchi, 2009). SCT seeks to understand mental development and learning by considering not only the contextual specifics but also the process over time, rather than focusing only on a particular moment of spoken or written production. SCT glasses are designed for both breadth and depth. They look back and forward in time, that is they *track development* (genetic method) and they look widely at the context in which the individual and the activity are situated as the source of development. These lenses encourage as much of the story as possible to be sought, observed, recorded and listened to when trying to understand phenomena like language learning and teaching. Stories told by language learners and teachers provide many of these dimensions which are not apparent (and not sought) in traditional experimental research.

Narrative tellings not only track development, but are sites of development themselves. According to Daiute and Lightfoot (2004), the imagination required for narrating stimulates complexities of memory, points out errors, transforms psychological and physical states, and often provides an opportunity for challenging mores. We move from telling stories in repetition in childhood to narrating new scripts during the process of becoming individuals. As a cultural tool, narrating is developmental.

In this textbook, SCT leads and the stories serve. That is, while invaluable, the stories are not the primary units of analysis in this book. We believe that the stories *mediate* particular SCT concepts which *are* the units of analysis in this textbook.

Narrative study

The use made of narratives in this textbook does not fit neatly under the heading of narrative analysis during which issues of form and of discourse are related, nor does it fit neatly under the heading of narrative inquiry, whereby narratives are created and listened to in order to explain and understand a phenomenon better. We elicited/solicited the narratives in circumstances separate from the conception of this textbook, and then studied these narratives to demonstrate particular SCT concepts-in-context. On the continuum of narratives-in-use that Georgakopoulou (2008) suggested, our work with narrative in this textbook may be described as closer to narrative inquiry or perhaps somewhere in the 'intermittent position'. Georgakopoulou observed

> ...an increasingly apparent need for the two camps of narrative analysis and narrative inquiry that have more or less happily lived apart to work together and cross-talk. The latter, in Freeman's terms (2003, p. 338), the expressivists (in my terms, the *narrative inquiry* scholars), use narrative as a means to an end (in my terms as a *method*) and on that basis their interest lies in the about, the what and the who of narrative: what stories tell us about the teller's self. Freeman reserves a rather (unfavourably) biased term (the productivists) for the other camp, the *narrative analysts* (in my terms), those who prioritise the how of narrative tellings and for whom the study of narrative can be an end in itself. But he [Freeman] is right to point out that this distinction should not be seen as a dichotomy that obscures any intermittent positions (2008, p. 1).

It could be said that for this textbook we use narrative as a heuristic. A heuristic is a device or a method that allows one to proceed fruitfully in finding information. Heuristics speaks of search spaces, i.e. how to locate or narrow down the space where a solution will be found. Our search space *for compelling, lived instantiations of SCT concepts* is narratives of language learning and teaching. In other words, this is not research *on* narrative; rather it is achieving/seeking understanding of phenomena (SCT concepts) *via* narratives.

SCT is a theory of mind

Sociocultural theory emphasizes Vygotsky's insistent focus on the *relationships* between the individual's physiological aspects and the social and culturally produced contexts and artifacts that transform the individual's cognitive or mental functions. Language is one such culturally developed artifact. According to Kozulin in his introduction to *Language and thought* 'Language and speech occupy a special place in Vygotsky's psychological system because they play a double role. On the one hand, they are a psychological tool that helps to form other mental functions; on the other hand they are one of the functions, which means that they also undergo a cultural development' (Kozulin, 1986, p. xxx). This relationship between socially and culturally produced artifacts and the transformation of individual psychological systems continues to fascinate current scholars and thinkers.

The chapters

For this concept-based textbook, we have selected as primary some of the concepts that Vygotsky introduced as part of his theoretical thinking. Although they are introduced separately, the concepts are interconnected in principled ways, one flowing from the other. Our coverage of concepts is by no means exhaustive and we direct you, wherever appropriate, to sources that delve into Vygotsky's work more comprehensively and at a more advanced level. However, the concepts we have selected are central to SCT and are of particular import to those who learn and teach languages. These primary concepts are mediation; zone of proximal development; languaging through private and collaborative speech; everyday concepts and scientific concepts; interrelatedness of cognition and emotion; Activity theory; and assessment. In each chapter, we typically add one or more concepts that are allied to SCT such as identity, scaffolding, dynamic assessment, and others. The allied concepts may not have been named by Vygotsky but are historically related to his theorizing.

Each story has a story: Data collection and analysis

Where do our stories come from and how do we treat them? Each chapter relates a story. Some are accounts from our own data from previous research (Grace; Sophie and Rachel; Mona) or from the data of others (Yang). Other stories have come our way in the form of class assignments (Madame Tremblay; Jody; Thaya; Sandra; Second Life; Beatles). The stories represent a variety of languages; language learning, teaching and using sites; people of different ages and at different stages of L2 development; and learners, teachers and researchers.

Each narrative was selected for inclusion in this textbook because it seemed to illustrate a particular SCT concept in a vivid way. Mona, for example, in *Mona: Across time and geography,* makes use of the affordances offered by a variety of people and artifacts to learn English in China, the USA and Canada, and this spoke to us of mediation. In *Sandra: a teacher's dilemma,* you will meet a language teacher and graduate student of applied linguistics who needs to make sense of her interactions with a particular Francophone student; her quandary brought to mind Activity theory. In *Grace: The effect of affect,* the author relates her story in which emotions and their contribution to cognition and identity are poignant. *Thaya, Jody* and *Madame Tremblay* each first appeared as an assignment in an expressive writing class. *Thaya: Writing across languages* illuminates a distinction made by Vygotsky between scientific and everyday (spontaneous) concepts. Jody talks to herself using private speech to sort out her dilemma, while in *Madame Tremblay,* a French immersion teacher and her student, Sarah, prompted us to examine the zone of proximal development (ZPD). Sophie and Rachel's interaction was extracted from a set of data that were re-interpreted as a dance of sorts between private speech and collaborative dialogue. Two final narratives are included without our interpretation. They are ready for your SCT interpretation. We assure you that there are no perfect interpretations or analyses and we are confident that you will be ready to engage in the process of examining phenomena through an SCT lens.

The individuals behind these stories are important to us and their larger stories would make valuable reading. Keeping in mind the affordances and constraints of this introductory textbook, we have selected parts/excerpts that were most relevant for our purposes without distorting the intent of the original authors. We offer them to you with the understanding that the story we deliver will be reshaped by you the reader because each of us responds to stories in individual ways.

SCT and allied social theories

We are convinced that thinking along the lines of sociocultural theory makes for a richer and deeper understanding of many phenomena, and particularly of second language learning and teaching. What distinguishes Vygotskian SCT from other more social and less psychological theories, is that Vygotskian SCT is a theory of mind (a psychological theory) and the connections between internal and external processes are explored. For example, in the chapter on languaging the relationship between cognition and private speech and social speech is examined.

The social turn in SLA, mentioned earlier in this introduction, has created a community of allied theories that look more widely at the phenomenon of learning and teaching. By virtue of participation in culture, meaning is rendered *public* and *shared* (Bruner, 1990). Thus, for example, when we discuss the concept of the zone of proximal development (ZPD) in Madame Tremblay's story, we show how Lave and Wenger's (1991) community of practice (COP) concept is closely related. The concept of a COP is an application of Vygotsky's ideas about learning and action. Vygotsky concerned himself primarily with the relationship between the individual and society with respect to development of the mind. Wenger (1998) focuses more on how a group shapes the practices of an individual through a combination of formal and informal situations. So while COP is more sociological in orientation, Lave and Wenger based their analysis and conclusions on Vygotsky's basic premise of learning through participation with more experienced and knowledgeable others.

Scholars in SCT

When you delve into SCT research and theory, the work of anthropologists, second language educators and researchers, and psychologists will come up. Readers will come across these scholars and their work in the chapters of this textbook. For example, Holland *et al.* (1998), have written eloquently using Vygotskian concepts of mediation and activity in their anthropological work. Wertsch (1991, 1998) approaches SCT as a developmental psychologist while Cole (1995, 1996) does so from the perspective of cultural psychology. Both Wertsch and Cole work with original (Russian) text and they problematize some of the translations from Russian to English (Cole, 2009). Notably, van Lier (1988, 1989, 2000) takes what he has termed an ecological approach to understanding language, language learning, language teaching, and research. SCT concepts are closely tied to his understanding of pedagogical contexts as ecosystems. Lantolf (2000), along with his students and colleagues, has extended SCT to research in second language learning and teaching (Lantolf & Appel, 1998; Lantolf & Poehner, 2008; Lantolf & Thorne, 2006). In addition, Lantolf has been responsible for the development of a center of excellence for SCT scholarship at Pennsylvania State University. Johnson (2009) has written extensively on second language teacher education from a sociocultural perspective. Hall and Verplaetse (2000) have done extensive research on interaction in the second language classroom drawing on both Vygotsky and Bakhtin.

Who owns Vygotsky and SCT?

Matusov in 2007 posed an interesting question: Who owns Bakhtin? The same question could be raised with respect to Vygotsky. Who owns sociocultural theory? Vygotsky died at a young age, before his theories and his studies were fully developed. Many scholars have interpreted Vygotsky and proposed what his reactions might have been to issues that have, since his death, become important in a particular field. In second language learning, for example, what Vygotsky might have said about identity formation is tackled by Penuel and Wertsch (1995). Although SCT was not originally intended as a theory of second language learning, applied linguists are leaders of SCT scholarship. Who else may participate in applying Vygotskyian theory and SCT concepts to their own fields of research?

Matusov (2007) argued that we generally hear of Bakhtin through philologists who are frustrated by what they consider to be the appropriation of Bakhtin by educators who use Bakhtin's theories to suit their (our) own purposes. Matusov suggested that we are already removed from the original Bakhtin by language (we read the translation), and by culture (he wrote in a time and a place and in a discipline quite different from our own). Similarly, Vygotsky, no longer alive, speaks through his published (and translated) works. Were he alive today, he would no doubt have moved in his thinking along with advances made in cognitive and social sciences. We believe that those who have a good understanding of his concepts may and should adapt Vygotskian concepts to suit the current state of knowledge. 'Vygotsky's theoretical claims are nothing if not tools, and tools must fit or must be fitted to the hands that use them.' (Belmont, 1995, p. 99).

Perhaps, the answer to who owns Vygotsky is a moot point because Vygotskian theory stresses the importance of *current context* and practices as well as history. Vygotsky's ideas cannot be passed unchanged from one scholar to another. No one can own Vygotsky's ideas; certainly they cannot freeze them. We have read some recent publications with the word sociocultural in the title but which make no reference to Vygotskian principles or concepts. SCT is much more than, and different from, a shortened form of social and cultural as applied to social behavior of individuals and groups. Umbrage may be taken when Vygotsky's name and/or the concepts Vygotsky introduced are claimed without evidence that the researcher or theorist attempted to understand Vygotskian sociocultural theory. The way in which some employ the concepts indicate how far the applications are from Vygotsky's original statements. The researcher or author may neglect to make evident how she has transformed the concept(s) and her own way of thinking in the process.

Scaffolding might be a case in point. The idea of scaffolding has been transformed into a set of mechanical steps and even programmed into computer testing programs. In contrast, the concept of scaffolding has also been transformed into dynamic assessment which seems much closer to Vygotsky's intent in proposing the ZPD. It seems important to consider the spirit, the soul of the ideas and not just the terms. We, too, have wrestled with how close we have stayed to the spirit of Vygotsky's theories. We believe we have maintained a respectful consideration of his work.

Chapter features

The title of each chapter juxtaposes the main character of the story (the teller) and the primary concept. The chapters exhibit the following features:

- **A front page** with key terms (glossed at the end of the textbook); **key tenets** of the primary concept as it informs SCT; the **context** of the story.

- We begin the chapter itself with a brief **introduction to the focus concept**.

- Then the **narrative itself** is presented followed by **our interpretation** of how the primary concept is illuminated by the narrative.

- The **allied concept** (if one is included in the chapter) is discussed.

- **Controversial issues** related to the primary concept are discussed.

- **Key studies** that relate to the concepts follow the controversial issues.

- Finally, we pose **questions** designed to provoke discussion of **implications for research and pedagogy**.

- All **references** appear at the end of the book following the **glossary**.

You the reader

As you read the narratives of teaching and of learning, you will bring your own schemata, your life histories and experiences to your reading. We hope that dialogue (maybe private, maybe collaborative) occurs as you interact with the characters, with Vygotsky and other scholars, and with the interpretations of the authors of this textbook. Vygotsky's life and times influenced his work. The life and times of the three authors of this textbook influenced the work you will read in this textbook. The life and times of each of you will influence how you make sense of what you read.

Mona: Across time and geography

Key SCT tenets related to mediation

- All higher mental processes (cognitive/affective) are mediated by material and symbolic artifacts

- In order to understand the 'now', we need to trace the process of how an individual got to that point. This is the genetic method

- Individuals do not have 'free will', but are rather 'persons-operating-with-mediational-means'

- Mediational means offer both affordances and constraints

- Through a process of internalization, intermental activity is transformed to intramental activity

- Individuals change artifacts, which, in turn, change the individuals

Setting of this narrative

Languages: home dialect, Mandarin, English

Context: English as a foreign language in China; English as a second language in the USA in an MA TESOL program, and later in Canada in a PhD program

Key terms in this chapter

(see glossary at the back of this textbook)

Mediation (material and symbolic)

Mediational means (tools, signs/symbols, artifacts)

Affordances and constraints

Internalization (mastery, appropriation)

Intermental (interpsychological) processes

Intramental (intrapsychological) processes

Genesis (ontogenesis)

Agency

Mediation

Through mediation the social and individual are brought together in dialectic unity

Mediation occurs when something comes between us and the world and acts in a shaping, planning, or directing manner.

Introduction

We interact with the **material** and **symbolic** world around us. Sometimes, our interactions are direct: a bee stings and we swat the bee. In this unmediated interaction, we use no **tools** or **mediational means**; nothing comes between us and the physical sensations (sting) and action (swatting). At other times, the interactions are **materially or symbolically mediated**. A bee circles, we take a book and swat the bee. In this mediated interaction, we use a **material tool** (the book) to extend our reach and protect us from the bee's sting. Yet another time, a bee circles, and we recall what we have read about bee behavior and move the plate of pineapple away. In this last scenario, we use a **symbolic artifact** – language written in a book about bee behavior – to plan and direct (mediate) our interaction with that annoying bee. That is, these **material and symbolic artifacts mediate** our interaction with bees.

Our goal in this chapter is to mediate your understanding of the concept of mediation! The most important artifact in accomplishing this goal is the narrative which follows these brief introductory remarks. The narrative includes reference to many artifacts that mediated the learning of an additional language, which in Mona's case, was English. By the end of this chapter, you should have an understanding of concepts such as **mediation**, mediational means, mediated activities and **artifacts: material** and **symbolic**.

In SCT, all human-made objects (material and symbolic) are artifacts. Examples include tables, clothes, books, numbers, languages, concepts and belief systems. But not all artifacts are mediating means; that is, they do not by virtue of their existence act as shapers of our interaction with the world. They have the *potential* to become mediating means, but until used as such, they offer only **affordances** and **constraints** to an individual. When that same book that was used to swat the bee is lying closed on a shelf, it is not a mediational tool. When used as a mediational means (tool), we need to consider the artifact itself and the where, why, when and how of its use.

Amply illustrated in the following story of Mona is the interweaving of artifacts as mediational means with Mona's changing and dynamic English learning goals. According to Lantolf and Thorne (2006, p. 62), within SCT, artifacts can be simultaneously material and symbolic aspects of goal-directed activity. Humans using artifacts to attain goals constitute an activity.[1] Perhaps Vygotsky's most important claim – because of its far-reaching pedagogical implications – is that all forms of human mental activity are mediated by material and/or symbolic means that are constructed within and through cultural activity.

Stories are a rich source of data and can yield new insights each time they are revisited. In this chapter, we will read of Mona's experience learning English across time and geography.

Her story was told as part of a research project in which participants were interviewed to uncover their individual language learning histories. Among many questions asked by the researcher (Linda), one included asking Mona to describe moments when she had felt competent in her use of the English language, what the researcher referred to as 'landings'. The information Mona provided relevant to her sense of being a capable user of English was fascinating and contributed much to that study (Steinman, 2007). Reading Mona's story again three years later, provided an opportunity to examine her experiences for evidence of mediation. As you read Mona's story, try to identify both material and symbolic mediational means that Mona used as she pursued her English learning goals.

This first chapter may seem packed because it is one in which we lay down the foundation for what is to come. It is one we expect you will return to often. SCT concepts which are discussed in this chapter will be revisited throughout this textbook. The essence of sociocultural theory is the interconnectedness of its concepts. In introducing sociocultural theory it is always difficult to know where to start as it is difficult to explicate any one concept without the aid, and an understanding, of the others. By the end of this textbook, we hope you will be able to grasp the 'wholeness' of the theory through an understanding of its concepts and their interrelationships.

Mona: Across time and geography

Highlights of Mona's life history

1959	Born in China
1971	Started to learn English (few affordances due to the Cultural Revolution) at age 12

1966–76 Cultural Revolution

1976	Moved to countryside. Began to teach English at age 17 at the village school. Continued to learn English from radio broadcasts
1978–80	Attended a machinery college
1980	Applied to teach English at the machinery college. Prepared for application by imitating tapes and studying a grammar book
1980–81	Taught English at the machinery college while taking a one-year teacher training certificate course
1981–84	Continued teaching at the machinery college and learning English from radio and TV in China
1984–87	BA, English major, China
1987–92	Taught EFL, China
1992–94	MA in TEFL, China
1994–97	MATESOL, United States
1998–05	PhD in an applied linguistics program, Canada

I began learning English at age twelve in a junior high school in China. At that time [in 1971], because it was during the Cultural Revolution [1966–1976], we didn't learn much English actually. After high school, when the Cultural Revolution was over, I settled down in the countryside and worked on a farm, and the village school needed an English teacher and I happened to know ABC. So that was how I became an English teacher, even though I didn't know much English! I listened to radio broadcasts designed to teach the English language. The opportunities to learn English were so limited.

I worked part-time in the village school. Mainly it was a primary school but it had a junior high class. I was 17. And I just taught "this is the blackboard" and "there are how many students?" "how many pupils?" "how many teachers?" and some things like that. Very simple. Then I attended a machinery college. When I graduated from the college, it needed an English teacher. I applied. I was 21. To prepare for the test, I listened to tapes so that I could imitate them. I don't know why, but then I could imitate much better than now. I have gotten old and now maybe I cannot.

I imitated so well that I passed that first test. Later there was a kind of interview and the final stage was to give a demonstration of teaching. I did it. I was bold when I was young. I feared nothing. Many professors from different universities were invited to choose the final person. I got the job.

I remember that to prepare that demonstration teaching, I didn't have systematic knowledge about English grammar so my father took an English grammar book one weekend and explained that to me from end to end. My father is a surgeon and in 1977 he started to study English by himself. At that time, when I wanted to apply for that job, he had only been learning for just a couple of years. He is a genius because later when some visitors from Canada and the United States came to visit the hospital, he could communicate with them, I guess because he studied medicine, and Latin can help him, right?

And I learned from that grammar book. So the next day when the examiner asked me some questions, I could answer. I was just preparing for that teaching examination. I was not interested in linguistics actually. I was just interested in the content. I liked to read stories. I studied the language for the purpose to use it. You can access another area. I thought that was the point of English learning.

The year 1980 was the year I really started to study English. I took a one-year teacher training course and at the same time I taught English in the machinery college. So I would prepare overnight and the next morning I would teach. So that's the point I really started my English learning. I think that I acquired English mostly by myself, and also transferred from my first language to the second language because discourse and communicative strategies are not isolated from language to language. You can borrow.

You asked me if I had positive feelings about learning English. When you sent me the e-mail about when I first felt that I had "landed" in the English language, I asked myself what was my landing moment. I searched my memory and found the first time I felt it was in 1983. I got married and we went to the Great Wall in Beijing. Before that my husband doubted about my English and we needed to take a picture and he said "Dare you ask that foreigner to take a picture of us?" So I approached that gentleman of some age and asked a favour to take a picture of us and he took a picture of us and my husband said "Oh now I believe you can speak English."

I was teaching English and I taught well at that time. My students loved me and my colleagues and everybody around loved me. I felt so good. I kind of got back the motivation for study. It became clear what I wanted. During that time the market economy was invading into China and most of the English teachers found another way to make more money. That changed many of my friends. Former classmates made good fortune at that time but I was poor. And I tried to change but whenever a big company or some institution wanted me, I didn't go. I just found I loved teaching. So I was the last one of my friends who stuck to being a teacher. It was a critical moment. I was frustrated. I was not clear what I wanted. Because the whole world around me changed, I doubted about the value of life – it kind of became meaningless.

Finally I found a solution – an answer for myself. I would stick with myself and just ignore the rest. In Chinese we say "unchange to face the change". I don't know how to put it in English? 以不变应万变 You must keep yourself. You let the environment around you change. You keep yourself.

*****

A problem was my English always had grammar mistakes and I didn't take it seriously until one class that I will tell you about later. The way you learn a language is very much influenced by your teacher. Probably I also affected my former students, I didn't know that. When I took my TESOL program – I took that in the U.S. – most of the professors were more interested in your content. So for international students at the very beginning, it was very positive. The teachers didn't correct me all the time, they just paid attention to my thoughts.

I wrote a paper and the first paper I remember the teacher said "you need to polish your grammar", and though he gave me a good mark, I argued with him about the grade. I was bold. I think people without knowledge are more brave. Another reason was I didn't know how to use a computer at that time – automatic spellcheck and things like that – but I began to realize 'okay you have a problem with grammar'. The professors were interested in the content and just mentioned the grammar. The weakness of that teaching strategy was that students didn't take it [grammar] seriously. That's not good. The teachers should have been tougher because you need to use the language in real life. Not everybody is like a babysitter, like the teacher.

*****

After doing my MA in the US, I moved to Canada to do my PhD. The first short assignment I had as a PhD student was a critical review, and I did very well, so I thought I could behave my way with English. But in the final paper – I thought it was good – the professor didn't like how I wrote. So I felt very disappointed about that, especially because I knew that my writing at that time, compared to other Chinese students in the same program, was not that poor. I just submitted the original work, my work, without editing, without polishing. But some peoples' content was poor, I thought. I mean it was poor for the thinking and content but they had perfect English because they paid for editing. That was a bad experience but I learned a lesson. It was good though, because psychologically I survived. And I became very cautious for the comprehensive examination, of course. I found a native speaker to keep guard for my grammar. Since then I pay more attention to my writing. I think the professors in my PhD program, they train students in a different way than in my MA program. But I appreciate the professors in our PhD program. In this profession, you need to have the skills. They have to prepare you, equip you. In Chinese, we say we give you tough lessons in order to protect you in the future.

I remember when I submitted my final draft of my thesis to my supervisor, the whole stack to him, and later I asked him "what do you think about it?" He told me it was excellent, and also he said "Your English improved so much".

I still don't think grammar is the most important thing. My grammar even now is not good. But I realize that grammar is important and also if we can do things better, why not? If you set up a room and decorate it with detail, which will make people feel comfortable, and organize it well, then it's much much better than in a mess. But it depends at which stage [of learning] you're at. Now my goals are to improve writing and speaking. I've learned in this interview that I wish to express a more authentic self in the second language.

*****

Mediational means in Mona's English learning

According to Vygotsky (1978), all forms of higher (human) mental (cognitive and emotional) activity – and that includes learning English – are mediated by culturally constructed material and/or symbolic means. What mediated Mona's learning of English? Some of the most obvious culturally constructed mediational means that Mona made use of were grammar books; computers; English language lessons played on the radio and TV in China; tapes; her first language; and her social interactions (e.g. with her father in China, her professors in the US and Canada, and highly proficient users of English (paid and unpaid)). As we will see, each of the mediational means used by Mona helped her, in varying degrees and ways, to learn English. Mona's learning was affected by the nature of the available artifacts and her changing (dynamic) goals for learning English.

In the first section below, we focus on the grammar book Mona used to mediate her learning of English. In the second section, we consider how her father mediated Mona's use of the grammar book as a mediational means. And finally, in the third section, we show how important other individuals were as they mediated Mona's English learning, *and* her sense of self – her identity, which also mediated her behavior. The changes that took place related to Mona's own changing goals.

Mona and the English grammar book

The grammar book used by Mona's father to teach Mona English gives us a relatively easy entry into understanding some of the complexities of the concept of mediation. Mona's short-term goal at that time (1980) was to know enough English to be able to pass an English-speaking test, be interviewed in English and do a demonstration English lesson, all as part of the process of being hired to teach English in a local college in China. She felt that she needed to improve her English grammar in order to prepare for the teaching demonstration. However, her heart was not really into learning grammar. As she acknowledged, her long-term goal was to learn English because she was interested in the content: 'I liked to read stories. I studied the language for the purpose to use it. You can access another area. I thought that was the point of English learning.'

Mona did not say much about the grammar book (material and symbolic artifact) her father used. According to Mona, 'My father took an English grammar book one weekend and explained that to me from end to end.' Our assumptions are that the book consisted mainly of rules and disconnected and decontextualized examples, including perhaps translations from Mandarin to English, and explanations in Mandarin. Certainly, it was unlikely to have been communicatively oriented because communicative methodologies had not yet been introduced into China on a wide scale. In any case, Mona set aside her long-term goal of learning English to access content (stories) in order to deal with her immediate, instrumental need to get a job. And she used the mediating artifact at hand, the English grammar book available at *that* time in *that* village in *that* culture.

Where and what was the grammar book before her father decided to help Mona learn English? The book was certainly a material (concrete) object – an artifact. During the Cultural Revolution, it had perhaps been used as a mediational tool, but not for its intended purpose. Perhaps it had been used to prop up a bedside table, or perhaps it had been used to swat a bee? In that sense, it was a tool. As a tool, it extended the capability of those using the book to make the table-top even, or to get rid of the bee. Used these ways, the book mediated between the users and the rest of the physical world.

Vygotsky (1978), in discussing mediated activity, distinguished between **tools**[2] which mediate our actions through material (concrete) objects, and **signs**[3] which mediate our actions through abstract, symbolic representations. Signs (symbols) include numbers, artistic forms, charts and diagrams, and most importantly, language. Tools and signs both have mediating functions. However, Vygotsky considered them to be quite different because of the way each orients human behavior:

> The tool's function is to serve as the conductor of human influence on the object of activity; it is *externally* oriented; it must lead to changes in objects.

> It is a means by which human external activity is aimed at mastering, and triumphing over, nature. The sign, on the other hand, ... is a means of internal activity aimed at mastering oneself; the sign is *internally* oriented. (italics in original, p. 55)

In other words, when the grammar book served to lengthen a leg of the bedside table so that its surface was level, it was a tool; through human influence, the bedside table was changed. Importantly, this change provided new **affordances** (opportunities) for those using the bedside table, for example, better lighting, easier access to a glass of water, medicine or books, leading perhaps to a better designed bedside table in the future.

As a sign (symbolic) system, the grammar book mediated Mona's learning of English through the language of the book (e.g. its grammar rules, explanations and examples). The extent to which Mona **internalized**[4] the grammatical knowledge symbolized in the book is the extent to which she would have gained greater control (regulation[5]) over her use of English. In other words, the extent to which Mona internalized the grammatical knowledge embedded in the book is the extent to which the book (and her father, see below) mediated change in Mona's higher mental (cognitive) processes. The outcome of this change would be a greater understanding and deeper conceptualization of English grammar.

Internalization (development) is the process by which symbolic systems take on psychological status.[6] That is, it is the internalization of symbolic systems that enable us 'to voluntarily organize and control (i.e. mediate) mental activity and bring it to the fore in carrying out practical activity in the material world' (Lantolf & Thorne, 2006, p. 62).

Although Mona got the teaching position she had applied for, her learning of grammatical rules fell short in her judgment: 'My grammar even now is not good.' Why? One plausible explanation is that the mediating artifact for her learning activity (the grammar textbook), constrained as it was by the history and knowledge of the culture that produced it, was inappropriate given Mona's long-term goal of learning English to access content.

Mona, the English grammar book and her father

Mona was proud of her father's English abilities, referring to him as a genius. He had taught himself English. She assumed he had been mediated in his learning of English by his knowledge of Latin, which he knew because he was a medical doctor.

Mona tells us only that her father 'explained' the grammar book to her from end to end over the period of one weekend. What did her father do? Did he 'talk at' her? In other words, did he provide explanations and continue to do so without checking on whether Mona understood them, or could apply them? Or did he 'talk with' her? In other words, did he engage Mona in a dialogue about the rules, providing and drawing out examples from her, asking her to explain the rules in her own words? And what language did he carry out his instruction in: Mandarin? Their shared Hunan dialect? English? How much of his teaching involved direct translation? How much involved making meaning as opposed to memorizing structures and forms?

The point we wish to make here is two-fold. First, as we have already pointed out, the grammar book mediated Mona's learning. It did so in a number of ways: by the conceptual content it presented; by the way it was organized; by the language in which it was written; and by the theory the author held of grammar in general, and the grammar of English specifically. Second, Mona's interaction with the book was mediated by her father who also held knowledge about English and held beliefs about how best to teach English grammar. These would have impacted on how he used the grammar book as a mediational means to mediate Mona's learning of English, and the nature of his interaction with Mona.[7] As we have seen, he could have interacted in many different ways, each of which would have had different consequences for Mona's learning of English. It was Mona's interaction with the artifacts and people in her social context that mediated her internalization of signs/symbols. (See also Chapter 3.)

It is important here to distinguish between the grammar book and Mona's father. The difference is that the grammar book does not change or adapt to Mona; if it is the wrong artifact given Mona's existing knowledge and goals, then it will not successfully mediate Mona's learning.[8] In other words, the artifacts we provide to our students may be poor choices. To make better choices as teachers, we need to better understand our students.[9] This moves us away from forms of transmission teaching and towards dialogic teaching (Wells, 1999b).

How might better choices by teachers be accomplished? Of course, direct questions by teachers to their students do provide some answers. However, Vygotsky's method was to observe individuals engaged in a task that they could not do on their own, provide them with material or symbolic affordances, and observe whether and how the individuals incorporated these tools as mediational means into their problem-solving activities. These affordances might well be in the form of dialogue with the individual. The dialogue would necessarily involve listening closely to the learner and responding to the learner's intent and displayed knowledge (see Chapters 2 and 7). In Mona's case, we do not know how her father responded to Mona, or if he paid heed to her at all. We do know that if he had, he might have been able to enact a ZPD with Mona (see Chapter 2) in which the grammar book might have become a more useful mediating artifact. The nature of the artifact, the nature of each person's interaction with the artifact, and where, when and with whom this interaction takes place will determine how useful it will be as a mediational tool.

We are beginning now to observe the complexity of the concept of mediation. In interaction with other human beings and artifacts, human behavior is mediated by sign/symbol systems. Also the meaning one makes of sign/symbol systems is mediated by those same sign/symbol systems in interaction with other human beings and artifacts. If these relationships seem circular, they are not. These relationships are reciprocal (bidirectional), thus allowing development in unpredictable trajectories. This reciprocity is an important aspect of SCT: it provides the connection between culture and individuals. Bidirectional (reciprocal) relationships represent the way in which individuals and cultural artifacts continuously develop. In other words, as we use the artifacts created by us or our predecessors, we change them, which then change us. To bring this back to our narrative, Mona's father transformed the English grammar book into a quick, intense tutorial. His use of the book transformed him into an English grammar tutor.

Mona, her colleagues, friends and students

Mona's long-term goal of learning English to mediate her access to content remained a theme in her story across time and geography. She reports that in response to the first paper she submitted in her MATESOL program in the US, the professor said 'You need to polish your grammar.' Even though he gave her a good mark, she 'boldly' argued that her grade should have been higher. So by the time Mona entered a PhD program in Canada (1998), her personal educational experiences (her **ontogenesis**; her life history) had convinced her that she 'could behave my way with English'. This belief, socially constructed through past dialogues (interactions, discourse) with her professors, initially mediated her writing activity in her PhD program. She wrote what she thought 'without editing, without polishing'.

However, through interactions with her professors and student colleagues in her PhD program, Mona learned how to improve her grades and pass her comprehensive examination. As did many of the other students, Mona hired 'a native speaker to keep guard for my grammar'.

We know from Mona's story that English was for the most part the symbolic system which mediated her interactions with her professors and other students (intermental processes). In all likelihood, her first languages (L1s) also mediated her interactions: with herself most certainly (intramental processes), as well as with other Chinese students. This means that English, along with her L1s, mediated both her learning of content and her learning of English through dialogic interaction.

Mona's story also shows that her dialogues with her students and colleagues in China mediated the construction of her identity as an English teacher, which in turn mediated many choices she made in the future. Recall that initially Mona taught English because the local village school needed an English teacher. She did not choose the job so much as the job chose her. When she was admitted to college, she learned about machines (tractors and other farm equipment), and English was not part of the curriculum. When she completed her college degree, the same college was looking for someone to teach English, and as we have seen, after some significant cramming, Mona got the position. Simultaneously with taking on this teaching position, Mona enrolled in a one-year English teaching certificate course. According to Mona, this was the point when she seriously started her English learning (1980–81), in part because she needed to learn more to teach it. After teaching for three years, she enrolled in a BA program with English as her major and then returned to teaching. 'I taught well at that time. My students loved me and my colleagues and everybody around loved me. I felt so good. I kind of got back the motivation for study.'

As Mona's story makes evident, her dialogue (interactions) with others mediated the construction of a strong professional identity and reinforced her goals to continue studying both English and teaching. In other words, Mona co-constructed with her colleagues, students and friends, a representation of herself as an excellent teacher which mediated her future actions. We can think of Mona as a 'person-acting-with-mediational-means' (Wertsch, 1998). In other words, Mona's choices are not 'free'; her actions are always affected by the affordances and constraints provided by her environment, and mediated by the symbolic artifacts she has internalized.

The identity Mona had co-constructed was a powerful force in mediating her future. Even though her colleagues and friends chose other paths 'to make more money', Mona 'stuck to being a teacher' because she loved teaching. But she did not stick to teaching without feelings of self-doubt as the world around her changed, leaving her wondering about the value of life, and of teaching. Her deeply felt sense of herself as an excellent teacher of English helped her to resolve this painful conflict. She 'kept' herself, letting the situation around her change. Mona's transformation from an English teacher who took a job teaching English because it was there, to an English teacher who *chose* to be an English teacher because she loved teaching English, was mediated by her dialogues (interactions) with colleagues and students.

To understand Mona's current behavior, one needs to know Mona's **ontogenesis** (life history) as it evolved in the particular sociocultural contexts in which she participated. Knowing Mona only as a PhD student is to understand her incompletely. The affordances and constraints her contexts provided, and the goals, knowledge, identity(ies) and beliefs she internalized, mediated her future trajectory. This is a point that Vygotsky made repeatedly and was the basis of his theorizing and research methodology: in order to understand a phenomenon, one needs to know its **genesis** (history).

> ... we need to concentrate not on the *product* of development but on the very *process* by which higher [mental] forms are established...Thus, the historical study of behavior is not an auxiliary aspect of theoretical study, but rather forms its very base. (Vygotsky, 1978, pp. 64–65, italics in original)

Vygotsky and his colleagues carried out most of their theoretical and empirical research in the ontological (life span) and microgenetic (moment-by-moment) domains in part because they can be observed in their entirety and are 'thus more "accessible" than phylogenesis and social history'[10] (Wertsch, 1985, p. 40).

Current controversy

To what extent did Mona internalize the grammar of English? Her thesis supervisor thought her English had improved considerably. However, the thesis draft he read had most likely been edited by someone else. So a question to ask is: 'to what extent did Mona internalize the grammar of English?'

Internalization is a contested term. Wertsch preferred not to use the term internalization because, in his view, the term has too great a variety of interpretations. Additionally, as Wertsch (1998) pointed out, the term sets up a dichotomy between internal and external, reflecting the mind-body dualism that Vygotsky argued against. Wertsch (1998) distinguished between internalization as **mastery** and internalization as **appropriation**. According to Wertsch, mastery refers to *knowing how to use* particular mediational artifacts.

Wertsch discussed a second meaning of internalization, of the relationship of agents to mediational means, as appropriation. He offered a translation of the Russian verb *prisvoit* as 'to bring something into oneself or to make something one's own' (1998, p. 53). He pointed out that there may be resistance on the part of the agent in appropriating cultural artifacts. A good example of this might be a person learning a second or foreign language who resists certain ways of saying something, or the meanings associated with direct translations. The important point here is that we must recognize the role of the active agent in the process of appropriation.

This distinction is illustrated in Mona's narrative. Mona resisted learning 'grammar', but as time and geography and circumstances changed, she came to think that '*Now my goals are to improve writing and speaking. I've learned in this interview that I wish to express a more authentic self in the second language*'. Perhaps only at this time in Mona's life might we think of her as appropriating English, even though she had mastered it years ago. Thus 'appropriation of mediational means need not be related to their mastery in any simple way' (Wertsch, 1998, p. 57).

In this textbook, we have continued to use the term internalization, but you may wish to keep in mind the distinction between mastery and appropriation.

Key research relevant to mediation

Lee's study is unique in describing the impact of the use of 'Cyworld', one of the most popular websites in Korea at the time of the study, on two Korean–English bilingual siblings. The language learning histories (ontogenesis) of the sisters differed somewhat, thus affecting their use of Cyworld's affordances and constraints in mediating their learning of Korean. Both their knowledge of and sense of self as Korean mediated, and were mediated by, their interactions on Cyworld.

> Lee, J. S. (2006). Exploring the relationship between electronic literacy and heritage language maintenance. *Language Learning & Technology, 10(2)*, 93–113.

Tocalli-Beller and Swain reported on a study with international university students who volunteered to participate in a course about humor. The students, working in pairs, collaborated to discover the meaning of jokes, riddles and puns, and then told (and if necessary) explained the jokes to the rest of the class. The students' collaborative dialogue mediated their internalization of the meaning of the 'semantic triggers' (the vocabulary essential to understanding the jokes, riddles and puns), as well as ways to approach the 'decoding' of jokes, riddles and puns.

> Tocalli-Beller, A. & Swain, M. (2007). Riddles and puns in the ESL Classroom: Adults talk to learn. In A. Mackey (Ed.), *Conversational interaction in second language acquisition: Empirical studies* (pp. 143–167). Oxford: Oxford University Press.

Questions to explore for research and pedagogy

1. Mona tells a brief anecdote ('small story') about how her husband became convinced that she knew how to speak English. Discuss this anecdote in terms of how it mediated Mona's identity as an English speaker. What is the relevance of Mona's small story for pedagogy?

2. As you will recall, Mona's first significant effort to learn English grammar occurred when her father taught her during an intensive weekend effort using an 'English grammar book' which we have assumed used a grammar translation methodology.

What affordances and constraints did the grammar book likely provide? How might the fact that it was her father, and not someone else, have changed Mona's experience?

3.   What can we now say about one of the artifacts that mediated Mona's English learning, that is, the grammar book? What if, at age 46 upon the completion of her PhD, Mona had had access to the same grammar book. How would she have reacted? How would it have related to her English goals at that time?

4.   How does knowing that all higher mental processes are mediated impact on your understanding of teaching? Learning? Consider this question with respect to Mona; yourself; and your students.

5.   If you were going to conduct a study about the impact of 'error correction' on second/foreign language learning, how would you conceptualize the role of mediation? Assume Mona is one of the participants in your study. Choose another area of research, for example, the relationship between identity and second language learning, and respond to the same question.

6.   What are the implications of the distinction between mastery and appropriation for second/foreign language assessment? You might want to wait until you have read Chapter 7 on assessment before considering this question.

7.   When you have read further in this book, come back to Mona's narrative to see if you can identify other SCT concepts in it. (See list of Key Terms in each chapter for SCT concepts.)

Notes

1.   Activity has a special meaning in SCT. See Chapter 6 on Activity theory.

2.   The word 'tool' is often used generically in the SCT literature to include both tools and signs/symbols. We will also use tools in this way. In this textbook we use tools and means as synonyms.

3.   In the SCT theoretical literature, sign, symbol and ideal are often used synonymously, and we will do so in this book. However, the field of semiotics distinguishes among them.

4.   Lantolf and Thorne (2006) use Vygotsky's term internalization. Wertsch (1998), however, distinguishes between mastery and appropriation, and uses those terms to replace internalization. See the Current controversy section at the end of this chapter.

5.   See Chapters 3 and 5. Note that mediate and regulate are often used synonymously.

6.   Mechanisms of internalization include language play, private speech, dialogue (see Chapter 3) and imitation (see Lantolf & Thorne, 2006).

7.   We wonder how Mona's father had interacted with the grammar book when he was learning English from it. How he used the book to mediate Mona's learning will be related to how he used it to mediate his own learning. This is an example of how culture

is carried across generations through artifacts, shaping individuals who in turn shape the artifacts.

8. In other words, she is unable to create a zone of proximal development (ZPD) with it. See Chapter 2.

9. This almost goes without saying in educating children, but tends to be forgotten in the second language instruction of adults.

10. Vygotsky discussed four different types of development in terms of 'genetic' domains: phylogenesis, sociocultural history, ontogenesis and microgenesis (Wertsch, 1985).

2

Madame Tremblay: A French immersion story

KEY SCT tenets related to ZPD

- The ZPD is collaborative and dialogic

- Learning leads development

- The expert may be animate or inanimate

- For Vygotsky, emotion and cognition are integrally related. At various times, one or the other may be highlighted, but the other is never absent

- A learner's trajectory during a ZPD is critical information for teachers and researchers

- The ZPD is transformative

Setting of this narrative

Languages: French and English

Context: Grade 4 (age 9–10); French immersion class in Ontario, Canada

The zone of proximal development (ZPD)

Introduction

Charged with educating children with special needs in Russia in the 1920s, Vygotsky believed that children could co-construct their learning and their eventual development with the assistance of an 'expert' and appropriate mediating artifacts (see Chapter 1). The difference between what an individual achieves by herself and what she might achieve when assisted is what is known as the zone of proximal development or the ZPD. The ZPD is arguably the most well-known of Vygotskian concepts (Kinginger, 2002; Mahn & John-Steiner, 2000) and is meaningful and attractive to those who teach. Because of its appeal, however, the term has not only frequently been used but also frequently misused (Chaiklin, 2003; Palincsar, 1999; Wells, 1999a). That is, some researchers and teachers use the term ZPD along with other sociocultural concepts when referring to social interaction and cultural awareness, but do not take into account Vygotsky's theory of mind.

In this chapter, entitled *Madame Tremblay*, we explore what can and what cannot be identified as a ZPD if one stays close to a Vygotskian representation of this concept. We will observe various interactions in this narrative that seemed to fulfill aspects of a ZPD as set out by Vygotsky. Other interactions seemed at first reading to evidence a ZPD, but upon deeper analysis, failed to do so.

Madame Tremblay was written by Sarah, a student in Penny's undergraduate Expressive Writing course. Sarah had experienced primary education in a Canadian (Ontario) French immersion program. This means that she entered school speaking only English but she was taught mostly through the medium of French. At the time of the story, she was in Grade 4 (age 9–10) and most of her content subjects would still have been taught in French.

In our analysis following the narrative, we will first focus on the ZPD and its relevance in *Madame Tremblay*. We then look to two other social theories and concepts that are relevant to this narrative, namely the concept of scaffolding (Wood *et al.*, 1976) and the theory known as community of practice (COP) (Lave & Wenger, 1991).

Madame Tremblay resonated with us immediately as it contains several interactions that seem representative of what we have often experienced in our own classrooms. Indeed, several previewers of this textbook who had been in French immersion programs said they recognized the dynamics of Sarah's classroom when they read the story. Although the ZPD is not represented to its full potential in any of the interactions that we describe in this narrative, the amount of discussion that the interactions in *Madame Tremblay* generated among us, and our struggle to determine what was and what was not indicative of a Vygotskian ZPD, convinced us to use the story. The discussions we had about *Madame Tremblay* served to create a ZPD for our further understanding of ZPDs.

Madame Tremblay: A French immersion story

"Silence classe. Silence." [Be quiet class. Be quiet.] Madame Tremblay pats her damp forehead, careful not to smudge her pencilled eyebrows. She moans. Her hand disappears into her wild red ringlets. "J'ai mal à la tête. Silence." [I have a headache. Be quiet.] The class shushes and whispers. Brock yanks one of my pigtails.

"Ow! Madame!" I whine, "Brock's bothering me!" I whack Brock in the stomach.

"Silence. Tout de suite!" [Be quiet. Immediately!] Madame Tremblay folds over and shakes her head. "Je demande le silence." [I insist on silence.]

Brock crawls to the carpet, crosses his legs, folds his arms, and pouts. We stare at Madame Tremblay.

"Madame?" Maggie flails her hand in the air. "Madame!"

"Oui, Maggie. Qu'est-ce que tu veux?" [Yes, Maggie. What do you want?] Madame Tremblay squints at Maggie from the couch.

"Madame, are you ok? Madame?" Maggie speed talks.

"Non, Maggie. J'ai mal à la tête. D'accord?" [No, Maggie, I have a headache. OK?] Madame Tremblay pushes her head deeper into the ragged couch.

"Madame?" Brock moves to the couch and whispers to her face, "Madame, should we call the nurse?"

Madame Tremblay presses her finger to her lips. "Shhh, Brock. S'il-te-plaît, juste pour un moment." [Please, just for a minute.] Madame Tremblay fans her face and waves Brock away.

"But, Madame! Are you okay?" Maggie continues.

"Madame, should we call Monsieur Dominique?" Clancy teases.

"Madame! Can we play?" Kyle fiddles with his untied shoelaces.

Madame Tremblay jolts up. Her black leather boots hammer the ground.

"Arrête!" [Stop!] She growls. "J'en ai marre. [I am fed up with you.] She raises her hand to the bridge of her nose. "J'essaie d'être patiente, mais vous bavardez, sans arrêt. Sans arrêt!" [I try to be patient, but you keep chattering, non-stop.] Her hands mimic mouths talking. "Je vais raconter vos chicaneries à Monsieur Dominique." [I am going to tell Mr. Dominque about your bad behavior.] Madame Tremblay tugs her ear. "Ouais, je vais lui dire que vous ne m'écoutez pas!" [Yes, I am going to tell him that you don't listen to me.]

The classroom door rattles. Madame Tremblay hurls the door open. A tall, grey-haired man in a grey suit leans against the doorjamb.

"Salut." Monsieur Dominique's deep voice trails into the class. "Comment ça va, la classe?" [How are you all?]

"Ça va bien, Monsieur Dominique." [We're fine, Mr. Dominique.] The class drones. Madame Tremblay blushes.

"Bon. J'ai besoin de votre professeur pour un p'tit moment." [Good. I need your teacher for a brief moment.] He pinches the air with his thumb and index finger.

The principal holds Madame Tremblay's arm and coddles her into the hallway. Madame Tremblay shuts the door behind her. Brock and Samuel scamper to the door and press their ears against it.

"She's telling on us." Brock whispers to the class.

"Elle raconte sur nous" I said, not thinking about my French.

"Elle dénonce de nous," worries Maggie.

"Elle nous dénonce!" cries Kyle.

"Elle nous dénonce! Elle nous dénonce!" cries everyone in unison.

"No she's not. No she's not." Samuel punches Brock in the arm. "She's telling him dinner would be nice..."

Smiles creep over the girls' faces. The smiles turn into giggles.

"Oh, Gérard, crois-tu au coup de foudre?" [Do you believe in love at first sight?] Maggie bats her eyelashes at Clancy.

"Parce que je crois que..." [Because I believe that...] Maggie pauses. She holds her heart.

"Je crois que..." [I believe that...] Maggie grasps Clancy's hand.

"Je suis en train de tomber amoureuse de toi!" [I'm falling in love with you!] Maggie hugs Clancy.

Laughter ripples from the class.

"Oh, Karen, je t'aime, mon amour" [I love you, my love.] Candice sidles over next to Karen and leans in.

"Et je t'aimerai toujours." [And I will love you forever.] Candice nods her head and holds Karen's hand.

"J'ai besoin de toi." [I need you.] Candice rests her head on Karen's shoulder.

"Tu es l'air que je respire." [You are the air that I breathe.] Candice presses her chest, "le seul..." [the only one...]

"Allez! Allez!" [Go! Go!] Samuel dashes back to the group. Brock trips over his shoelaces and sprawls onto the couch. The doorknob shakes. Samuel crosses his legs and folds his hands in his lap. Brock's face contorts in pain. The door inches open.

"Merci Gérard." Madame Tremblay croons.

*****

Students rush in from afternoon recess, the last recess of the day. Monsieur Dominique bellows from his office, "Viens ici!" [Come here.] He eyes a first-grader running through the hall, and points to the boy to come. The boy shuffles over to Monsieur Dominique. Brock darts past me and plows into Monsieur Dominique. Brock rights himself and cowers at the tall man glowering at him. Monsieur Dominique waves the first-grader away and focuses on Brock.

"Sorry, Sir." Brock whispers.

"Pardon, Monsieur Tanner?" Monsieur Dominique blinks at Brock.

"Um." Brock's sneakers squeak. He twists his feet and clasps his hands behind his back. "Um. *I'm* sorry, Sir?"

"Monsieur Tanner, tu sais bien que nous parlons français dans cette école." [Mr. Tanner, you know very well that we speak French in this school.] Monsieur Dominique wags his index finger at Brock and sucks his teeth. "Essaie encore, Monsieur Tanner." [Try again, Mr. Tanner.]

"Je...m'a...je..." Brock stutters. "Um. Je...m'e..sccusix?" Brock bites his lip and catches my eye.

"Je m'excuse," [Excuse me.] I whisper to Brock and continue past.

"Je m'excuse, Monsieur Dominique." [Excuse me, Mr. Dominique.] Brock says.

"Bon. Va à ta classe." [Good. Go to your class.] Monsieur Dominique sighs. "Et, Mademoiselle Sarah."

I freeze just before the first step down the corridor to Madame Tremblay's class. I turn my head to Monsieur Dominique.

"Oui, Monsieur?" [Yes, Sir?] I swallow and shiver in my puffy purple snowsuit. I inch around and stare at Monsieur Dominique's grey eyes.

"Merci." [Thank you.] Monsieur Dominique smiles.

"De rien." [You're welcome.] I stammer.

"Dis à Madame Tremblay, que je vais lui rendre une visite bientôt. D'accord?" [Tell Mrs. Tremblay that I'm going to visit her soon. OK?]

"D'accord." [OK.] I shuffle back to the steps. Monsieur Dominique disappears into his office. I scuttle to my classroom. I stare at my closed classroom door. *I'm late!*

I tap on the door.

"Un moment," Madame Tremblay's sharp voice pierces through the door. I step back and wait. The door flies open. Madame Tremblay glares at me.

My eyes widen. "Madame, Monsieur Dominique said he's visiting the class," I whisper.

"Pardon?" Madame Tremblay cups her ear. "Parle plus fort, Sarah. Et en français." [Speak more loudly, Sarah. And in French.] Madame Tremblay rolls the 'r'.

"Monsieur Dominique," I cough, "dit qu'il visite la classe." [Mr. Dominique says that he's visiting the class.] I gaze at my wet boots.

Madame Tremblay huffs at my wet boots. "Change tes bottes." [Change your boots.] She waves her arms and sighs.

"Oui, Madame." [Yes, Madame.] I kick off my boots, grab my sneakers, and hop back to the door. Madame Tremblay drags me into the class and closes the door.

Clancy and Maggie flip through French picture books in the centre of the classroom. Karen, Janelle and Candice play French hangman on the chalkboard. Kyle, Brock and Samuel whip French grammar flash cards at each other.

Madame Tremblay kneels down in front of me and rests her warm hand on my shoulder. "Alors, répète après moi. Monsieur Dominique m'a demandé de vous dire qu'il rendra visite à la classe." [OK, repeat after me. Mr. Dominique asked me to tell you that he will make a visit to the class.]

"Monsieur Dominique m'a demandé..." I nod, "Um..."

"...de vous dire qu'il rendra visite à la classe." Madame Tremblay squeezes my shoulder.

"Monsieur Dominique m'a demandé de vous dire qu'il rendra visite à la classe." I beam.

"Bon. Alors, quand?" [Good. OK, when?] asks Madame Tremblay

"Bon. Alors, quand?" I raise my eyebrows and stare at Madame Tremblay. Brock, Maggie, Clancy and Samuel giggle. Madame Tremblay glares at them.

"Silence!" [Be quiet!] Madame Tremblay hisses. "Kyle, Samuel, et Brock, ne jetez pas ces cartes!" [Don't throw around those cards.] Her voice pierces my ear. "Sarah, quand vient-il?" [Sarah, when is he coming?] She shakes her finger at me. "Et, ne me regarde pas fixement." [And, stop staring at me.]

"Je m'excuse. Monsieur Dominique ne dit pas quand." [I'm sorry. Mr. Dominique does not say when.] I stammered.

"Non. Répéte. Monsieur Dominique ne *m'a pas dit* quand." [No. Repeat. Mr. Dominique didn't tell me when.]

The classroom door rattles.

"Reste ici." [Stay here.] She rises and opens the door. Monsieur Dominique smoothes his grey suit and clips past Madame Tremblay.

"Salut les enfants." [Hello students.]

*****

The ZPD

Despite its popularity, Vygotsky's ZPD is viewed in conflicting ways. It has sometimes been referred to as an unfinished concept. (There is some validity to calling all of Vygotsky's work unfinished in light of his early death in 1934 at the age of 37.) Chaiklin, for one, noted the paucity of specific references to the ZPD in Vygotsky's writings: 'There is not an extensive corpus of material from which Vygotsky's true meaning or official definition or official interpretation can be found' (2003, p. 43). Van der Veer and Valsiner (2003) also downplayed the importance of the ZPD in Vygotsky's work. In contrast, Del Río and Álvarez (2007) emphasized that close reading of Vygotsky's writing indicates that the ZPD, although late to actually be named, was nevertheless a strong concept underlying much of his work. Guk and Kellogg (2007) concur.

Before examining *Madame Tremblay* for evidence of a ZPD, we would like to review some of the differing ways in which a ZPD is understood by people in the field of second language learning.

How has the ZPD been conceptualized? It has been called a metaphor by John-Steiner and Mahn (1996); an opportunity for learning by Swain and Lapkin (1998); a heuristic by Del Rio and Álvarez (2007); the distance between being and becoming (Holzman, 2002); and a **dialectical** (balanced tension) unity of learning and development by Dunn and Lantolf (1998). Often it is described as a place. The authors of this textbook feel most comfortable thinking of the ZPD as an activity rather than a place, but we find it somewhat clumsy to 'syntax'. The preposition most often used with ZPD is 'in'; however, if one is referring to an act, then the corresponding preposition should be 'during' as in 'during the ZPD'. So we will be using grammar and lexis that correspond to an activity.

Holzman (2002) touched on syntax as well as she made personal sense of the ZPD. She suggested a small change in preposition, zone *for* proximal development instead of zone *of* as this makes it sound less linear – less stage oriented. Similarly, Negueruela (2008) expressed concern about the linearity implicit in the term; he took issue not with the preposition but with the adjective 'proximal' as if the next step were part of a lockstep progression. More flexibility seems possible in Negueruela's term 'zone of *potential* development'. Chaiklin (2003) considered carefully the four-word label of the concept and reminded us that Vygotsky chose proximal *development* instead of proximal *learning* to indicate that the focus was on the individual growth not on the skill/task (p. 42). Mercer who also writes from a sociocultural perspective, bypassed the term ZPD and referred to an intermental development zone (IDZ) (2002, p. 143). He conceived of the IDZ as a shared understanding and activity that, if successful, leads to transcendence of current knowledge. If not successful, the IDZ collapses and the construction halts. So, he suggested, the addition of 'intermental' emphasizes the mutual nature of the achievement.

Perhaps the elements of a ZPD might be described best by contrasting it with another theory that is familiar to many second language (L2) teachers and researchers: Krashen's *i+1*. (For those not familiar with *i+1*, Krashen (1985) suggested that language improvement occurs when language input is pitched just a little higher in difficulty (+1) than the current interlanguage stage of the individual *(i)*.) Often (and incorrectly according to Dunn and Lantolf, 1998) the two concepts, ZPD and *i+1*, are thought of as the same. Dunn and Lantolf pointed out that when creating or analyzing a ZPD, the focus is on *all* dimensions of the activity whereas during *i+1* the language *level* is the focus. ZPD is aligned with the participation model of SLA, while *i+1* supports the acquisition model. That is, during a ZPD, the relationship among the participants matters as does the context. In contrast, the context and relationship are not part of *i+1*. In a ZPD, the 'expert' and the 'novice' interact and negotiate but during *i+1*, the expert transmits considering only the interlanguage stage of the learner.

Thorne wrote of 'collaborating bodies' during a ZPD and a 'passive body listening' during *i+1* (2000, p. 226). During a ZPD, the trajectory is unknown; this is not so during *i+1*. Vygotsky described learning as preceding and leading to development. In contrast, because Krashen's *i+1* is more stage oriented, development is required before learning. In other words, using an SCT perspective, we do not wait for development to occur; rather, instruction and learning are the means by which we can encourage development to occur. Development includes the ability to transfer learning across multiple contexts.

Certainly, the ZPD and *i+1* are distinct from one another.

So where can we find a ZPD enacted in the *Madame Tremblay* story? That is, what is it or who is it that assists the learners to move further than they could have moved if working alone? We look first to tangible resources in the classroom; to gesture; and to student–student interaction. We then look to interactions between Brock and M. Dominique; between Sarah and Brock; and between Mme Tremblay and Sarah.

Tangible resources as potential for learning

The expert other during a ZPD need not be animate but can be cultural artifacts as well. (You will remember that artifacts are symbolic and material, and are created and used by a particular culture. Language is an artifact as are beliefs, attitudes, books, and the like. See Chapter 1.) The author of *Madame Tremblay* recalled her own French immersion classroom as filled with charts, flashcards, books, puzzles and no doubt other artifacts designed to mediate the learning of French. By equipping the classroom in this way, Mme Tremblay created the possibility for an individual or for a whole class ZPD (see Guk & Kellogg, 2007, for a description and analysis of a whole class ZPD). If selected appropriately by Mme

Tremblay, and if interacted with by the students, then both the artifacts and Mme Tremblay herself helped to mediate learning and subsequent development during the ZPD.

Gesture as potential for learning

Gesture and other paralinguistic phenomena are intriguing areas of research in second language acquisition in general and SCT in particular. Gesture has been discussed by, for example, Gullberg (2006) Harris (2003) and Lantolf and Thorne (2006). For research on gesture used as a cognitive tool by the person who gestures, see Gullberg and McCafferty (2008) and McCafferty and Stam (2008).

Madame Tremblay however evidenced gesture in a somewhat different manner. Consider the effects of gesture on the learners. When analyzing the story, we noticed that at the beginning of the class, Mme Tremblay made excellent use of dramatic gesture. We surmised that this was probably part of her character and not part of a purposeful teaching routine at that moment. We visualized the scene where Mme Tremblay 'ran her hands through her ringlets', 'pushed her head deeper into the ragged couch'; and 'fanned her face'. The students may not have understood the words 'mal à la tête' [headache], but their teacher's accompanying gestures likely would have made the meaning quite clear to them. A more intended gesture on her part might have been 'tugging at her ear' when threatening to tell the principal that the students in class never listen to her. Similarly, M. Dominque 'pinches the air with his finger' as he says 'p'tit moment' [just a moment]. This gesturing accompanying the target language is quite typical of French Immersion teachers who, in principle, are expected to avoid using English in the classroom.

Student play/drama as potential for learning

When Mme Tremblay left the classroom to speak with M. Dominique, the students dramatically mocked the couple, imagining and then narrating the romantic dialogue between the two 'lovers'. The extracurricular-but-in-the-classroom exchanges took place entirely in French (the one exception was quickly corrected by the peer group). An excerpt from the students' playful interaction follows.

> 'Oh, Gérard, crois-tu au coup de foudre?' [Do you believe in love at first sight?] Maggie bats her eyelashes at Clancy.
> 'Parce que je crois que...' [Because I believe that...] Maggie pauses. She holds her heart.

The use of French in this exchange was unprompted and the exchange became an unintended (by the teacher) opportunity for learning. Did any learning take place? Guk and Kellogg (2007), among others, suggested that student–student interaction can constitute a vigorous ZPD. Perhaps 'coup de foudre' [love at first sight] was unknown to some of the children but they may have been impressed by their classmate's use of the idiom and filed the idiom away for future use.

Brock and M. Dominique

For Vygotsky, emotion and cognition were integrally related. At various times, one or the other may be highlighted, but the other is never absent. The following interaction from the narrative illustrates how emotion (affect) can impede rather than advance learning.

Recall the scene when Brock literally ran into M. Dominique in the hall of the French Immersion school. M. Dominique expected Brock to apologize in French and he uttered a sarcastic '*Pardon*'. Brock thought that his mistake was that he had not used a complete sentence.

> 'Sorry, Sir.' Brock whispers.
> 'Pardon, Monsieur Tanner?' Monsieur Dominique blinks at Brock.
> 'Um.' Brock's sneakers squeak. He twists his feet and clasps his hands behind his back.
> 'Um. *I'm* sorry, Sir?'

But M. Dominique clarified the transgression: 'Monsieur Tanner, tu sais bien que nous parlons français dans cette institution.' [You know that we speak French in this institution.] Surely Brock knew how to say a simple 'I'm sorry' in French given the level of French being used in his class. He appeared unable to do so at that moment of interaction, however. Perhaps he was intimidated and M. Dominique continued to act in a manner that might well have seemed threatening to Brock.

Being unable to speak in the face of fear (or ridicule) is a strong theme in much of the research on anxiety and failure in language development, and appears frequently in first person accounts of language and culture learning (Bailey, 1991; Schumann, 1998; Steinman, 2004). Brock made some efforts to call up 'I'm sorry' in French but his language skills appeared to have fallen apart in the face of M. Dominique's 'wagging finger' and 'sucking teeth'. No ZPD emerged here.

Those particularly interested in affect and learning/teaching should note interesting research conducted on emotion and the ZPD by Holzman (2002, 2009) working from a background in psychological therapy who considered 'therapeutic relationships as construction sites' (2002, para. 5). Newman and Holzman (1993) wrote of 'emotional ZPDs' while Mahn and John-Steiner (2000) referred to the 'affective ZPD'. We can grow emotionally with the help of others; we also seem to regress in the presence of negative interactions with those who have power as is evidenced in the M. Dominique–Brock interaction discussed above. See Chapter 5 for a more detailed description of emotion/cognition.

Sarah and Brock

During Brock's interaction with M. Dominique, when Brock appeared unable to speak even the simplest phrase in French, along came Sarah. She quickly assessed the immediate situation, understood what Brock needed at that very moment and provided it. '*Je m'excuse*' she whispered as she passed Brock in the hall while he was squirming under M. Dominique's glare. This was not a time for admonitions like 'don't you remember what we always say when we come into class late?' or a didactic 'what's the conjugation of a reflexive verb with je?'. Sarah, more capable than Brock at that moment (her confidence and ability had not been destabilized by M. Dominique), provided just-in-time assistance which we consider to be the enactment of a brief ZPD.

Magnan (2008), in considering communicative goals, called up Hymes' (1972) distinction between short-term and long-term goals for communicative performance. We suggest that what Sarah provided for Brock had a short-term goal, was a 'just in time ZPD'. We further contend that it remains unknown and unpredictable whether Brock learned at that moment. (See Chapter 1 for the distinction that is made in SCT among internalization, appropriation and mastery.) However, dramatic moments of language interaction – such as the fear Brock experienced and the enormous gratitude he felt towards Sarah and for that particular phrase – may well have resulted in Brock calling up 'je m'excuse' accurately, vividly, and independently in the future. Technically speaking, if Brock had known the correct phrase 'je m'excuse' (as we suspect he did) but had been unable to produce it at that time, then Vygotsky would have denied that a ZPD had been enacted since the linguistic learning had taken place previously. However, if we interpret this interactive slice more deeply, *development* might have taken place in the sense that Brock continued his socialization into the use of French on school grounds. He also might have internalized that peers are a resource for language and support.

Sarah and Mme Tremblay

It was the interaction between Sarah and Mme Tremblay which brought the ZPD concept to our minds when we first read the story. We were impressed at how the interaction between Sarah and Mme Tremblay prompted our vigorous and fruitful discussion of the conditions necessary for Vygotsky's ZPD. When Sarah returned from meeting Brock and M. Dominique in the school corridor, she was bursting with important information for her teacher. She was the sole bearer of knowledge regarding M. Dominique's intentions to visit the class. At the same time, Mme Tremblay was quite firmly engaged in her teacher role. The class was well underway; students were looking at books, playing games, using the flashcards, and the histrionics of the earlier moments of the class seemed to have disappeared. Sarah announced breathlessly, 'Madame, M. Dominique said he's visiting the class!' But Mme Tremblay wanted Sarah to follow school rules – not only to use French but also to use French accurately.

Remember that a ZPD requires co-authorship or co-construction. Even between an 'expert' and a 'novice' there needs to be some level of intersubjectivity – enough common ground – to proceed. This was not the case during the interaction under discussion. Sarah, in her excitement, spoke English to Mme Tremblay. Either she had forgotten the rules, or else she believed that the content in this case was more important than the form. But Mme Tremblay ignored Sarah's message (although she may have been intrigued by it – was she perhaps somewhat embarrassed that her student knew of and was becoming involved in her private life?). Sarah did not share her teacher's understanding of the interaction as a student–teacher moment of pedagogical possibility. Instead, she felt that she was a conspirator in the relationship (real or imagined) between her teacher and the principal.

You may have noted from various incidents in the narrative that Mme Tremblay was not shy to speak about her personal feelings to the class (remember how she complained of her headache and announced her irritation at the beginning of the class). We also know that French immersion practice traditionally has avoided focus-on-form (grammar-driven) types of activities with their concomitant error corrections, so Sarah's confusion over the nature of her dialogue with Mme Tremblay is understandable. She expected that her teacher was commenting on content. Not so. Mme Tremblay momentarily ignored the import of the breathless announcement and instructed Sarah to speak French and to put away her boots. She then recast Sarah's message in French.

Sarah submitted to the lesson on syntax although her mind was clearly on the dramatic content/meaning of the message. This distraction was evidenced by Sarah's mindless repetition of Mme Tremblay's *'Bon, alors, quand?'* [Good. Okay, when?]. Mme Tremblay had finished with the accuracy lesson and had switched to really conversing with Sarah. When Sarah finally realized that it was content she was now being asked about, she gave her news and Mme Tremblay immediately corrected the form of this new utterance. We interpreted the exchange as one that lacked intersubjectivity because the two interlocutors were on different planes, one talking about form, the other about content at different times.

We deliberated whether this interaction between Sarah and Mme Tremblay would better illustrate activity theory (see Chapter 6) than it would a ZPD. Indeed, it might best be considered a ZPD within an activity. Although Mme Tremblay and Sarah were in the same environment, i.e. the French immersion classroom, at the moment of this interaction they were engaged in different actions and activities. Sarah was the knower of news and Mme Tremblay the knower of language; each needed the other but was confusing the other. So indeed there was an 'opportunity for learning' (Swain & Lapkin, 1998) albeit 'missed opportunities' as Storch (2002) would name these particular interactions.

Limits/boundaries of a ZPD

What constitutes a ZPD – how wide do we cast the net? Do we stop at the 'pedagogical duet'? (Vygotsky, 1997, p. 50) the class? the semester? the first year? the university experience? How do we know when the ZPD has ceased? Perhaps the ZPD enacted by a teacher–student or student–student or during group interaction in a particular class is continued out of sight of the initiating agent, whether it be a teacher or other person or artifact. That is, one of the participants during a ZPD may experience a situation in her next class where her learning and consequent development and ultimate transformation continues. A learner may engage in homework or watch a film that extends the learning. The original partner in the ZPD is gone. But the ZPD may continue in new contexts.

Scaffolding and community of practice

Next, we would like to describe the concept of scaffolding, followed by the theory community of practice; both are social in orientation, as is the ZPD.

Scaffolding

Scaffolding is another teacher-friendly concept that is associated with Vygotsky although not named by him. The meanings assigned to scaffolding have ventured from the original mention in Wood *et al.* (1976). Wood *et al.* did not reference Vygotsky in that article, but their definition of scaffolding as 'a kind of process that enables a child or novice to solve a problem, carry out a task, or achieve a goal which would be beyond his unassisted efforts' (p. 90), is close to the Vygotskian ZPD.

Scaffolding can occur without classroom teachers. Not only teacher–student, but also student–student scaffolding can be powerful. (So can self-scaffolding not evidenced in this story, but investigated by Knouzi *et al.*, 2010). When the children in *Madame Tremblay* engaged in their mini-drama of what they predicted was being said by their teacher and M. Dominque, they created what Fernandez *et al.* (2001) called an intermental zone where students, in effect, scaffold one another.

The ZPD and scaffolding support each other both conceptually and syntactically. How do we 'verb' a ZPD? Scaffold seems a helpful verb to operationalize the meaning of a ZPD (Wells, 1999). The metaphor of a scaffold (noun or verb) or scaffolding (noun or verb) is a vivid one. In co-construction of knowledge, assistance is given when needed and in the quantity and quality needed, and is then gradually dismantled when the structure/individual can mediate (regulate) itself. We see some scaffolding in action during the 'dénoncer' incident.

> 'She's telling on us.' Brock whispers to the class.
> 'Elle raconte sur nous.' I said, not thinking about my French.
> 'Elle dénonce de nous,' worries Maggie.
> 'Elle nous dénonce!' cries Kyle.
> 'Elle nous dénonce! Elle nous dénonce!' cries everyone in unison.

Brock initiated the scaffold when he provided the English sentence. Sarah made it more appropriate by translating it, albeit incorrectly, into the expected language of the classroom, French. Maggie, who has more experience in French relative to the other students, continued the construction, scaffolding Kyle to a well-formed and appropriate 'Elle nous dénonce.'

Daniels (2001), however, argued that a scaffold can be interpreted as a one-way act, that is, as an experience constructed by the expert alone, whereas the ZPD is construed as a negotiated activity. Further, Daniels suggested that the experience would be different depending on whether it was a *rigid* or a *flexible* scaffold (p. 59). Some have argued that the term scaffold justifies a direct and heavy-handed intervention by teachers (Verenikina, 2003). The metaphor's weaknesses have been addressed in the literature. It seems to us that as popular as it is, the scaffolding metaphor, like almost all metaphors, falls apart eventually (pun intended). For example, strictly speaking, the withdrawal of the scaffold is a planned, systematic act. That is how it works in construction. But in teaching, the support sometimes falls apart rather suddenly and at inopportune times. The lesson may end without time for debriefing; the supply teacher who perhaps began the process leaves and does not return;

the dictionary that provided the scaffold disappears, the student changes classes and the new teacher does not continue the construction of the scaffold.

Scaffolding as a metaphor may have its weaknesses but it does have the quality of stickiness (Heath & Heath, 2007). (See the explanation of 'stickiness' in the Introduction.) We suggest that a more extended reflection about how we conceive of and operationalize scaffolding in our own practice, asking if co-construction and language development are included, would be enlightening to teachers and researchers.

Community of practice (COP)

From acquisition to participation. From cognition to social practice.

COP is as appealing a concept as ZPD in education (and across other fields of study as well). The idea that learning involves a gradual and deepening process of participation in a community of practice has become influential in many fields, including second language learning. One may grow into greater and more legitimate participation in a linguistic community, a professional community or other type of community where there are preferred structures, routines, lexicons and values.

Lave and Wenger (1991) referred to the ZPD in their description of COP. COP and ZPD are not synonymous, however. SCT is a theory of mind and COP is not. COP as a theory pays less attention to cognitive processes themselves and more to social practices that facilitate cognitive processes. However, both are squarely situated among social theories and complement one another in many ways. Both during a ZPD and in a COP, people develop and learn through interaction. 'Learning implies becoming a different person' (Lave & Wenger, 1991, p. 53) which certainly is congruent with Vygotsky's notion of transformation in learning. COP theory sees learning as participation in the cultural, historical, political life of the community. COP intentionally moves away from school-centred discussion because learning happens beyond schools. Traditionally, what happens in schools and what schools are known for stand somewhat in opposition to Lave and Wenger's less structured conceptualization of learning, so they strive to keep learning and intentional instruction distinct. School is a particular form of learning and context of learning, but is not the only or perhaps even the most important learning site. The ZPD, however, most often is presented in a schooling-related context. Vygotsky would argue that school learning is where the intentional teaching of systematic and generalizable knowledge (scientific concepts) should occur (see Chapter 4). Both during a ZPD and in a COP, participation is always situated (that is, integrated with context and local negotiation). Neither ZPDs nor COPs focus only on the intramental (individual); rather they rely on the intermental (social). For these reasons, we present COP as a theory allied with SCT generally and ZPD specifically.

Where do we see a potential or a realized COP in *Madame Tremblay*?

- The class speaks French unforced and uncorrected.

- Sarah knows the rules of the hall when interacting with M Dominique – Brock does not.

- Teachers teach – students do not nominate topics! (as Sarah tried to do).

COP can certainly be used to describe phenomena in *Madame Tremblay*.

The social order is made evident at various times in the story *Madame Tremblay*. We can see what the children in this French immersion classroom know. They know about romance and the language of such; they know that if Mme Tremblay truly is ill they are responsible for getting help; and they know that if a teacher insists upon a certain form of behavior, then they had better listen. These are the rules of the local COP. In the classroom, Mme Tremblay is free to announce her personal sense of well-being or frustration to her students. She insists on the use of French although does not demand the use of French when the children respond to her personal statements of distress (her headache, for example). Mme Tremblay is positioned in the middle of the school-as-community hierarchy; the students are at the bottom and M. Dominique at the top (at least of the part that we can see) and it is to him that Mme Tremblay 'denounces' or at least is suspected of denouncing the students. Sarah may not speak until she has put away her boots and may not nominate topics such as the message she is carrying from the principal without first submitting to the French instruction of her teacher. Other breaches in the practice of the community such as Brock speaking English in the hall are dealt with promptly. The 'we' that M. Dominique uses when he says 'tu sais bien que nous parlons français dans cette institution' [You know quite well that we speak French in this institution] temporarily excludes Brock, suggesting that conformity will make him one of them.

One weakness of COP, according to Tusting (2005), is that critical discourse analysis (which examines issues of power/dominance/ideology evident in talk) is not often examined. Tusting called for the inclusion of discourse analysis, particularly critical discourse analysis, in extending the COP theory. In Mme Tremblay's classroom, the children are a community themselves, electing to speak French for the most part in the absence of any authority. Barton and Tusting (2005) and their contributors would call for investigation into the position of this class in this institution, and this institution at varying levels of the society beyond it. That is, understanding a community of practice should require looking outside the immediate grouping to examine the impact of the larger community. A comprehensive analysis of this narrative would have to take into consideration what lies beyond this Grade 4 classroom. With respect to a ZPD, interrogation of what the larger contexts are – i.e. the various levels of institutions and the hierarchy beyond the immediate school – would be analyzed as an Activity system network (see Chapter 6).

Current controversies about the ZPD

Kinginger (2002) distinguished between the *prospective* (future-oriented) and the *retrospective* (conservative) orientations to education and discussed how both orientations seem to have appropriated/co-opted the ZPD for their own purposes. The latter appropriates the zone as a place of transmission of predetermined goals, with the expert playing the lead role and the outcomes well-defined. Kinginger suggested that for these users of the ZPD, the ZPD = $i + 1$ (p. 253) and cited studies in which this interpretation is developed. Because Vygotsky saw the ZPD as a revolutionary, transformative space, Kinginger supported the use of the ZPD by the former group, the prospective camp, who honors the ZPD's flexibility, its negotiated nature, its 'co authoring' (Kozulin, cited in Kinginger, 2002, p. 242) and its unpredictable outcomes.

Most often, we argue, teaching requires a judicious blend of transmission and co-construction. To perpetuate the dualism that one's teaching must be either one or the other seems simplistic and reductive.

How far will a teacher go when it comes to sharing the responsibility and the floor with students? Kinginger (2002) cited Hall whose work showed an end point when students tried to introduce their own topic (p. 252), something to think about with respect to our own practice.

Key research relevant to the ZPD

Alijaafreh and Lantolf use SCT to 'analyze the interaction between error correction and the learning process as it unfolds during the dialogic activity collaboratively constructed by learner and tutor' (p. 467).

Aljaafreh, A. &. Lantolf J. P. (1994). Negative feedback as regulation and second language learning in the zone of proximal development. *The Modern Language Journal,* 78(4) 465–483.

Individuals in the above study are working with a tutor. The study is unique in that the goal was to determine if, when, and how the learner began to internalize the learning, i.e. to move from intermental to intramental – i.e. from other to self-regulation (you will read more about this in Chapter 5) .

A regulatory scale is provided indicating the steps from other to self-regulation and the nature of the assistance is provided for each step.

We see how various levels of feedback are necessary for three different students – the feedback (scaffold) that helps one student is not appropriate for another. Individualization is critical to creating a ZPD.

We see within a particular learner the microgenesis (history) of learning as the individual begins to appropriate the feedback in subsequent sessions.

A debated issue in second language acquisition studies is whether feedback should be explicit or implicit. In this study, the answer is not either/or; rather, it depends on where you are during the learning/teaching process. In other words, the focus is not explicit OR implicit, but WHEN during the ZPD one uses implicit or explicit feedback.

This work was further developed in:

> Lantolf, J. P. & Aljaafreh, A. (1995). Second language learning in the zone of proximal development: A revolutionary experience. *International Journal of Educational Research*, 23(7), 619–632.

This next study draws on Aljaafreh and Lantolf (1994) and documents the importance of contingent graduated assistance in order for self-regulation to happen:

> Nassaji, H. & Swain, M. (2000). A Vygotskian perspective on corrective feedback in L2: The effect of random versus negotiated help on the learning of English articles. *Language Awareness* 9, 34–51.

In the following study, no one has the title of teacher. The collaboration is peer–peer and the roles assumed by the two students shift during the writing revisions.

> de Guerrero, M. C. M. & Villamil, O. (2000). Activating the ZPD: Mutual scaffolding in L2 peer revision. *The Modern Language Journal* 84, 51–68.

In his empirical study, Toth noted the confusion experienced by students when they were unclear as to whether the teachers were responding to what they were saying (content) or to how they were saying it (form). (This is similar to Sarah's confusion in her interchange with Mme Tremblay over the planned visit of M. Dominique.)

> Toth, P. D. (2004). When grammar instruction undermines cohesion in L2 Spanish classroom discourse. *Modern Language Journal*, 88, 14–30.

Questions to explore for research and pedagogy

In order to make the ZPD, scaffolding and COP relevant to teaching and research, we encourage consideration of the following questions.

1. Is the approach to the teaching (or the curriculum) retrospective **or** prospective? (See Kinginger's distinction above)

2. Does the envisioned ZPD have an outer limit? – if so, what is it and importantly WHY is it?

3. How negotiated are the turns or the progress? When does a ZPD cease to be one?

4. Are 'pedagogical duets' the only possibility or are students encouraged to enact their own ZPDs.

5. Is transformation during the ZPD co-experienced?

6. How, when, and why are scaffolds constructed?

7. How rigid are the supports in the scaffolds?

8. When is the scaffold dismantled once it has been constructed? And how? Kick it away? Piece by piece? Is it a back and forth process?

9. How does the most local COP shape and get shaped by the eddying circles of COPs in the wider contexts in which we conduct our lives?

10. What other SCT concepts might be identified in the *Madame Tremblay* narrative? (See the Key Terms at the beginning of each chapter for SCT concepts.)

3

Narrative 1: Jody (talking to self)
Narrative 2: Sophie and Rachel (talking to others and self)

Key SCT tenets related to languaging

- The origins of higher mental processes are social

- Languaging (private speech and collaborative dialogue) mediates complex thinking

- Private speech originates from social interaction

- Language learning and teaching can both be studied microgenetically and ontogenetically

Key terms in this chapter

(see glossary at the back of this textbook)

Languaging

Private speech (self-directed speech; speech for the self; self-talk; intrapersonal communication)

Collaborative dialogue (interpersonal communication)

Regulation (object; other; self)

Microgenesis

Higher mental processes

Setting of Narrative 1

Jody
Languages: Cantonese and English

Context: bilingual university student on a bus in Toronto

Setting of Narrative 2

Sophie and Rachel
Languages: English and French

Context: Grade 8 (ages 13–14) French immersion students in Canada doing a dictogloss task as part of an action research study

Languaging: Private speech and collaborative dialogue

Introduction

We bounce ideas off each other, and in doing so, create, negotiate and solve problems. In effect, we engage with others as a joint endeavor in meaning-making. We also talk with ourselves for similar purposes. Indeed, it is not unusual for us to talk out loud to ourselves. Often we do this as part of an internal dialogue, and it usually happens when we are engaged in cognitively/affectively complex tasks. These two activities – talking with others and talking with the self – are connected theoretically and in practice. The first is often referred to as **collaborative dialogue**, and the second as **private speech**. These two concepts, collaborative dialogue and private speech, originated with Vygotsky, though he used neither term. In this chapter, we address these two different forms of **languaging**.

There are two narratives in this chapter. The first is a short narrative written by a Cantonese–English bilingual student, Jody. We chose this narrative from many written by Penny's students because it illustrates an aspect of private speech that will be familiar to most of us, the 'speaking-out' of frustration. But most importantly, we see in Jody's private speech, how she learns the meaning of *sei*; that is, we see the **microgenesis** of Jody's internalization (learning and development) of the meaning of this one Cantonese word. We are constantly internalizing aspects of language in our everyday lived experiences, unconnected with a formal educational setting. For Jody, the context of her learning was downtown Toronto, heading south in a bus which she often took to get home.

The second narrative has at its center a short dialogue that takes place between Sophie and Rachel, two Grade 8 French immersion students (see Glossary). Their social dialogue occurs in a radically different context to Jody's inward-focused dialogue: a classroom in a school. Sophie and Rachel are participating in a research study investigating the role of collaborative dialogue in language learning. In Sophie and Rachel's interaction we are able to observe both collaborative dialogue and private speech. The boundaries between social speech and speech for the self are often blurred, and what looks like collaborative dialogue may on closer inspection also be considered as speech for the self. Our intention in using this story is, in part, to illustrate the value of multiple gazes on data. First the data were looked at through the lens of the 'input-interaction-output' metaphor (Block, 2003). Next the data were looked at through the lens of SCT. Overall, this narrative traces an experienced researcher's (Merrill's) development across more than a decade as she re-cognizes Sophie and Rachel's interaction.

The overarching goal in this chapter is that the combination of the two narratives mediates your understanding of languaging, which includes private speech and collaborative dialogue. To comprehend the intricate relations among SCT concepts, it is particularly important to understand the theoretical connections between speech for the self and speech for others. Among other reasons, such an understanding will lay a foundation for discussing several pedagogical implications of languaging for second and foreign language learning and teaching.

Narrative 1: Jody (talking to self)

The #63 bus loads at the front of Ossington subway station. The crowd swarms the bus doors, inching forward, as people fight to get on one by one.

I jump down from the 94 bus, just arrived at the station, and dash across the cement sidewalk to join the edge of the crowd. The wind blows hair into my face and scatters dead maple leaves along the platform. I pull my jacket collar to my neck, and tuck in my arms to squeeze into the crowd. A girl's huge blue backpack gets in my way. Through the dusty windows, I see that the bus is nearly full.

Someone touches my arm. I look back to see a stocky Chinese man. I catch a brief glimpse of graying hair and laugh lines. I catch one word. "Sei?"

I rattle off the four directions in my head. *Dong, lam, sei, bach*. A set of words, ingrained in my head from childhood. Like a melody, like a rhythm. *Dong, lam, sei, bach*.
North, east, south, west.

I think the man is asking if this bus goes south. I nod my head quickly, "Yeah, yeah."

The crowd pushes forward; the man fades away. I push into the back of the bus and lodge myself between a tall, large woman and a young boy. The bus bounces down Ossington Avenue. I strain to grip the overhead bar tighter, to keep from falling on the boy. The strap of my schoolbag digs into my shoulder. The air in the bus is heavy, tired. Everyone wants to get home.

Dong, lam, sei, bach. A set of words ingrained, a melody and rhythm ingrained.
Dong, lam, sei, bach. As the words play back in my head, I start to feel uncertain.
Sei. South.

Is that right? That doesn't seem right.
Dong, lam, sei, bach.

The bus halts at Dewson Street, the third stop from the station, in front of an empty schoolyard. A few people push through to catch the doors before they close. I stand on tiptoes to look for the old man. I'm almost sure he got on the bus right after me.
Dong, lam, sei, bach.

The bus continues its way through traffic. It stops at College Street, in front of a takeout shawarma joint. The bus starts to empty. I plop down in one of the hard, plastic seats.

Dong, lam, sei, bach. Damn. I realize my mistake.
Dong, lam, sei, bach.
East, south, west, north.
Damn, damn, damn.

I scan the bus again. I don't see the old man. Did he get off already? Is he lost?
Damn, I gave him the wrong directions.

At each stop, the bus gets a little emptier. I get a little more discouraged. There are only three people left when I reach my stop, the last stop, and he's not one of them.

*****

Private speech

What is **private speech**, and where does it come from? Private speech is speech addressed to the self. It is intrapersonal communication that mediates thinking processes; that is, it is a cognitive tool that helps to structure and organize our own thinking. It is 'that form of externalized [but possibly subvocal] speech deployed by adults to regulate their own mental (and possibly physical) activity' (Lantolf & Thorne, 2006, p. 75). Labels for private speech include: '**self-directed speech**' (Vygotsky & Luria, 1994); '**speech for the self**' (Lantolf, 2000; Lee, 2008); '**self-talk**' (Vocate, 1994); and '**intrapersonal communication**' (Lantolf & Thorne, 2006). The term private speech, that is, speech that is social in origin and form but psychological in function, was first used by Flavell (1966) to differentiate it from the term egocentric speech which Piaget used to refer to the speech of young children who developmentally did not yet distinguish between the self and others. Vygotsky (1987) adopted Piaget's term, egocentric speech, to cover both Flavell and Piaget's meanings.

In our presentation of Jody's narrative, we have italicized her private speech. Jody wrote, 'I rattle off the four directions in my head'. This covert speech that she 'rattles off' in her head is her way of trying to answer the question the Chinese gentleman has just asked her, which is whether the bus they were boarding is going *sei* (west). In order to answer the question, Jody repeated the four directions in Cantonese (*dong, lam, sei, bach*), a routine memorized years ago in her childhood. But this melodious memorized chunk did not help her in figuring out the meaning of *sei*. To do this, she tried comparing the set of Cantonese directions with her less routinized list of directions in English: 'north, east, south, west'. This allowed Jody to make a direct comparison: sei = south. This comparison was probably strengthened by the fact that both words began with 's'. And so, in response to the man's question, she confirmed, that, yes, the bus was heading south. Unfortunately, the man was asking if the bus was going *sei*, west.

We do not know if Jody actually spoke '*dong, lam, sei, bach*' or 'north, east, south, west' out loud while on the bus. In a more solitary context, she might well have. We imagine that later, as her frustration rose, she might have voiced 'damn'. In fact, it is not at all difficult to imagine Jody saying 'damn', and then realizing what she had done, looking sheepishly around to see if others had heard her. Or she might have externalized parts of words, or parts of the phrases, but they were meant for no one but herself.

Whether Jody spoke the words covertly to herself, or out loud, her purpose was to solve an everyday problem that she faced as she headed southwards along Ossington Avenue in Toronto. Jody used private speech to gain control of her thinking processes, her cognitive activities. Private speech provided her with both the process and product that allowed her to compare across her languages to quickly solve the problem, albeit incorrectly. Private speech transformed her thought into words that, once produced, served as artifacts (objects, products) for Jody to reflect on.

And reflect on them she did. Jody continued to repeat those Cantonese directions in her head, hoping to retrieve their meaning: 'As the words play back in my head, I start to feel uncertain.' Jody focused her attention on the two key words, isolating and comparing them: '*Sei. South.*' She engaged in a dialogue with herself, by first questioning herself and then answering her own question: '*Is that right? That doesn't seem right.*' This externalization of **higher mental processes** in the form of a dialogue with the self is part of the evidence Vygotsky used to argue that the source of higher mental processes is found in the external world of social interaction between individuals. In other words, much of the private speech that emerges when one is faced with a cognitively complex problem to solve, is indicative of an internal 'I-me' dialogue, which could only have been internalized from observation and participation in interactions where such question/answer strategic patterns occur in 'I-you' dialogue (Vocate, 1994).

In Jody's case, she continued to repeat *dong, lam, sei, bach*, three more times in fact, hoping that in repeating those words she would realize why *sei* = south did not seem right. With Jody's '*damn*', we know she had figured it out. It marks a 'eureka' moment. At the same time, it evidences the emotional nature of thinking. Jody was not just saying, 'I figured it out' which would more likely have been signaled through 'Oh', but she was signaling that she figured it out and felt bad about giving the wrong information to the Chinese man.

It would seem that with each repetition, Jody was able to further disentangle the meaning from its melodic rhythm (a movement from sense to meaning; inner speech to private speech), evidenced by her ability to now translate from Cantonese into English: *dong* = east; *lam* = south; *sei* = west; *bach* = north. Through repeated verbalization of Cantonese, Jody was able to retrieve the Cantonese meaning allowing her to move from Cantonese to English. Her accomplishment? She internalized (learned) the meaning of *sei* making use of knowledge and a cognitive tool (private speech) at hand. While going about her everyday activities, Jody mediated a solution to a problem by languaging. Languaging focused her attention, retrieved stored information, and created artifacts for her to compare and question.

Private speech has been identified as speech that does not appear to be directed to anyone in particular (though, of course, it is directed at 'me', the self). It has the empirical characteristics of: (1) no eye contact is established; (2) voice is lowered often to a whisper and sometimes it is not audible at all; and (3) utterances may be short (often limited to a few words or less) (Ohta, 2001; Saville-Troike, 1988). However, as we will see in the next narrative, much that is private speech appears as social speech, making the boundary between speech for the self and speech for others permeable, and demonstrating the close link between the two as manifestations of higher mental functioning.

Origins of private speech

We have examined briefly what private speech is. But where does it come from? Why is it so important in Vygotsky's sociocultural theory of mind? It is important because language, in this theory, is considered to be the most crucial mediating artifact in the creation and functioning of higher mental processes. Language is a semiotic tool that mediates thinking and learning. Vygotsky argued and demonstrated through his experiments with children, that during a child's development (ontogenesis), language and the ways it is used in the child's environment, are internalized to become tools for self-regulation and mental functioning in general.

> Symbolic signs... serve the child, first and foremost, as a means of social contacts with the surrounding people, and are also applied as a means of self-influence, a means of auto-stimulation, creating thus a new and superior form of activity in the child. (Vygotsky & Luria, 1994, p. 111)

Initially, children are regulated by objects in their environment. That is, concrete objects control children's behaviour, a phenomenon known as **object regulation**. For example, a parent tells his child to go and get her favourite ball. On the way, the child sees her teddy bear and picks up the bear to play with (regulated by object bear) instead of getting the ball. But, as children learn language, their behavior comes to be regulated by it. Thus, later in the child's development, when her parent tells her to go and get her favorite ball, she does so. This is known as **other regulation**, regulation by an other. Over time, children come to use language to regulate their own behavior, so the child might say to herself, 'where is my favorite ball?', and go off searching for it, undistracted by all her other toys, including her teddy bear. This is known as **self regulation**. Speech becomes 'the instrument of the problem's organized solution' (Vygotsky & Luria, 1994, p. 121). When language comes to take on these mediating (planning and organizing) functions, a qualitative 'leap' takes place, making humans a unique species. The genius of Vygotsky and Luria was that they traced this process ontogenetically.

The development of an individual (ontogenesis) is seen both in the individual's increasing ability to use language to mediate cognition, and in the transition from speaking-after-action to speech/action unity to a speaking-before-action. Through a series of experiments, Vygotsky and Luria (1994) studied this forward movement of speech. Their intent was to developmentally trace the role of speech in a child's cognitive development. In doing so, they noted that initially a child's speech follows his action; speech and action are independent. Then the child's speech begins to accompany action so that action and speech occur simultaneously. Action and speech become integrated. Vygotsky (1978) stated, '...as soon as speech and the use of signs are incorporated into any action, the action becomes transformed and organizes along entirely new lines.' (p. 24). But then, the child's speech begins to move forward, that is, it begins to appear *before* an action is taken. Language now intervenes to mediate (organize and plan) the child's behavior. Spontaneous behavior has been transformed into planned and organized behavior with the aid of speech: 'Where is my favorite ball?', readying the child to begin the search; or Jody's 'That doesn't seem right', readying her to focus on figuring out what *sei* means.

> At an early stage speech *accompanies* the child's actions and reflects the vicissitudes of problem solving in a disrupted and chaotic form. At a later stage speech moves more and more toward the starting point of the process, so that it comes to *precede* action. It functions then as an aid to a plan that has been conceived but not yet realized in behavior. An interesting analogy can be found in children's speech while drawing. Young children name their drawings only after they have completed them; they need to see them before they can decide what they are. As children get older they can decide in advance what they are going to draw. This displacement of the naming process signifies a change in the function of speech. Initially speech follows actions, is provoked by and dominated by activity. At a later stage, however, when speech is moved to the starting

point of an activity, a new relation between word and action emerges. Now speech guides, determines, and dominates the course of actions: *the planning function of speech* comes into being in addition to the already existing function of language to reflect the external world. (Vygotsky, 1978, p. 28; italics in original)

As we have seen, according to Vygotsky, speech for the self (what he referred to as egocentric speech to differentiate it from social speech) has its source in speech with others. Vygotsky argued that developmentally, speech for the self goes 'underground' to become inner speech.[1] On its way to being transformed into inner speech (pure meaning), it is abbreviated, agglutinated and fragmented. It is from this inner speech, this 'melody and rhythm' of sense, that Jody draws. 'As the words play back in my head, I start to feel uncertain.' Jody needs to make meaning of this ingrained sense. To do so, she voluntarily (intentionally) repeats and repeats, pulling the sense of the words to the surface, transforming them into words, into private speech. As private speech, they help Jody regain control of her cognitive activity. Voluntary action is 'where we find *the mastering of one's own behaviour with the assistance of symbolic stimuli*'. (Vygotsky & Luria, 1994, p. 135, italics in original).

Voluntary action constitutes the activity of our higher mental processes, such as focusing attention, solving problems, evaluating, planning, memorizing, and thinking logically, all of which together form human consciousness. Without language, it is difficult to imagine how we could carry out these mental activities. As Mercer (2000) pointed out, we use language for 'thinking together, for collectively making sense of experience and solving problems' (p. 1). And according to Vygotsky, it is through participation in these activities that children internalize them, transforming them into psychological tools. In other words, the genesis of private speech is: *social speech* → *egocentric speech* → *inner speech* → *private speech*.

We often assume that private speech occurs when we are alone, anonymous, unseen and unheard. Jody was not alone on the bus, and the dialogue that we were given access to in her story was between Jody and herself. Sophie and Rachel, about whom you will read below, on the other hand, are in school working together on a task assigned by the teacher. Sophie and Rachel are talking with each other about solutions to the task for which they have constructed a goal even more challenging than that offered by their teacher. Their talk – their collaborative dialogue – mediates their problem solution. As we examine Sophie and Rachel's collaborative dialogue, we will begin to see in its ebb and flow, that social speech and private speech perform similar cognitive/affective functions. What prompted Merrill to recognize the dialogue that emerged between Sophie and Rachel was the social and private speech she had engaged in over the years about the Sophie/Rachel example.

Narrative 2: Sophie and Rachel (talking to others and self)

In 1997, Maria Kowal and I published a paper (Kowal & Swain, 1997) based on data from Maria's doctoral research (Kowal, 1997). Our goal was to show how it was possible to encourage French immersion students (see glossary) to focus on form *and* meaning through the use of a dictogloss task (Wajnryb, 1990).[2] Maria was the teacher of the grade eight French immersion class in which this action research was carried out, so she knew her students well. Sophie and Rachel were two of Maria's high achieving students who made rephrasing dictoglosses a main feature of their work with this type of task. As Maria noted, this was Sophie and Rachel's self-chosen means of making the activity more challenging. Maria's goal in designing the particular dictogloss that Sophie and Rachel were working on in the episode provided below was to have them focus on the present tense. However, as we pointed out (Kowal & Swain, 1997), one result of Sophie and Rachel's approach to dictogloss tasks was to increase the scope of the grammatical features they discussed beyond the teacher's intended focus. In the episode below, we observe Rachel and Sophie focussing on the correct form of partitive articles[3] and gender agreement.

In the dictogloss that Sophie and Rachel had heard, the phrase was *de nouveaux problèmes* (some new problems), but Rachel instead suggested using *menaces* (threats) for *problèmes*, and Sophie, in turn 2, congratulates her on this good idea. But the phrase *des nouveaux menaces* is not well-formed. To be well-formed, the partitive *des* needs to be changed to *de* because it precedes an adjective, and *nouveaux* should be *nouvelles*, because *menaces* is a feminine noun. By producing *des nouveaux menaces*, Rachel has created a phrase, an artifact, that they both can now reflect on.[4]

1 Rachel: des nouveaux menaces [*some new threats*].
2 Sophie: Good one! {congratulating Rachel on finding a synonym for 'problèmes'}
3 Rachel: Yeah, nouveaux, des nouveaux, de nouveaux. Is it des
          nouveaux or de nouveaux?
4 Sophie: Des nouveaux or des nouvelles?
5 Rachel: Nou... des nou...de nou
6 Sophie: It's menace, un menace, une menace, un menace, une menaceay ay ay!
          {exasperated}
7 Rachel: Je vais le pauser [*I'm going to pause it*]{i.e., the tape-recorder}
          {Sophie and Rachel look up `menace' in the dictionary}
8 Sophie: C'est des nouvelles! {triumphantly}.
9 Rachel: C'est féminin...des nouvelles menaces.

Rachel wonders if the partitive form she has produced is correct. In turn 3, she verbalizes the possibilities out loud to see what sounds best, and then explicitly asks the question: "Is it *des nouveaux* or *de nouveaux*?", that is, "Should the partitive be *des* or *de*?". As indicated below, we need to ask to whom is Rachel addressing this question? To Sophie? To herself? She continues to test out her hypothesis in turn 5, "*nou...des nou...de nou*".[5]

Sophie meanwhile is caught up with whether this new word that her friend has introduced is masculine or feminine. As we see in turns 4 and 6, Sophie, too, tests alternatives, but relating to the gender of *menaces*.

Sophie and Rachel resolve the gender issue by turning to a readily available tool, their dictionary, and discover that *menaces* is feminine. Triumphantly they give the implications of this discovery, that is, that the adjective should be *nouvelles*: in turn 8, Sophie provides the correct form of the adjective, and in turn 9, Rachel confirms

Sophie's choice and provides the reason for that choice -- that *menaces* is a feminine noun. In their delight with this discovery, the issue of the partitive is laid aside.

What follows is an account of my changing interpretation of Sophie and Rachel's dialogue. The theoretical framework which guided our interpretation in Kowal and Swain (1997) was the Output Hypothesis (Swain, 1995). The Sophie and Rachel episode was presented under the heading of "noticing a gap" because as soon as Rachel suggested substituting *menaces* for *problèmes*, they noticed things they did not know, for example, the gender of the noun *menaces*, and started to fill the gaps in their knowledge.

In our 1997 paper, Maria and I drew the conclusion based on this episode and other data presented in the paper that: "...the dictogloss has been a successful vehicle for encouraging students to create meaning and process language syntactically; the students are hypothesizing about language, using the tools at their disposal... It has also allowed the students to go beyond the assigned grammatical feature and to follow their own agenda, based on their specific learner needs." (p. 299). We took it for granted that "their own agenda" was a jointly held one: to produce correctly the phrase *de nouvelles menaces*.

In Swain (2000), I re-examined the Sophie and Rachel dialogue within a sociocultural theoretical framework, focusing particularly on the concept of "collaborative dialogue". I defined collaborative dialogue as dialogue in which speakers engage jointly in problem solving and knowledge building, a concept quite different from the concept of "negotiation for meaning" which is part of the input-interaction-output model (Block, 2003). Negotiation for meaning occurs when learners anticipate or experience difficulties in message comprehensibility (e.g. Pica, 1994). Through negotiation, comprehensibility is achieved as interlocutors repeat and rephrase each other, and this *leads to* second language learning because the input has been made more comprehensible (Krashen, 1985; Long, 1985).

During collaborative dialogue, however, the issue is NOT one of making a message more comprehensible, but rather of building, and building on, what each interlocuter has said to create new knowledge and solve problems. The issue is of "growing the meaning." *Sophie and Rachel did not interact because they misunderstood each other; they did so because they identified linguistic problems and sought solutions.* Their output, in the form of collaborative dialogue, mediated their knowledge building and problem solving.

It became clear to me that what my co-researcher Maria and I had observed in the dialogue of Sophie and Rachel was not *leading to* language learning but was *language learning in progress* (Vygotsky's **microgenesis**; see also Gutiérrez, 2008). In sum, what was occurring in Sophie and Rachel's collaborative dialogue – their "saying" (process) and responding to "what is said" (an artifact/product) – *is* language learning (knowledge building). Languaging mediated this process. What we observed in Sophie and Rachel's interaction as they participated in problem solving were developmental processes derived from and constituted in dialogue (Donato & Lantolf, 1990). We observed "tool and result", not "tool for result" (Holzman, 2009).

Now, in 2010, I still consider this to be a satisfying interpretation – that Sophie and Rachel's collaborative dialogue mediated their problem solving and knowledge construction. This interpretation is based on a richer theoretical base than the information processing one that lies behind the negotiation-for-meaning interpretation. Also, knowing that Sophie and Rachel are friends, that they chose to turn the task into a challenging one for themselves, and that they enjoyed working together, supports the position that, overall, they were working collaboratively, with a common set of goals in mind. Without each other, they would not likely have set their goals so high and might not even have completed the task. Their bond of friendship keeps them oriented and enjoying the activity through to completion. In other words, that they are collaborating is not really in question. But what else might be gleaned from another look?

******

Languaging: Private speech and collaborative dialogue

Now, with our SCT eyes wide open, we might add that some of what Sophie and Rachel say is more for themselves than for the other as they sort out a response to their own self-set agendas within the broader collaborative activity in which they are engaged. This is in keeping with Wells (1999), who questions the distinction that has been made between social and private speech:

> ...all overt speech uttered in a context of social interaction is necessarily speech available to both speaker and hearer(s). On the one hand, speech deliberately addressed to another can also be significant for the speaker in extending or clarifying his or her understanding of the topic or of the conversation so far or in directing his or her concurrent or future action. On the other hand, speech intended primarily for the self can also function to inform or direct a co-participant and thus play a significant role in how the interaction proceeds. In either case, the sharp distinction between social and private, inter- and intrapsychological, breaks down, since all speech in a dialogic context has both functions simultaneously. (pp. 348–349)

Once Rachel suggested *menaces* as a synonym for *problèmes,* then, in effect, each tends to her own agenda. Although they spoke out loud, it would appear that Sophie and Rachel *each engage in private speech; i.e. speech for the self.* Even though they are physically in each other's presence, Rachel is concerned about the form the partitive should take (turns 3 and 5); Sophie is concerned about the form the adjective should take, which depends on the gender of the noun *menaces* (turns 4 and 6).

Rachel's question in turn 3 'Is it *des nouveaux* or *de nouveaux*?' is most likely addressed to herself, not to Sophie. This interpretation is reinforced by Sophie's non-response, and Rachel's abbreviated speech in turn 5. In turn 5, Rachel does not complete the word *nouveaux.* She does not need to as there is no intended audience but herself. She uses private speech to focus her own attention on *de* versus *des.*

Sophie, too, asks a question: *des nouveaux* or *des nouvelles?* (turn 4). Who is this question addressed to? Is it to herself or Rachel? Perhaps the important point here is that, effectively, it is addressed to herself, as Rachel is absorbed in the *de* versus *des* issue. In any case, it is Sophie who answers her own question by trying to settle on the gender of *menaces* by repeating it with first a masculine article, then a feminine article, then masculine, then feminine, hoping she will 'hear' the solution. This is much like Jody repeating *dong, lam, sei, bach* in her search for meaning. Jody turned to her other language to mediate a solution; Sophie turned to a dictionary.

In turn 7, Rachel indicates that she is going to press the pause button on the tape recorder. We do not know why. Perhaps she was frustrated with their non-collaboration? Perhaps she wanted to look up the rule concerning partitives? Perhaps Sophie's more social-like speech was interfering with her ability to concentrate? (See Borer, 2005.) Maybe she thought that tape-recording silence was not of interest to the teacher-researcher? In any case, in the last two turns, they return from their private worlds and again, after turning the tape recorder back on, collectively consolidate their new knowledge by providing the correct form *nouvelles*, giving *c'est féminin* as an explanation, and putting it all together in the phrase *des nouvelles menaces*.

As the narratives in this chapter have illustrated, both private and collaborative talk functioned to mediate cognition; they helped Jody, Rachel, Sophie and Merrill to control and organize their thinking when faced with tasks that were cognitively complex for them. Languaging is a term that covers both the private and social use of (spoken and written) language to mediate the process of thinking.

We usually language with others as a form of shared cognition. Take a minute to think about what you do when you are faced with a cognitively complex problem to solve. Out of school, you are likely to turn to a friend to help you 'talk it through'. (In class, we hope you are allowed to make use of this affordance too. And we hope that you, as a teacher, provide such opportunities.) Together you may come up with a solution you would not have been able to on your own (through collaborative dialogue). Or, just by talking to your friend, you may work out the solution yourself (private speech although it occurs in a social context).

The concept of languaging is based on Vygotsky's claim that language is one of the most important symbolic systems we have at our disposal in the development and mediation of voluntary actions. Languaging is one of the mechanisms of internalization. But languaging is also a means of externalization: it completes our thoughts (cognition, ideas) and transforms them into artifacts that allow for further contemplation, which, in turn, transforms thought. While we speak or write, we often achieve new or deeper understanding of complex phenomena, and plan and organize for the future based on past experiences.

Vygotsky distinguished between the social function of language and the intellectual function. As a means of communication, Vygotsky (1978, p. 28) said: 'Signs and words serve children first and foremost as a means of social contact with other people.' It is the intellectual function of language that corresponds to languaging. As language is internalized, it provides the means to be free of the immediate present, to solve difficult problems, to impede impulsive behavior, to plan, to focus attention, in sum, to master one's own behavior. Languaging mediates these cognitive (intellectual, higher mental) processes.

It is important to understand that not all speaking or writing can be considered languaging. Speaking and writing that is routine, that has the social function of passing along a simple message, of being friendly, of showing support, and so on, is not languaging because that language is not being used as a cognitive tool to mediate thinking.

Some pedagogical implications

From these narratives and their analyses, we are able to draw several implications for pedagogy. They suggest a conception of second and foreign language learners as meaning makers, as users of the target language to create meaning, to 'grow meaning', to organize and plan, to remember, to focus attention, and so forth. Once we envision our learners in these ways, then it seems necessary to reconceive how we teach them. Both the goals and the pedagogical means of teaching an additional language need to be recognized.

The narratives suggest moving beyond teaching communicative skills – a teaching orientation that tends to focus attention on the practicing of language as a set of rather inflexible grammatical and syntactic rules, and a slightly more flexible set of appropriacy rules. Carrying out tasks, often with trivial, unchallenging content unrelated to learners' needs, and which are designed to 'force' the learner into practicing a particular grammatical form or structure, is unlikely to push learners into using the target language as a cognitive tool. As we saw, Sophie and Rachel found the task assigned to them inconsequential. They, themselves, turned it into a more challenging activity, one in which they needed to language to solve their self-made linguistic problem.

There are at least two ways in which we might encourage learners to go beyond merely transmitting (communicating) an already existing message. One way is to ask them to engage with non-trivial content. Rather than working with content that is assumed to be known, teachers could actively create with learners their zones of proximal development (see Chapter 2), for both content and language, and their integration.

Teachers are able to discover these emerging ZPDs partly by *listening* to their students as they engage in meaning-making activities. Teachers will hear collaborative dialogue and private speech, like that of Sophie and Rachel, which may offer them insights into what learners know and what they do not know, what they want and do not want to know, and what they need to know to move forward developmentally. An important consequence for teachers of listening to their students' languaging as they struggle to accomplish classroom activities is that the teachers may learn about their students' goals, affective reactions and cognitive challenges. This knowledge could form the basis of an emerging curriculum for those students.

A second way in which we might encourage students to go beyond using language merely to transmit information is to encourage students to play with language, to try out old and new forms and see what meanings they are able to create with these forms, and importantly, to reflect on this process (Cook, 2000; Tocalli-Beller & Swain, 2007). As Lantolf (1997) and Lantolf and Thorne (2006) have argued, language play is a mechanism of internalization (see Chapter 1). Vygotsky (1978) saw play as one means by which the conceptual abilities and imagination of children are developed. 'In play a child is always above his average age, above his daily behaviour, in play it is as though he were a head taller than himself' (p. 129). Play, like instruction, leads development.

In much current second and foreign language teaching, focus is placed on the constraints that language imposes. It seems important to encourage learners to use language to expand their worlds, and to understand their new language as a tool which can serve them affectively and cognitively. Students need to see themselves as agents in an emergent process of meaning-making.

Current controversies

In this section, we discuss two controversial issues. The first issue is related to the differences between inner and private speech. The second is related to the use of one's first language in second and foreign language teaching and learning.

Vygotsky (1987) distinguished between meaning (*znacheniye*) and sense (*smysl*). For him, meaning is the equivalent of a dictionary definition, that is, the meaning for which there is consensus across individuals within a cultural grouping. But words and concepts accrue personal, idiosyncratic meanings according to each individual's experiences (*smysl*). The combination of a culture's meaning and an individual's personal experiences with any particular word or concept is what Vygotsky referred to as inner speech. According to Vygotsky, inner speech is 'pure meaning'. All language has been stripped away. It is thought without words, without structure. Wertsch (1980) has argued that Vygotsky referred to this 'pure meaning', this meaning abstracted from speech, as inner *speech* because its *origins* were found in dialogue.

The controversy lies in what is to be considered inner speech. Some (e.g. Guerrero, 2005) assume that inner speech is already in a languaged form. We, like Vygotsky, assume that once inner speech is languaged, it is already private speech. In other words, private speech is inner speech made conscious through the symbolic mediation of languaging. This means that private speech may be covert or overt, but it IS speech, unlike inner speech.

A second controversy lies in the language of languaging! Often the idea of languaging has been resisted by teachers, and even students, because 'it may happen in the first language' in a second or foreign language classroom. True, it might. But if it does occur in the first language, the question to be asking is whether this helps or hinders second/foreign language learning. (See, for example, Turnbull & Dailey-O'Cain, 2009.) From the perspective of the learner, it may be the case that he or she has no other option. That is, if the activity requires complex cognitive processing, then the best (or perhaps, only) way for the learner to engage in the activity is by 'talking it through' in the first (strongest) language.

Let us look at an example reported in Behan *et al.* (1997). In this example, a teacher of a Grade 7 partial French immersion program[6] was concerned that although her students would have no difficulty engaging with content material in English that she was required to teach in French, the students did not have the ability to express their ideas adequately about it in French. So she decided to try a small classroom experiment. Her students, in small groups, worked collaboratively to combine individually held information about the lifestyle and environment of First Nations people. The next day they would have to give an oral presentation on their 'findings' in French. The teacher considered this to be a cognitively complex activity.

All groups were instructed to use French in their groups, but two groups were closely monitored by the researchers who reminded the students to use French whenever they slipped into English. Both the talk of the students as they collaborated on this task and their oral presentations were taped. Not surprisingly, the groups of students who were not monitored for their use of French used more English than the monitored groups. Interestingly, and seemingly paradoxically, the oral presentations given the next day in French by the groups who spoke more English were judged to be better than those who spoke more French during the preparation time. Why would this be?

Behan *et al* argued that it is because the unmonitored students used their first language, English, to mediate their task understanding so that they could then work with the ideas in French. And, in fact, the researchers were able to demonstrate that instances of task management, information sharing and vocabulary searches where English had been used in task preparation were carried forward into the final oral presentation in French. Behan *et al.* (1997) concluded that 'L1 use can both support and enhance L2 development, functioning simultaneously as an effective tool for dealing with cognitively demanding content' (p. 41).

A key, relatively unexplored research and pedagogical question is, from an SCT perspective (in which language is considered as a cognitive tool), what is the optimal level of first language use in the second and foreign language classroom? And in order to begin to address this question from an SCT perspective, we would need to understand the context and the history of the learners, teachers and institutional program of which they are part. This opens up a multitude of research possibilities.

Key research relevant to private speech

Centeno-Cortés and Jiménez-Jiménez were interested in the question of the importance of the L1 in an L2 (Spanish) classroom with respect to the process of reasoning. To this end, they examined what they referred to as private verbal thinking (PVT),[7] the externalization of the process of reasoning during problem-solving activities. The participants were required to answer cognitively challenging questions (including logic or mathematical problems, visual-spatial problems, and kinship questions) in Spanish. The participants were intermediate and advanced university students of Spanish as well as L1 Spanish speakers. The PVT of the intermediate students was mainly in English; they could not use Spanish for reasoning. The advanced students used a combination of L1 and L2 PVT, and much more L2 PVT than the intermediate students. The L1 Spanish speakers mostly used Spanish PVT. From these findings, we can conclude that language learners rely heavily on their L1 to mediate complex problem-solving, and only at a later stage of target language development is the target language likely to be spontaneously used for problem solution.

Centeno-Cortés, B. & Jiménez- Jiménez A. (2004). Problem-solving tasks in a foreign language: The importance of the L1 in private verbal thinking. *International Journal of Applied Linguistics, 14*, 7–35.

Ohta studied the private speech of adults learning Japanese in a university classroom setting. Ohta observed some students using repetition, vicarious responses and manipulation of form and meaning in their private speech. For example, some students whispered answers to themselves to questions directed at other students, completed or provided alternatives to their peers' responses, anticipated what would come next, made difficult words or phrases salient through repeated practice, and manipulated and segmented grammatical structures and morphology even when the class was not discussing those structures.

Ohta, A. S. (2001). Private speech: A window on classroom foreign language acquisition. Chapter 2 of *Second language acquisition processes in the classroom setting: Learning Japanese*. Mahwah, NJ: Erlbaum.

Saville-Troike video-taped nine ESL learners in their classroom setting over an extended period of time. The children were from three to eight years old. Six of the children went through a silent period during which they stopped using their L1 before beginning to use English, their L2. However, during the silent period, private speech (PS) mediated their L2 development. PS was defined as the child not having eye contact or any apparent expectation of response. During PS, the children repeated others' utterances, practiced routines, created new linguistic forms, made paradigmatic substitutions and syntagmatic expansions, and rehearsed for overt social performance. The amount and complexity of PS depended on age and context.

Saville-Troike, M. (1988). Private speech: Evidence for second language learning strategies during the "silent" period. *Child Language, 15*, 567–590.

The students in this next study made use of both private speech and collaborative dialogue. The study was designed to explore the relationship between languaging and second language learning. Students were attending a second-year university French as a second language (FSL) course. Each student was asked to read aloud and explain his understanding (languaging) of each sentence from a passage about active, middle and passive voice sentences in French. Findings showed that the quality and quantity of languaging was related positively to post-test and delayed post-test scores measuring their knowledge and use of active, middle and passive voice contextualized sentences.

Swain, M., Lapkin, S.,Knouzi, I., Suzuki, W. & Brooks, L. (2009). Languaging: University students learn the grammatical concept of voice in French. *Modern Language Journal*, 93, 5–29.

See also, Knouzi, I., Swain, M., Lapkin, S. & Brooks, L. (2010). Self-scaffolding mediated by languaging: Microgenetic analysis of high and low performers. *International Journal of Applied Linguistics*, 20, 23–49.

Key research relevant to collaborative dialogue

The participants in Donato's study were third-semester university students of French. Using microgenetic analysis, Donato demonstrated how the students were able to construct collectively a scaffold for each other's performance. As Donato stated, 'the speakers are at the same time individually novices and collectively experts.' (p. 46). Overall, the study demonstrated how social interaction in the classroom resulted in the internalization of linguistic knowledge by individuals.

Donato, R. (1994). Collective scaffolding in second language learning. In J. P. Lantolf & G. Appel (Eds), *Vygotskian approaches to second language research* (pp. 33–56). Norwood, NJ: Ablex.

The students in this next study were ESL adults. Storch was interested in the nature of the collaborative dialogue between pairs of students over time and different tasks. She distinguished four types of interaction patterns: expert/novice, collaborative, dominant/passive and dominant/dominant. The first two patterns of interaction were more conducive to second language learning. Watanabe and Swain (2007) found a fifth pattern of interaction: expert/passive.

Storch, N. (2002). Patterns of interaction in ESL pair work. *Language Learning*, 52, 119–158.

Watanabe, Y. & Swain, M. (2007). Effects of proficiency differences and patterns of pair interaction on second language learning: Collaborative dialogue between adult ESL learners. *Language Teaching Research*, 11, 121–142.

In Swain and Lapkin, the researchers were interested in how students would respond to a reformulation of a story they had jointly written and what they would learn from the process. The participants in this study were two Grade 7 French immersion students. They were asked to write a story collaboratively. The story was then reformulated, that is, rewritten to make it more target-like without intentionally changing the meaning, and the students were asked to compare the two versions and notice what changes had been made. Later, they watched a video of themselves noticing and were asked to comment on each change they had noticed. Then they were individually given a copy of their original story and asked to make any changes to it that they wished. The findings demonstrated that the changes the students made, i.e. what they had internalized from the activities, which had been spread out over two weeks, could be traced back to their collaborative dialogue (operationalized as language-related episodes), and that they were agentive learners in that they did not accept some of the reformulated changes because they did not agree with them or because the reformulation had changed their intended meaning.

> Swain, M. & Lapkin, S. (2002). Talking it through: Two French immersion learners' response to reformulation. *International Journal of Educational Research, 37*, 285–304.

Gutiérrez drew on Vygotsky's methodological construct of microgenesis to refer both to the tool and object of her study. Brief language learning episodes were the *object* of her study. She used microgenetic analysis as a *tool* to analyze the process of internalization of the language in these language learning episodes. Her research was conducted with intermediate level (undergraduate) students of Spanish as a foreign language. She demonstrated the importance of language as a mediational tool for co-constructing meaning and learning opportunities.

> Gutiérrez, A.G. (2008). Microgenesis, *method and object:* A study of collaborative activity in a Spanish as a foreign language classroom. *Applied Linguistics, 29*, 120–148.

Questions to explore for research and pedagogy

1. Many individuals upon hearing or reading about private speech giggle a bit (an interesting reaction which probably references embarrassment or discomfort). Yet, on reflection, these same individuals will nod knowingly. There is evidence that the meaning of overt use of private speech may be socially constructed, for example, the belief in some cultures that only 'crazy' people talk aloud to themselves. What did private speech signify to you before you read this chapter? Have your views changed?

Have you since noticed yourself or others using private speech? What role might private speech play in your classroom or in your research?

2. Consider your own personal experiences and practices as a user of an additional language. In what language(s) do you use private speech? Why? When you converse with someone who knows the same languages as you, what language(s) do you talk in? Why?

3. The emphasis in this chapter has been on oral languaging. Do you think writing can have the same (or greater or lesser) power to create and transform thinking? What are some concrete examples of how languaging (written or oral) has mediated your problem-solving or led you to new insights?

4. What uses of language would NOT be languaging? Can these decisions be determined independent of the context of use?

5. Consider a language classroom where you have taught, learned or researched another language. What activities provided affordances (opportunities) for private speech and or collaborative dialogue? As a teacher, what did you learn about your students' language learning processes from listening to their languaging? How might you have taken more advantage of these affordances? As a student, how might you have taken more advantage of these affordances? As a researcher, how might you take into account private speech and collaborative dialogue?

6. What other SCT concepts might be identified in the narratives found in this chapter? (See the Key Terms at the beginning of each chapter for SCT concepts.)

Notes

1. Piaget argued that egocentric speech preceded social speech and disappeared once social speech was fully developed.

2. A dictogloss is a passage that includes a particular grammatical structure that the teacher wishes to focus on. The teacher reads the passage twice, out loud, and at a normal speed. Students jot down notes of what they hear, and then are asked to reconstruct the passage alone or in pairs.

3. Partitive articles *du, de l', de la, des* are used with nouns where English uses 'some' or no article at all.

4. Transcription conventions used: { } = transcriber's commentary; [ ] translation; ...pause.

5. It should be *de* because the partitive *des* is reduced to *de* in front of an adjective+noun construction (Grevisse, 1980, p. 353).

6. These students had only studied French as a second language for short daily periods before they entered this content-based program taught in French.

7. We have used the term private speech for private verbal thinking.

4

Thaya: Writing across languages

Key terms in this chapter

(see glossary at the back of this textbook)

Scientific concepts

Everyday or spontaneous concepts

Complexes

KEY SCT tenets related to scientific and everyday concepts

- Scientific and everyday concepts are symbolic means (tools) used to solve problems

- Scientific and everyday concepts are both necessary for development

- Everyday concepts are experience-based and partially transferable, unconscious and unsystematic

- Scientific concepts are conscious, systematic and generalizable

- Scientific and everyday concepts inform and shape each other

- The dialectic between scientific and everyday concepts creates a ZPD

Setting of this narrative

Languages: English and Tamil

Context: Writing classroom at an Ontario university

Everyday and scientific concepts: Establishing connections

Introduction

Vygotsky was fascinated both by the ways children and adults solved problems and by the symbolic tools and material tools they used to solve those problems. For Vygotsky, this problem-solving constituted learning and development. Much of his research and thinking focused on understanding this developmental process with the intent that it would lead to more effective ways to educate children. He looked at the ideas and understandings children brought to the classroom from their experiences outside of formal education. He saw young children not as empty vessels but as minds that had already noticed and constructed working explanations of the various phenomena they had experienced. He considered these explanations to be a child's spontaneous or everyday concepts. Everyday concepts are 'situational, empirical, and practical' (Vygotsky, 1986, p. 145). In school, children are presented with 'scientific concepts' (1986, p. 135) or abstract, systematic relationships and definitions.

Three key differences distinguish scientific from everyday concepts. Scientific concepts are conscious (and consciously applied), systematic and not bound to a context. Everyday concepts are intuitive, unsystematic and situated. Vygotsky saw everyday and scientific concepts working together, not one replacing the other. He saw well-designed instructional activities and practices mediating interactive and transformative dialogic relationships between scientific and everyday concepts. The story you will read in this chapter shows how one student, Thaya, developed his understanding of the scientific concepts of writing and translation. You will see a young man take his everyday concepts and the scientific concepts introduced in Penny's writing class, make sense of these concepts and apply them to tell his best friend's story. The two-part discussion that follows the story examines this transformation and how classroom discussions, scholarly readings, writing and revisions mediated it.

Thaya emerged from Penny's experience with Thaya in a course she initiated for students in a professional writing program at her university. In this story, note how the students, especially Thaya, move between their everyday and scientific concepts to build their writing skills and sensibilities as well as a more conscious understanding of the writing process. The students use these symbolic tools, (e.g. concepts) to solve their writing problems. This scientific understanding and application strengthened their intuitive practices.

The course was designed as a response to the cultural and linguistic diversity of the students in the writing program. The students commonly drew on their experiences from their other languages and cultures for the content of their writing. However, the students had not examined, from either a theoretical or a practical writing strategy perspective, how the changes they had made to the original story had transformed those experiences. The course challenged students to consciously examine the process of moving their stories across linguistic and cultural borders. Penny chose to use *re-languaging* (see Chapter 3 for a discussion of languaging) in the course title because she felt it expressed better than *translation* the complex processes students engaged in when they worked to bring readers into unfamiliar contexts without violating the authenticity of the original experience. Meeting those goals meant they had to solve a great many cognitively complex writing problems.

Thaya, the student at the centre of this story, chose to use the stories of his friend Kajan. The two young men had first met in Grade 8. Both young men are Tamil from Sri Lanka. In Canada, Thaya had dropped out of high school only to return to complete his requirements for high school graduation and move on to university. Kajan never finished high school, but Thaya held a deep respect for his friend's character, intelligence and Tamil literacy.

We welcome you into Penny's classroom and into her office to witness her interactions with Thaya and the other students, their responses to one of his stories, and their deliberations on solving writing problems. It is through these conversations that you can glimpse the interaction of everyday concepts of writing and translation with scientific concepts of writing and translation.

Thaya: Writing across languages

Thirty-five undergraduate students had signed up for the new course, *Re-languaging: Writing Across Languages and Cultures*. Thirty-five students sat each week in a windowless classroom where they discussed course readings, read and critiqued one another's work and grappled with fundamental questions of meaning across languages and cultures. All but four of the students spoke languages other than English on a regular basis outside of the classroom. Those languages included Mandarin, Cantonese, Korean, Portuguese, Italian, French, Urdu, Hindi, Spanish, Finnish, Arabic, Tagalog and Tamil. All of the students had taken a number of writing courses where they had practiced producing readable, engaging, non-fiction prose drawn primarily from their own experiences. They all knew how to manipulate parallel structures.[1] They were adept at constructing dialogue and showing actions. They could insert text boxes to provide readers with definitions or a bit of background. But they had not analyzed what happened to an experience lived in their other language and the meaning they had made of that experience when translating it into English for English-speaking readers. Penny challenged them to do so with each reading and in each of the seven pieces of writing they would draft and revise in the course.

   Thaya sat in the same seat in the back of the classroom each week. He had taken courses with Penny before. He liked ideas. He liked questioning the way language gets used. But he struggled to turn in the weekly reading journals where students tried to make sense of an idea or two from the readings or apply the ideas to their own writing practice. Much of the time, Thaya managed a paragraph or maybe two in his reading journals. But he would drop in during office hours to talk through his questions and insights. About a third of the way through the term, Thaya had fallen behind on his reading journals, turned in patchy first drafts but attended class every week.

   The students had recently completed two of the required readings, an interview with Ngugi wa'Thiong'o that appeared in *Writing Across Worlds* (Trivedi, 2004) and Thiong'o's narrative that appeared in *Genius of Language* (Lesser, 2004). Thiong'o's narrative, *Recovering the Original,* begins with a vivid scene of a student being whipped by a teacher because he had been caught speaking Gikuyu in the English medium school he attended in Kenya. Since many of the students had experienced English as a Second Language classes in their own linguistic histories, Thiong'o's story released many of their stories of teachers' attempts to bribe, coerce and control classroom language use.

Thiong'o used that classroom scene to contextualize his own linguistic and political conflicts as a writer and eventual decision to write his stories and novels in Gikuyu rather than English. Thiong'o's decision partly reflected a political statement about language and partly Thiong'o's understanding that the story is in the language as well as in the characters, setting and dialogue. This insight prompted more debate among the students about the possibility of ever being able to bring readers completely into a world experienced in another language and culture. Student comments ranged from attempts to find accurate translations of the names of foods to questioning the authenticity of replacing Chinese relationship titles with given names in order to avoid clunky English sentence constructions. Thaya sat silently attentive during the discussion. After class when he went to Penny's office for a writing conference, he had a question, "Can we use someone else's story? Can I use interviews?"

"Of course..."

"I need to write this in Tamil first. Thiong'o's right. The story is in Tamil. I have to write it in Tamil."

"If that's where you need to start, do it. Let's see how it works."

Thaya showed up at Penny's office a couple of weeks later with a sheaf of closely written pages. His blue ballpoint pen had imprinted the graceful Tamil script on both sides of half of the papers. The other half were inscribed with the English. "These are two of the stories from my friend Kajan. I have to wait for him; he doesn't always want to talk or have the time. But then he'll call me up and he'll start to talk. I meet him and listen and write in Tamil, because that's where his memories are, that's where the story is. And then when we're done, I go home and I write it all down in English. The English, it's just a rough draft yet, but the story, I think it's there."

"I noticed, I don't know if this is true, but Tamil seems to be much better for expressing emotions than English. Kajan says I'm butchering Tamil spelling. I know I'm making mistakes, I just write it the way I hear it and I'm making mistakes, but he'll fix them up. This is really making me practice! I feel like I'm back in grade 3." He laughed and grinned. "I've forgotten so much. I have to work at putting all the sounds and symbols together. I hope it gets a little easier. But this, writing it in Tamil, it helps me understand the story to its core."

Penny started reading the first story. It had no setting and described only the action of a young boy, getting on the back of a bicycle to leave home.

"I stuck pretty much to what Kajan said. It's his story. I can't go far from what he said, right?"

"You're right, you can't change the meaning of his story. But, remember, most of your readers won't ever have been to Sri Lanka. We don't know what it looks like, what it feels like, what it smells like. I would guess many won't even know about the war, the fighting that's been going on for so long. We won't get the full impact of this boy getting on the bicycle and watching his mother disappear without at least some of that. Remember what Baker[2] wrote about the public narrative? This is when you have to bring in the public and use it with the ontological narrative. Can you get Kajan to give you more details?"

"I'll try. I guess I have to wait it out and let him tell me the story he wants to tell me. I don't have the first-hand experience, like Kajan. I can't really fill that stuff in. I'll try to get him to tell me more, maybe some dialogue. And sometimes, some of the stuff, it's pretty sensitive, I don't think I can include it all, at least not exactly the way he's told me."

"Hmm, you do have to respect his story and his privacy. That's sometimes the trouble with telling a friend's story. What's in the public narrative you might be able to use? When you've done a revision, would you consider reading this for a class seminar?"

"Really? You think it's good enough?"

"I think it will be 'good enough' and I think you will see what's working and everyone can help you with what needs to work better."

Thaya agreed to read his story to the class the following week.

*****

Kadase Naal (Last Day)[3]

I looked outside my house. Pawan, Ravi, Vinoth and Nishanth from school were playing cricket on the street. I sat with my newly bought gray shorts and red t-shirt. I stared at the ground. My heart felt sadness that I never experienced before.

"Kajan, Appa took all your stuff and sent it with your Chithappa, Thambi also went with him," Amma told me as she sat beside me.

"Appa will take you on the bicycle, so hurry up and get ready," she said.

"Neenga? Are you not coming Amma?" I asked eagerly.

"Illa chellam, I can't take your other brothers and go that far, Appa will take you."

I remember that day as the last time the smell of morning sandalwood graced my nose. The last time the bright red sand graced my feet. I was leaving my beloved Analatheevu for an unknown Canada. I knew why I was leaving but I could not really understand it. We are to leave the War and blood torn Jaffna with some strangers, for our protection and the future of my family.

"Paru Kajan, you are the eldest of the house, your Appa is deaf and you have two younger brothers here. We are all dependent on you. Go to Canada, study well, succeed in life and bring us to you." Amma trembled as the words came out of her mouth.

"Thambi is only five years old; you have to look after him Kajan," she held my hand softly.

"Seri Amma," I said with a slight smile of approval.

Appa arrived a few minutes later. I saw the bicycle stop in front of the house. Appa hopped from the bicycle and walked inside the house. I slowly got up and hugged my brothers good bye and turned to Amma and hugged her tightly. Appa smiled at me from the front of the house. I sensed the timing and walked toward him. Appa grabbed my left hand and walked me to the bicycle. I hopped onto the back of the bicycle. Appa turned the bicycle around and slowly started to pedal. Hari trailed behind the bicycle; Amma held Neethan in her arms and chased the bicycle. They were crying.

I turned around and stared at my family. The bicycle started to pick up pace. Amma started to get smaller, her eyes full of tears. Suddenly my heart realized what was happening. My hands clenched onto my father's shoulder. Amma was now out of my sight. The tears in my eyes ran down my cheeks.

The class sat in silence after Thaya finished reading. Mandy[4] raised her hand, "I like the way you just jump into it. I liked the detail of the new shorts and shirt while he watches his friends play cricket."

Theo added, "The bicycle and how he looked back while he rode away on the bicycle, that's a great image."

Vibhuti asked, "How did you choose which words to leave in Tamil and which to translate?"

Thaya responded with his own question, "Did you understand? Was the meaning clear enough?"

Rob nodded, "Yeah, I think I got most of it, it's like mostly words for mother, father, right?"

"Mostly. I think the Tamil words give a sense of family and closeness that is not completely there in English, so I left those in Tamil."

Claudia asked, "So you started with these stories in Tamil?"

"Yeah, I wrote them in Tamil first. That's how Kajan told me the stories. I really had trouble writing the stories in Tamil as I am not too literate in it. But, especially after reading *The Genius of Language* I wanted to get the original in Tamil then write the English version. I was quite lucky to have my grandmother live with us. As I grew up she forced us to speak the Tamil language and really helped me understand things through stories, but I did not have the first hand experience like others."

Sarah raised her hand, "I get most of it, but I'm not sure yet about this *"Illa chellam."* There's just not enough context around it."

"I didn't want to translate that. Because if I was busy trying to explain what *chellam* is—because *chellam* can be interpreted so many ways. It can be used for someone you love or a mother can say it to her son or so many other things. By the time I explained all that, I would actually move away from the story. So I left the *chellam* in there but even without it, I hoped you would still get it. That was one of the things I had to choose. But I left it in there because it sort of shows the connection with his mother."

Ana nodded in agreement, "Yeah, some words just don't translate, you really have to show it and don't try to explain it."

Theo raised his hand again, "Maybe you need to give us a little more of the background, you know, the public narrative."

Claudia nodded, "Yeah, and more about what the place looks like. I think it needs more detail about the streets and the house, maybe. I can't quite picture it yet."

Thaya made a note on his paper, "But I don't want to interrupt the flow of the story by trying to fit in too much information. How do I avoid interrupting here?"

Several students spoke up at once. They argued about the advantages and disadvantages of using textboxes or adding a public narrative voice to the first person narrator in the story. "Can you do that?" asked Karen. Vibhuti and Rob pulled out their copies of *Genius of Language* to find examples of how the writers had combined the two. Over the next fifteen minutes, the student writers urged Thaya not to clutter the story with too much background but at the same time asked him to add more detail that would locate the story unmistakably in Sri Lanka and Kajan being sent off to safety just because he was Tamil Thaya listened, answered his classmates questions and posed questions of his own before Penny halted the discussion and the class ended.

At the end of the term Penny received, on time, Thaya's portfolio of six stories and a reflection on the process of languaging and re-languaging stories across linguistic and cultural borders.

*****

Everyday and scientific concepts

Conscious awareness and the presence of a system are synonyms when we are speaking of [scientific] concepts, just as spontaneity, lack of conscious awareness, and the absence of a system are three different words for designating the nature of the child's [everyday] concept. (Vygotsky, 1987, pp. 191–192)

In this story we will examine two sets of everyday/scientific concepts. They are concepts related to: (1) the writing and construction of non-fiction narratives for a public readership; (2) translation as it relates to multilingualism and narrative writing.

Vygotsky wrote:

...a concept is not an isolated, ossified, and changeless formation, but an active part of the intellectual process constantly engaged in serving communication, understanding, and problem solving. (1986, p. 98)

It is important to keep this dynamic character of concepts in mind. Concepts are not well-formed definitions or explanations students must learn to produce on demand; rather, Vygotsky presented them as cognitive tools that students can use to mediate various problems inside and outside of formal schooling contexts. Vygotsky first broke concepts into two categories – **everyday** (or spontaneous) and **scientific**. In exploring both sets of concepts, Vygotsky concerned himself primarily with finding more effective ways to school all children to meet the goals of a new Russian society. He also made the point that although he did his research with young children, adults also move back and forth between everyday and scientific concepts depending on the topic; none of us ever live entirely in the world of scientific concepts.

Just where do these concepts come from, how are they formed? How are they related to one another?

Everyday concepts are internalized from concrete, face-to-face experiences and contexts. They are not very portable from one experience or one context to another. While there may be a loosely organized system about them (**complexes**, in Vygotskian terms), they lack an overall system that allows the individual to use them in relation with other concepts. Think about the 'rules of thumb' students bring with them (and that we often teach) such as

'Never begin a sentence with "but"' and 'never end a sentence with a preposition.' These everyday concepts work some of the time but the student does not always think to apply them in a different situation or applies them indiscriminately.

Scientific concepts are systematic, hierarchical and subject to *conscious* manipulation. Perhaps more than any other characteristic, consciousness, the ability to hold the totality of the phenomenon in mind and a systematic application of the concept in diverse contexts separates the everyday from the scientific. Vygotsky differentiated being conscious of an action and being conscious of the *how* of that action, 'We use *consciousness* to denote awareness of the activity of the mind – the consciousness of being conscious' (Vygotsky, 1986, p. 170). We can use scientific concepts to help us solve problems such as structuring a sentence or a paragraph to make a meaning clear. We use the higher cognitive functions of reflection and analysis as we simultaneously use the relevant scientific concepts to solve a variety of problems.

Both scientific and everyday concepts have their strengths. They are both necessary for the development of the other and for a student's cognitive development. Vygotsky did not value one over the other. He wrote that 'The strength of scientific concepts lies in their conscious and deliberate character. Spontaneous [everyday] concepts, on the contrary, are strong in what concerns the situational, empirical, and practical' (1986, p. 194). He did not advocate replacing the everyday concept with a scientific concept. Instead, he understood that the two in interaction were necessary for development. He wrote, 'We believe that the two processes – the development of spontaneous and of nonspontaneous [scientific] concepts – are related and constantly influence each other. They are parts of a single process...' (1986, p. 157).

Another important aspect of the relationship between everyday and scientific concepts involves language. According to Vygotsky, the formation of both everyday and scientific concepts develops through '...the functional use of the word, or any other sign, as a means of focusing one's attention, selecting distinctive features and analyzing and synthesizing them' (1986, p. 106). However, the way language is used with scientific concepts differs from the way language is used with everyday concepts. Whereas everyday concepts depend on experiences and words (concrete plus abstract), scientific concepts are understood, used and expressed primarily in words (abstractions alone). The words take on different and unique meanings when used as scientific concept words.[5] They function differently. Words are no longer used for communication alone but 'as a part of a system of knowledge' (Minick, 1996, p. 41). The learning is mediated not by experience but by words and symbols.[6] In Penny's classroom the students used words in both everyday and scientific ways when they talked about their writing practices. According to Daniels, '...scientific concepts are developed through different levels of dialogue: in the social space between teacher and taught; and in the conceptual space between the everyday and the scientific. The result is the production of webs or patterns of conceptual connection' (2001, p. 53).

One of the mechanisms by which scientific and everyday concepts are transformed is imitation. Vygotsky differentiated imitation from automatic copying. In Vygotsky's view, imitation is a potentially transformative mechanism that is applied consciously and is goal-directed. Intentionality of the imitation, the reflection and examination of the results, and the subsequent revisions differentiates the action from simple mimicry. He appears to have based this on the work of James Mark Baldwin who wrote:

...imitation to the intelligent and earnest imitator is never slavish, never mere repetition; it is, on the contrary, a means for further ends, a method of absorbing what is present in others and of making it over in forms peculiar to one's own temper and valuable to one's own genius. (quoted in Valsiner & Veer, 2000, p. 153)

It could be argued that students sometimes mimic or copy the scientific concepts introduced to them in formal learning contexts. It is problematic when these reproductions are assumed to be evidence of a student's development. In Newman and Holzman's terms, this would be the use of a tool-for-result, e.g. a reproduction of a scientific concept used to pass an exam. In contrast, imitation that is deliberate, reflective, and accompanied by some kind of instruction can potentially be transformative. It is the tool *and* result (Newman & Holzman, 1993). Imitation in this way contributes to the internalization of the concepts (see Chapter 1). In the *Thaya* story we can see imitation in the ways in which the students consciously used in their narratives rhetorical devices and strategies they had been exposed to. Many of these devices, e.g. the different types of narrative, were first presented as scientific concepts. Students reflected on the effectiveness of their attempts through the in-class and private editing sessions and refined their understanding of the concepts.

Many of the students had chosen the initial course in the writing program hoping to improve their essay writing skills. Instead, they were introduced, through practice, to some of the scientific concepts of writing non-fiction narratives. Some of these students realized these concepts, including parallelism, could successfully be used with essays, short stories, research papers or newspaper articles. In other words, they were able to transfer the concepts across contexts to solve different writing problems. In this new course Penny introduced them to additional concepts through both practice and theoretical writings.

Writing and construction of non-fiction narratives

Parallelism in everyday and scientific terms

Fortunately, the understanding of writing has moved beyond the idea that it simply encodes speech, that once a person learns a sound–symbol relationship pattern she can write. As Vygotsky stated, 'Written speech is a separate linguistic function, differing from oral speech in both structure and mode of functioning. Even its minimal development requires a high level of abstraction' (1986, pp. 180–181). Thaya's classmates had all studied writing personal narratives or incident-based non-fiction prose in at least four previous courses in the writing program. Most of the students were drawn to the program by their own interest and compulsion to write. Most were intuitively good writers with a sense of what makes a good sentence or paragraph. They had what Vygotsky would call **complexes**, a loosely organized, context-specific variety of everyday concepts that had not been worked into a larger system or consistently and consciously applied. When they started the program, most could not analyze what worked or did not work in a piece of writing when asked to revise. Nor could most of the students repeat a successful or effective sentence or paragraph on demand. They most often depended on 'inspiration' and not conscious control of their writing. They had not developed a systematic set of writing concepts that they could consciously use to analyze and revise their writing across discipline or audience contexts.

Parallelism is one scientific concept writing students had had the opportunity to develop through an instructional unit in the initial course of the program. When asked to explain the appeal of a sentence like 'Brian eats, drinks and dreams rugby' students would talk about the rhythm. Those same students could recite a quick definition of verb as an 'action word' but they could not use both of those bits to explain the rhythm in the sentence – a simple present tense verb repeated three times. Most students had memorized parts of speech definitions at some point in their primary or secondary education. However, those remained just labels or definitions used to complete worksheets or fill in blanks on tests.[7] The knowledge was useless to them in addressing writing problems.

Our work with parallelism illustrated one connection between scientific and everyday concepts. The most efficient way of talking about the structure of parallel series is to use grammatical labels and point out repeating patterns. This is a clear case of the words functioning as part of a system of meaning that Vygotsky associated with scientific concepts. 'Verb' or 'Subject' or 'Object' each calls to mind a set of relationships that are part of the totality of 'grammar' that students might use as they work with their writing. As teachers, we call upon that particular function of the words (as concepts) to help teach parallelism. We also call on the students' everyday concepts, which in this case was the recognition of the curious and effective rhythm of a parallel series that enables students to quote examples from advertising or favorite songs.

Using the names of the grammatical elements, putting different combinations of these elements in certain relationships with one another in the abstract, for example, $[n] + [n] + [n]$ or $[s + v] + [s + v] + [s + v]$,[8] mediated the understanding of how certain rhythms students had experienced were constructed. Students had the opportunity to transform an everyday concept (pleasing rhythms in sentences) into a scientific concept (grammatical elements in repeating patterns). They gained an abstract understanding and ability to consciously apply this knowledge to their writing practice to achieve specific goals.

The following is an instance of how this transformation can happen. Thaya and the rest of his classmates had been introduced to abstract explanations of parallel structures in their introductory writing course. They had all been given a series of practice exercises that included most of the possible combinations of grammatical elements. Students deliberately imitated specific parallel structures of increasing complexity. In fact, some of the students commented as they progressed through the parallelism exercises, 'So *that's* what an adjective is!' The exercises had been critiqued allowing the students to examine the ways in which their own imitations reflected and played with the parameters of the concept. Next, students had been challenged to use parallel structures in their own prose. Over time the students had added parallel series to their repertoire of writing strategies. The everyday experience of a strong rhythmical list had been transformed into a scientific concept the students could use consciously and purposefully to solve a variety of writing problems from efficiently setting out an academic argument to setting up an unexpected image in the mind of a reader. This transformation had been mediated by the use of specific words (grammatical labels for parts of sentences), drawing attention to the phenomenon, imitating it, analyzing it, applying it, and reflecting on the results its use produced in different contexts. Thaya and his classmates could now call on this concept and apply it for a specific reason in their writing. The list of names, 'Pawan, Ravi, Vinoth and Nishanth' at the beginning of Thaya's story is an example of a single element (noun) parallel structure. Thaya has used that to efficiently locate Kajan as a child with friends who play games together in the opening sentence of his piece. The list of imperatives he has Kajan's mother say, while not a perfect parallel series, carries a strong enough rhythm that it works to emphasize the profundity of expectations, '*Go to Canada, study well, succeed in life and bring us to you.*' Neither of these structures was in the first draft of Thaya's story. They appeared after he moved from getting his friend's story down on paper to consciously composing the story for a specific set of readers.

In a formal learning context, the teacher presents the learner with a formal, abstract, objective statement of an everyday concept that the students bring with them to the classroom. In this case, definition of parallel structures is linked with the experience of memorable, rhythmic phrases. The intellectual process that follows as the two manifestations of the concept (i.e. scientific and everyday) interact, takes the learner through a series of transformations as the learner builds a conscious understanding of the patterns and relationships expressed in the concept of parallelism. The learner who has repeated or imitated the words in the scientific definition of the concept gradually begins to use the words with the same meaning as the teacher so that the words comprise similar, if not exactly the same, sets of categories, relationships and implications. Or, as Daniels describes, '...the systematic, organised hierarchical thinking that [Vygotsky] associated with scientific concepts becomes gradually embedded in everyday referents and thus achieves a general sense in the contextual richness of everyday thought' (2001, p. 53). Sometimes teachers refer to this as 'transfer' such as when a student can employ irregular past tense forms or vocabulary in paragraphs unrelated to the original contexts in which they were introduced. This process is mediated by both the students' experience and interactions and the teacher's goal-oriented, structured and conscious presentation and use of the scientific concept.

The teacher used the scientific words to draw students' attention to the link between their experience and the concept, creating a dialectic between the two. 'Spontaneous concepts that confront a deficit of conscious and volitional control find this control in the zone of proximal development, in the cooperation of the child with adults' (Vygotsky, 1986, p. 194). By now, you should begin to see how this relates to the process of a developing ZPD (see Chapter 2). In the *Re-languaging* course, the words 'parallel series' or 'parallelism' were used by the teacher and the students with a full understanding of the scientific concept they referred to, including the references to grammatical structure, grammatical elements and functions, and the possible effects the use of such structures could create for readers.

Translation

Multilingualism and meanings

The second set of everyday/scientific concepts that we will consider is part of those that comprise translation, in particular, those concepts that relate to multilingualism. The *Re-languaging* course that Thaya was enrolled in emerged from the results of a focus group study of bilingual students in the writing program at Penny's university. The demographic of the focus group was representative of the campus. Thaya and most of the other students in the writing program used two or more languages on a regular basis. They were bilingual in that they used a language other than English with family and certain sets of friends. Some students were also biliterate; they could read and write their other language as a result of at least some formal literacy instruction. However, most of the students had not been formally educated in their other languages. They had **everyday concepts** of their other languages as well as everyday concepts of the translation process. Students used language in certain contexts without conscious awareness of the linguistic system. They were not usually conscious of the *how* of their language construction and use. They just 'did it'. They had certain 'rules of thumb' that guided their use of the language but those rules could be unreliable outside of specific contexts. In Thaya's case, he could converse with his friends in Tamil, he could enjoy movies in Tamil, he spoke with his grandmother and with the older men and women who attended his grandmother's meditation practice in Tamil, but his use of Tamil was limited to these contexts.

Thaya and the other students in the class had not consciously addressed the complex issues of culture, translation, cultural accessibility or authenticity before taking the *Re-languaging* course. They had not thought about what happens when they took an incident that had occurred in Chinese, Urdu, Polish or French and constructed a first-person narrative of that incident in English for English readers. Vygotsky wrote in *Thought and Word*,

> The structure of speech does not simply mirror the structure of thought; that is why words cannot be put on by thought like a ready-made garment. Thought undergoes many changes as it turns into speech. It does not merely find expression in speech; it finds its reality and form. (1986, p. 219)

Most of the students thought of translation as merely putting on another 'ready-made garment', not creating a new reality and form. The process of change from thought to written word is a complex, cognitive/emotional one, further complicated when the change crosses linguistic and cultural borders. It requires that a person solve the many problems of identifying physical, sensual and emotional meanings in the story and transforming those meanings into a form that both the writer and the readers can comprehend. The everyday concepts that most of the students relied on to move their narratives from the original language to English solved only superficial problems of meaning. The everyday concepts did not help students when they tried to express the same *sense* (see Chapter 3) of a word or phrase. They did not help students express how the original story was so funny, poignant or tense. They did not help students make decisions about setting or character details or why those details were even necessary. They did not help students recreate the story so the reader could experience it as an insider. As the students explored the issues they found, for example, that substituting 'little brother' for 'thambi' simply did not work.

In the story *Kadase Naal* Thaya had to re-present and create understanding and empathy for people involved in an incident which occurred in a language, a time and a place unfamiliar and perhaps incomprehensible to most of his readers. Thaya experienced his stories in Tamil, the language he and his friend Kajan most often used together. But he had to produce his stories in English because his potential readers read English and because his university course was in English. Thaya and the other students in the class had depended on their everyday concepts of translation to write narratives. Sometimes these narratives worked and sometimes they fell flat because the students had no reliable, systematic way to analyze what worked when they crossed linguistic and cultural borders. In order to write across their languages and cultures confidently and consistently, Thaya and his classmates needed to develop scientific concepts in translation.

Penny had worked out a hierarchical relationship among the concepts she had identified as critical to help students who wished to deliberately introduce and use aspects of their other language(s) and culture(s) into their English-language narratives. These elements were systematically introduced. She began with culture and related it to stereotypes in order to develop students' understanding of the concepts of culture beyond the 'foods, festivals and costumes' level. Students engaged in discussions about the implications of using physical descriptions, representing accents in dialogue, showing gestures and using activities.

Next, she introduced a typology of narrative. Most of the students in the course had worked exclusively in first-person narratives. The typology introduced them to other categorizations of narrative, making first-person or ontological narratives only one element in a larger system of narratives, all of which might be used to accomplish a writer's goals. Examining the characteristics of the different categories opened up students' thinking to consciously include audience as part of the conceptual system. Claudia's suggestion to include more detail about the setting of Thaya's story reflected this awareness, as did Theo's suggestion to include something of the public narrative.

Translation was introduced as a transformation that included the requirement of both linguistic and emotional equivalency. Most of the time students searched for ideal words that had identical meanings in both English and the students' other language. The students would become frustrated when the precise words eluded them. This was especially true when dealing with humour, shyness, shame, embarrassment, pride or fear – that is, emotions. Students read academic discussions – symbolic mediational tools – of culture, narrative and translation. They participated in class discussions about the readings where they would refer to their own experiences to make sense of the conceptual discussions. They practiced the conscious application of these concepts to their writing-in-progress in assigned exercises that were shared and critiqued in class. Towsey and MacDonald (2009) described this process of developing scientific concepts as '...the developing partnership of the ability to generalize and to abstract systematically, to make consistent use of these cognitive functions that have grown out of the earlier prototype versions of these abilities' (p. 237). The process was mediated by the language, the reading, the languaging, and the exercises.

According to Daniels (1996, p. 11), 'Scientific concepts are formed on the basis of systematic, organized and hierarchical thinking,' characteristics that can be associated with formal instruction in an educational setting. Wardekker (1998) described this process of moving from everyday to scientific concepts in terms of reflection and practice. He wrote powerfully about the dialogic quality of the relationship between everyday and scientific concepts rooted in the process of becoming conscious of decisions and actions taken.

> For Vygotsky, consciousness is an activity: becoming con-scious of something. I think this comes close to what we normally call *reflection*, except that in the context of

Vygotsky's theory, the *con* in *conscious* should be taken quite literally ('knowing together'): It points to the contribution of other people in this activity. (Wardekker, 1998, p. 144)

After Thaya read the required *Recovering the Original* by Thiong'o (1986, 2004), he developed a consciousness of the differences in the experience of meanings between his two languages. The class discussion of the reading added to this growing understanding of the relationship between the language in which an experience occurred and the language in which it was written. The class requirement that students respond to these weekly readings added yet another opportunity for the interaction of the scientific conceptualization of meaning and the everyday concept of meaning in translation. For Thaya, this combination of activities produced an 'Aha!' moment which he shared with Penny when he came into her office with his reading journal and announced, 'I need to write this in Tamil first. Thiong'o's right. The story is in Tamil. I have to write it in Tamil.'

In other words, the abstract ideas, the scientific concepts, organized and presented in the course were transformed as students reflected on their own related experiences. A combination of the class discussion and the reading journal had helped Thaya to language (see Chapter 3) the connection he had made between Thiong'o's decision to write in Gikuyu and the trouble Thaya himself was having composing his own stories or those of his friend in English. Thiong'o had written, 'What happens to this original text, since in fact it exists only in the mind and it is not written down? It is lost, and we can access it only through English' (2004, p. 106). This insight had given Thaya permission to go back to the original Tamil where Thaya felt he 'understood the core of the story.' Thaya wrote this in his reading journal and reiterated it in his discussion with Penny. In both contexts, Thaya made use of the concepts of ontological and public narratives, linguistic equivalency and cultural context, to mediate the connections between his storying experience and his everyday concept of translation. He added his observation from working from the Tamil version of the story to the first English draft that 'Tamil seems to be much better for expressing emotions than English.'

This observation made reference not only to Thaya's observation about his developing conceptual understanding of his two languages as he consciously worked with meaning and not just words, but also to a related concept, emotional equivalency. Thaya had read and participated in discussions about *Bilingual Selves* by Pavlenko (2006) and *Language and Emotional Experience: The Voice of Translingual Memoir* by Besemeres (2006) – texts that Penny had included in the course. These are scholarly writings that discuss in scientific conceptual terms the phenomenon of experiencing life in two languages. Besemeres explored the relationship between the meanings associated with an emotional label in one language and the meanings associated with the label in a different language. In her article, Besemeres argued that the emotional experience represented by the words are not simply transferable across the linguistic and cultural landscapes. Rather we must look for equivalents between the two experiences and work to find the closest linguistic equivalencies. This both acknowledged the students' experiences as they struggled to retain the authenticity of an experience, e.g. the humour or the pathos of a parental spat or the eyes of a beggar child outside a closed car window, and provided them with a conscious, systematic way of going beyond a bilingual dictionary.

The class followed a similar pattern of engagement with these concepts as they had with the Thiong'o readings. The students read and responded to the scientific concepts first in their reading journals. In class discussions they continued this interaction, drawing again and again on their everyday experiences to explicate, illustrate and explore equivalency. They were assigned exercises that challenged them to apply this concept to their own writing and then shared and discussed those. The series of interactions between the everyday and scientific concepts in which Thaya and his classmates engaged supported the development of the concepts of bilingual experience, of emotion and expression of emotions. Thaya expressed this understanding when he talked about the reason he chose not to translate *chellam* in the class editing session and Ana agreed with him. Thaya had imitated Thiong'o's, Dorfman's (2004) and others' use of words in the original language in their narratives. Discussions such as the one Thaya participated in with Ana, Vibhuti and Rob were part of that transformative imitation process.

Thaya now had a way to recognize, talk about and deal with a writing problem – the emotions and their expressions in Tamil and English were not the same.

Narrative and context across languages and cultures

Related to the challenge of moving across languages, Thaya and the other students had to develop an understanding of the role of context in their narratives. On a simple level, context would help explain the meanings of the 'foreign' words and phrases they included in the narratives. On a more complex level, in order to establish emotional equivalency, students needed to create a more detailed setting (physically and emotionally) in order to nudge readers into a more authentic interpretation of what they read, to ensure a more culturally, emotionally and linguistically authentic reading. It meant helping the reader to have a Tamil experience rather than a Canadian experience in the proximity of Sri Lanka. This meant the writers needed to develop their concepts of narrative and of culture. Although narrative and culture are considered separately in the following analysis, it is important to note that students struggled with the consequences of this interactive relationship as they searched for equivalent linguistic expressions for the incidents and settings in their stories.

Creating context is one of the biggest challenges beginning writers face. Thaya and his classmates had previously written their stories without reference to the meanings different contexts might imply. Without being aware of how the languages and contexts differ, writers cannot make decisions about the kinds of details they need to include in order to present the writer's experience. In the course readings, two chapters from Mona Baker's book (2006) were included as one expression of the scientific concepts of context in narrative. In these two chapters, Baker presented a typology of narrative based on Somers and Gibson's (Somers, 1992, 1997; Somers & Gibson, 1994) work. She presented definitions of ontological, public, discipline and meta-narratives with examples of how they work or do not work across languages. This typology presented an excellent example of the systematic, hierarchical set of relationships Vygotsky described as scientific concepts. Baker used the words associated with narrative, language and culture in specific ways to talk about these concepts. When students first read these chapters, they often accurately reproduced the definitions but struggled to see the relevance or application to their own writing. The everyday and the scientific remained separate.

One exercise that mediated students' understanding required that they examine their own drafts for reference to ontological, public, discipline or meta-narratives. Reviewing these in class prompted vigorous discussion as to whether certain details referenced ontological or public narratives, whether it was a public or discipline narrative or perhaps a meta-narrative and what purpose that reference served in the story. These discussions forced the students to isolate, abstract and relate a particular detail to the entire conceptual system of Baker's narrative typologies.

This, in turn, produced discussions on just what kind of detail or references a writer can use with their imagined or intended audience. This brought culture and stereotypes back into the discussion. The discussion of building context with detail and background information created a tension, a dialectic, with the students' concepts of storytelling and background or context. When did the context-building get in the way of the story? How do you know? How do you find the balance?

Theo's comment, 'Maybe you need to give us a little more of the background, you know, the public narrative' directly referenced the concept and its relationship with the cognitive problem to be solved. Theo's comment also showed how the understanding he and his classmates had established allowed them to reflect on, analyze and propose a solution for a writer's dilemma that was not specific to one concept. Theo proposed adding detail about the public narrative of Sri Lanka's civil war as a way to both physically and emotionally build a context readers could empathize with. It also opened a discussion of how much Thaya could assume most of his readers would know of this public narrative, referencing the concept of audience. Claudia added to this with her suggestion 'Yeah, and more about what the place looks like. I think it needs more detail about the streets and the house, maybe. I can't quite picture it yet.' Here, Claudia used her own experience to connect with the concept of audience and how an audience builds images from their own experiences and what they need to build a more authentic image, a Sri Lankan and not a Canadian image.

The problem was transformed from finding interesting details to add to the story that would hold a reader's attention, to one of considering what a reader needed to know to understand and empathize with the motivation of Kajan's mother and father. This discussion had transformed and now referenced a deeper understanding of the meanings of culture, of the complexity of narrative and how readers construct meanings from the details the writer chose to provide.

Dialectic

The writing class activities offered students the opportunity to step back and examine, in order to become conscious of and regulate the process they used to construct narratives for an audience. Through these activities, Thaya discovered that the story had to be in Tamil before it could be in English and that the Tamil language could be included in the narrative. Along with the reading and discussion of Pavlenko and Bessemere, an additional activity was assigned. In the activity, students had to use a word, phrase or complete sentence from the original language of the story and make it comprehensible in an English version. They could use a parenthetical translation, a repetition in English before or after the non-English word or phrase, or build a context that would make the meaning evident, much as Thaya had done with his use of *Amma* and *Appa*. This exercise, along with the other activities, mediated the bidirectional movement John-Steiner *et al.* (1998) described between everyday and scientific concepts (in this case, narrative and translation):

> Vygotsky described the interfunctional reorganization in concept formation as a process in which scientific concepts grow downward from the domain of conscious awareness and volition 'into the domain of the concrete, into the domain of personal experience' (p. 220), whereas everyday concepts, which begin in the concrete and empirical, 'move toward the higher characteristics of concepts, toward conscious awareness and volition.' (p. 128)

Thus, Thaya's everyday concepts of narrative and translation had interacted with the scientific concepts that Penny had presented through readings, mini-lectures and students' languaging. Both the everyday and scientific concepts were transformed in the process. Thaya became conscious of *how* he was making decisions about writing, about recreating experiences for readers unfamiliar with either the language or the culture in which the original experience had occurred. As a result, he consciously made specific choices about the details, actions, dialogue and language he used to express Kajan's experience.

Current controversies

Practical experience also shows that direct teaching of concepts is impossible and fruitless. A teacher who tries to do this usually accomplishes nothing but empty verbalism, a parrotlike repetition of words by the child, simulating a knowledge of the corresponding concepts but actually covering up a vacuum. (Vygotsky, 1986, p. 150)

Teaching with concepts: Why, what, when, how?

Why?

A concept-based approach to teaching is an issue that extends beyond the boundaries of second language learning and teaching. Why teach concepts for complex skill-based practices is an open discussion. Does everyone need to know the concepts that govern arithmetic operations in order to keep a monthly budget; the principles of chemistry, physics and engineering in order to drive a car; the concepts of tense and voice in order to carry on workplace communications?

Vygotsky was clear that both scientific and everyday concepts had roles to play in student learning. Linking the scientific and everyday concepts led the development of conceptual thinking – thinking that allowed students to face any number of novel problems and mentally work through possible solutions. Development might be domain-specific to begin with but the cognitive functions resulting from that development could transfer into other domains. The scientific concept, in the form of a properly reproduced definition, has often become the object of our language teaching. This contrasts sharply with the cultivation of the relationship between everyday and scientific concepts that Vygotsky emphasized.

Memorizing rules and definitions rather than nurturing conceptual thinking has often become the goal for both students and teachers.

It is important to ask questions about the everyday concepts students bring to a learning context – from experience outside of school or from other learning contexts – because the school and the teacher face the challenge of establishing and guiding an educational dialogue between those everyday and scientific concepts. This is part of the *why* that Vygotsky addressed in *Thought and Language*:

> School instruction induces the generalizing kind of perception and thus plays a decisive role in making the child conscious of his own mental processes. Scientific concepts, with their hierarchical system of interrelation, seem to be the medium within which awareness and mastery first develop, to be transferred later to other concepts and other areas of thought. Reflective consciousness comes to the child through the portals of scientific concepts. (1986, p. 171)

Often, students bring either from outside the classroom or from another classroom 'simple word meanings at a very basic level of generalization' (Haenen *et al.*, 2003, p. 247) and the teacher has the responsibility for finding and using appropriate mediational means to employ those everyday concepts. Scientific concepts and an educational dialogue are two of the most important mediational means. However, why we would teach concepts is not so clear in an age that emphasizes accountability and gatekeeping through high-stakes standardized testing. The issue is further complicated by controversy over *what* to teach.

What?

Language learning and teaching has been primarily organized around skills and the acquisition of vocabulary, syntax and knowledge of different sets of rules. Attempts at **concept-based learning** and teaching (Brooks *et al.*, in press; Gibbons, 1991, 2003; Negueruela, 2008; Negueruela & Lantolf, 2005) do not fit the traditional curricular designs nor the assessment practices associated with them. Negueruela and Lantolf (2005) made the point for texts used to teach Spanish (and we would add English) that the grammatical explanations 'consist by and large of incomplete and unsystematic rules of thumb' (Negueruela & Lantolf, 2005, para. 15). These rules of thumb are much closer to the everyday concepts that are grounded in specific contexts and often fail learners in different contexts adding to their frustrations.

Although the field of Cognitive Linguistics approaches the study and research of language through concepts, the transformation of those concepts to practical teaching and learning materials teachers and students might want to use has been minimal. Halliday's (2002a, 2002b) work with Systemic Functional Linguistics has perhaps contributed the most to attempts to teach and learn language conceptually. But most of this work concentrated on teaching students specific genre rules. This keeps the focus on the performance of the task rather than on the dialogue between everyday and scientific concepts.

Another contentious area in both the *what* and *how* involves the use of students' first languages (L1s). In second language education, the L1 has often been understood in terms of its interference with rather than its possible contributions to L2 learning. Instead, we could ask what everyday L1 concepts a student might bring as resources to mediate L2 concepts.

Characterizing an L1 as an interfering factor has contributed to the political decisions such as the one in California to limit bilingual education in favor of English-only education.[9] In contrast, Cummins (2000, 2001, 2006) and others have argued that the L1 directly contributes to the learning and development of the L2 and thus should be recognized, used and developed along with the L2.

When?

The confusion of which language concepts along with the pressure to accurately measure language competency or proficiency have muddled the conversation and tangled it up with another issue – when.

Vygotsky did not discount the importance of minimum levels of biological maturity including ability to attend to something and memory. However, he disagreed with Piaget[10] and others who based instruction on levels of maturity. Vygotsky postulated a relationship between everyday and scientific that moved cognitive development along. Learning was not laid over a foundation of maturation but instead it was the systematic interaction (or educational dialogue) that developed memory and deliberate systematic, abstract thinking. Vygotsky's writing does not answer the question with regard to learning another language, although he did differentiate between the way a first and a subsequent language was learned, arguing for a much more conceptual approach with a second or foreign language. But what does that mean in terms of the content and the activities a teacher uses? Does it mean to teach students the concepts of a language from the first day they step into a second or foreign language classroom? Or does it mean to introduce concepts once the student has a rudimentary vocabulary and control of syntax? Can a teacher use the same approach for students at age 5, age 15 or 50? Will such an approach apply to students without literacy in a first language, children or adults? These questions prompt passionate discussions but few conclusions.

How?

Interpretations of Vygotsky have produced various classroom practices centered on discovery or inquiry methods, communicative and even immersion methodologies in language teaching. The central criticism of these approaches is that students, without explicit mediation from teachers or more knowledgeable peers, will form their own, often mistaken, conceptualizations. Stensenko and Arievitch (2002) have argued that students need help to take the implicit rules of language they 'pick up' and develop a coherent system they can apply in contrast with Krashen's argument against direct instruction and the constructivist approach that privileges student discovery. Karpov (2003) provided a provocative critique of discovery learning that may prompt teachers to reconsider their use of this technique. He argued, among other points, that students often discover misconceptions and are not provided with appropriate mediational means to test and correct their conclusions.

Examining the development of concepts creates similar dilemmas for researchers. We too often study the end product, the definition of a concept that a learner can produce but not the thinking that produced that definition. Research methods that focus on collecting and conducting microgenetic analyses of observations, audio and video recordings of student activities and discussions offer the most promising way to capture this dynamic process and better inform our teaching/learning decisions.

Defining and implementing more concept-based language instruction is challenging as discussed above. Moving away from a strictly skill-based approach to language learning means that we would: (1) reconceptualize language as a meaning-making tool that can be acquired through use and explicit instruction; (2) redesign curricula to include attention to concepts; (3) reconceptualize the role of L1 in learning another language; (4) educate teachers to think in terms of concepts in addition to skills; and (5) encourage the development of curricula and materials that reflect attention to concepts and skills.

Including concept-based instruction has implications for teacher preparation and development, for material development, for curriculum design and for assessment. We do not expect these controversies to be settled easily or quickly. We do hope that they will be discussed, debated and investigated by teachers and researchers together.

Key research relevant to scientific and everyday concepts

Gibbons traced the teacher's deliberate and careful support of student language from everyday to scientific in a primary ESL class in Australia. Gibbons analyzed the dialogue between children and the dialogue between the teacher and children to show how the students changed their use of language. Although Gibbons did not explicitly address the interaction between everyday and scientific concepts, her choice of language interactions from peer–peer, teacher–peer interactions and student writing showed this interaction as it occurred in classroom dialogue.

Gibbons, P. (2003). Teacher interactions with ESL students in a content-based classroom. *TESOL Quarterly*, 37(2), 247–273.

Northedge modeled the teacher's role as 'discourse guide' in this reflection on and discussion of teaching and designing Open University courses. He showed how a student may respond when confronted first with the scientific concepts and the language in which they are expressed. Working from that initial narrative, he showed how a teacher, the materials, assignments and responses the teacher provided mediated a student's participation in specialized discourse communities through the development of scientific concepts particular to the discourse of the discipline.

Northedge, A. (2002). Organizing excursions into specialist discourse communities: A sociocultural account of university teaching. In G. Wells & G. Claxton (Eds), *Learning for life in the 21st century* (pp. 252–264). Oxford: Blackwell Publishing.

This microgenetic analysis of two university-level students of French focused on how the materials, the students' languaging and the researchers' questions mediated the development of the concept of voice. The students moved from 'rules of thumb' they had memorized to the (mostly) successful ability to consciously choose an appropriate voice for the meaning they wished to construct. The analysis showed the interactive development of everyday and scientific concepts.

Brooks, L., Swain, M., Lapkin, S. & Knouzi, I. (2010). Mediating between scientific and spontaneous concepts through languaging. *Language Awareness*, 19(2), 89–110.

Although this next article did not directly deal with language teaching and learning, it provided an accessible and sophisticated explication of Vygotsky's classification of concept development from heaps, chains, complexes and pseudoconcepts to scientific concepts. Fleer's observations of the children, their interactions with various mediational means and their dialogues with one another and the teacher showed the role that deliberate teacher mediation played in helping students develop scientific concepts.

Fleer, M. (2009). Understanding the dialectical relations between everyday concept and scientific concepts within play-based programs. *Research in Science Education, 39,* 281–306.

In contrast with the Fleer article, Shepardson found that even with the best intentions, without problems to solve or appropriate teacher (and peer) mediation, concept development did not occur. The research provided fascinating examples of the *possibilities* or affordances that well-designed school activities can provide and the important role a teacher can play.

Shepardson, D. P. (1999). Learning science in a first grade science activity: A Vygotskian perspective. *Science Education, 83,* 621–638.

Questions to explore for research and pedagogy

1. Trace the genesis of one of your own concepts from everyday to scientific (or vice versa) in teaching, in writing, in research or in language learning.

2. Consider a class you have taught, observed or have been a student in. How can you recognize everyday and scientific concepts in use? When have you noticed and appreciated when a student has begun to use scientific concept terms in the way that you use them?

3. How does a teacher facilitate the movements between everyday and scientific concepts? What is the relationship between these movements and the ZPD?

4. What do you consider to be scientific concepts in language learning and teaching?

5. Other than the internalization of everyday and scientific concepts what else may have mediated Thaya's development as a writer?

6. Is teaching based on concepts always appropriate or necessary? When would it be appropriate? When would it not be appropriate?

7. How would teacher education, both pre-service and inservice, have to change to support concept-based instruction?

8. What other SCT concepts might be identified in the *Thaya* narrative? (See the Key Terms at the beginning of each chapter for SCT concepts.)

Notes

1. Students learned to write single and multiple-element parallel series in their initial writing course. This means they could effectively compose sentences such as *John, Farah, Jacques and Roberta joked, composed, quarrelled, rehearsed and performed a one-act play for Nuit Blanche.* Or *The Conservative party advocates a balanced budget and tax cuts while the Liberal party advocates a balanced budget and tax reforms.*

2. Baker, M. (2006). *Translation and conflict: A narrative account.* London: Routledge. Students had read two of the chapters that set out a typology of narrative and the roles of the four types of narrative in translation. Baker named (1) ontological or personal stories we tell ourselves (2) public or narratives shared by a group or community (3) discipline or the stories scholars construct about their field and what they study—quantum particles or graffiti artists and (4) metanarrative or a more encompassing contemporary narrative where individuals are participants.

3. This is a draft; no changes have been made.

4. All names of class members are pseudonyms except for Thaya.

5. Bernstein has developed this idea in his work on vertical and horizontal discourses (Bernstein, 1999).

6. According to John-Steiner (1985) concepts can also be visual (think of artists, photographers), auditory (think of musicians) or a combination (think of film-makers or choreographers).

7. It is interesting to note that for the one or two international students in the course who had studied English as a foreign language, the relationship between scientific and

everyday concepts was different. They had the scientific concept but their everyday experiences with the rhythm parallel structures produced was not well developed. In this case, just as Vygotsky described, the scientific concept enabled these students to develop the everyday concepts.

8. N=noun, s=subject, v=verb.

9. In 1998 California voters passed Proposition 227 that mandated all English language learners be put in English-language immersion classrooms with the goal of moving into regular English-only classrooms at the end of one year. The program was meant to replace bilingual programs in the public schools.

10. Vygotsky had the opportunity to read Piaget's work long before most North Americans. Chapter 2 of Vygotsky's book, *Thought and Language*, served as the introduction to the Russian translation of Piaget's first two books, *Le langage et la pensée chez l'enfant* and *Le jugement et le rasisonnment chez l'enfant*. The books were not published in English until 1959 and 1969, respectively.

5

Grace: The effect of affect

Key SCT tenets related to the interrelatedness of emotion and cognition

- Thinking and feeling are integrally related. Separating intellect from affect restricts understanding the fullness of life

- Learning in the ZPD affects all aspects of the learner – acting, thinking and feeling (Wells, 1999b, p. 331)

- Emotional responses are mediated by culture

Key SCT tenet related to regulation

- The trajectory from other-regulation to self-regulation is not one way and permanent. Particular contexts can return us to other-regulation after a period of self-regulation and vice versa

Setting of this narrative

Languages: Greek and English

Context: Over time (ontogenesis) – childhood to adulthood in Greece and Ontario

Key terms in this chapter

(see glossary at the back of this textbook)

Affect/Cognition

Regulation

Perezhivanie

Interrelatedness of cognition and emotion

Introduction

When Grace participated in the two-hour interview from which this narrative is drawn, she had just turned 50 but her reflections cross all stages of her life (see timeline). Grace's emotions with respect to her languages were not the focus of the interview when it was conducted. However, when the authors of this textbook began to look for a story demonstrating the interrelatedness of **cognition** and emotion as an important SCT concept, i.e. **affect** as key in the development of mind, Grace's story came back to us as a particularly rich demonstration. Evident in the narrative is Grace's frequent anxiety when using each of her languages, English and Greek. Grace also introduces the strategy of silence – when emotion is so strongly felt that language participation ceases.

The affect (emotion) and cognition link is strongly supported by Vygotsky and forms the key concept of this chapter. Two other concepts relevant to SCT and closely allied to emotion are also discussed. The first, regulation, often referred to by Vygotsky and the second, **identity**, alluded to, but not named by Vygotsky, are evidenced in Grace's narrative. Regulation refers to monitoring, controlling, or evaluating; Lantolf and Thorne (2006) used the term interchangeably with mediation in some instances. Self-regulation, considered an advanced stage of development, refers to the ability to monitor oneself. When very young, we all are first object-regulated, and then other-regulated as our caregivers model for us and tell us what is right and wrong, do-able and not do-able. As we mature, we move towards self-regulation – that is, the locus of control is transferred to ourselves (see also Chapter 3). We noticed that Grace, in many instances, seemed to be regulated by others with respect to her perception of her language performance.

In the second part of this chapter (the theoretical discussion) you will read that other-regulation and self-regulation are not permanent states. That is, with a change in context or increasing complexity of a known context, we once again need to seek the help of others (other-regulation).

The third concept evidenced in this story is identity which appears as multiple, multifaceted and shifting. Only some of Grace's multiple identities are discussed explicitly in this story but her movement among identities is referred to often. Note how she affiliates herself at various times as learner, as teacher, as sister, as daughter, as mother of bilingual sons, and more, and how these identifications relate to language issues. Note also how she is ascribed affiliations by others.

At the beginning of the interview, when asked as a matter of record what her mother tongue was, Grace replied, '*I don't know. You tell me, is it English or Greek?*' From that moment, it was clear that Grace's story would be an interesting account of hybridity of language and culture.

Grace: The effect of affect

Chronology		
0–24	24–44	44–50 yrs old
Small town in Canada	Greece	Big city in Canada
Spoke Greek at home	Taught EFL	Attended graduate school
Greek school on Sat.	Spoke English at school	Taught ESL
English at school	Spoke Greek to her husband	Spoke Greek and English to family
	Spoke English to her children	

The teacher had just shown a picture and asked the class what sort of thing the people in the picture were eating. Eight-year-old Grace said, 'They're eating salad'. 'And what sort of things do you put in a salad?' asked the teacher.

I was all excited and I said 'aggouri' and she said 'What?' and everyone started laughing and I realized I didn't know the English name for cucumber. I went home crying. It was so embarrassing. I was just very mortified.

They stay with you, those moments, don't they?

Yes, that word – aggouri. Everyone laughed

Grace went on to say that as a result of that incident, she went to the supermarket with her mother and made sure to learn the name and correct pronunciation of cucumber and other similar items.

Grace explained that the matter of language dominance has been confusing in her case. When she lived in Greece, which was from her mid-twenties until her mid-forties [see timeline] she still felt that English was her dominant language but it was a special kind of English—classroom English.

That's the sort of English the people that I chummed around with used. In Greece, talking with friends like me – expats – we would get together for coffee and we used to laugh at how our English had deteriorated. I mean we would use phrases from the other language and say "My God that's terrible!"

When she moved back to Canada in her mid-40's, Grace enrolled in a graduate program in education where she became painfully aware of the gaps in her knowledge of English, particularly academic English. She was not familiar with terms like "literature reviews" nor with a lot of the specialized vocabulary that her classmates used and her professors expected. She was "*too embarrassed*" to ask her classmates for help and so she attended some writing workshops because she was "*scared*" about her writing.

My first month in the grad program I was in a terrible state. I think it all clicked when I presented a proposal for a research paper. I really worked hard on it. Initially, the professor had thought I couldn't handle the writing but I guess I really knew what I wanted to do. When I got the mark back she said she was so impressed that she wanted to keep the paper as a model for future students in the course. That's when I realized that English once again had really become dominant.

How did you know she had thought that you couldn't do it?

She told me! She told me when she handed it back.

And you were assuming that it was because of your language or because you didn't seem acculturated to graduate work?

*Maybe a lot of people thought that I was Greek – you know **Greek** Greek – because I had been away for so long and you know maybe it was my accent. In all those years in Greece I think my accent [in English] changed. I never spoke [English] like this and maybe everyone thought "she couldn't do it because English isn't her L1". And I was also very conscious when I had to make my first presentation. Wow!*

Conscious of language?

Everything.

Do you remember specifically what you worried about?

*I was trying to find the vocabulary that would be at **their** level. Because it was far different.*

So you wanted to up it a bit?

Yes, and I'm still doing that. I had come back one summer and someone was speaking English and I was just so impressed. Wow! and then when I sat down to think about it, I realized that I used to speak like that at one point but then if you don't use the language at that level for 20 years – I mean it's there, but it has to be brought back to the surface and I'm still conscious of that all the time. Yes, I needed the...the encouragement from my profs. Maybe I was being really strict with myself but I could see the other foreign students managing and I thought: "What's wrong with me?" Maybe I was harsh on myself.

But I think a language teacher is more aware and you're thinking "My God, what are people going to think?" And my brothers laugh and they say "You sound like a teacher" because after all these years it was just school English that I spoke and it's a different kind of English.

*With Greek, it's funny. I grew up in a household where we used Greek—my father insisted we speak only Greek. At 16 years old you don't really think a lot about language. I thought I was fluent in the language and when I went for the first time [to Greece] it was a real eye-opener—I was not fluent! I was using Greek that was more than 40 years old and saying things my Grandma would have said and again I became more conscious and I really made efforts so that I could speak like **them** and learn the vocabulary. When I moved to Greece, I realized just how proficient I wasn't. I couldn't understand a TV show or a news report and I really had to work at it.*

And you worked at it by yourself?

By myself. But I had friends – you know I would say to my husband "If I'm not saying something correctly please correct me". Even today I am still asking "Is this appropriate in this context?"

In Greek?

Yes. All the time.

So is it more related to register?

Register and vocabulary, appropriateness – a lot of things. You think you grow up with the language and you know it but you don't, and now I'm watching my children because I am interested in their code switching and I can see that now English is their dominant language and I'm hearing very little Greek at this time. Only if they're very excited or they want to tease one another, but everything else is English and about 4 years ago it was the complete opposite.

Now for them I don't know when things clicked. I think for the little guy...the first time he ever did a presentation in high school and I asked him how it went, he said "It was good. People understood" so I think they are very comfortable with English now. But I wasn't with Greek and I wasn't with English when I came back.

I know that my accent is funny when I speak English and I'm trying to figure it out and I'm wondering is it because I was listening to British tapes all the time? Well it doesn't sound Canadian.

Is this feedback you get from people?

Yes, my brothers.

Grace spoke of how her inability to time her interruptions appropriately in English caused her grief and embarrassment (and embarrassment to her brothers).

Greek has almost a non-existent wait time between turns and when I was in that environment I was so often left out of the conversation. So you have to pick up on cues. What you have to do is as soon as you think someone is going to stop you jump right in. Coming back to Canada I do that because you get into the habit and I realize that sometime it comes out a bit rude. The wait time isn't the same—and I want to say 'excuse me'.

I didn't realize it but I had come over one summer and I was with my brother at an office and the woman there had her head bowed. She was writing. Now in Greece you just say "Can I have my papers?" and I did that and my brother said: "You're supposed to wait until the woman raises her head and says 'Yes, can I help you?'" He said to me: "Do you know how it seemed to her? I'm embarrassed."

Grace, I know you are ambivalent about naming your mother tongue, but do you consider yourself a native speaker of English?

I thought I did but then I realized that so many things in discourse are cultural and that's where I'm not coming across as a native speaker. I am very conscious of that and sometimes I say "Okay, count – count to 3. And then say something." Or when I go to the front office and I want to ask one of the girls something, I say: "Stop, think, and then speak".

And I use my hands a lot which I get from Greek. My brothers say: "Sit on your hands when you're with us because it's embarrassing". But when I go there [Greece] I have to use those skills or nobody will pay attention.

But then they [in Greece] hear my accent and **they'll** say "she's not one of us so let's not pay attention".

At this point, Grace surprised me.

You know, now that you've asked me, and I am thinking about it, I would consider English my mother language. That's the language I've been educated in and the language I work in and the language I communicate most in, but there are so many times when I am conscious I am not using it properly.

I asked Grace if she were able to write in Greek.

I haven't had formal instruction in Greek and Greek writing uses a lot of pompousness and it's not part of my character. I can't write that way and I can't speak that way either and I think if I were to write in Greek I would have to be retrained. I can write a letter or a note or send an e-mail but I can't do a piece of writing...no. When I am in the classroom, English is my language but when it's for emotions or feelings, it's Greek. I can't express myself in English.

The only really unequivocally positive feedback with respect to language that Grace included in our interview was proffered by a friend of Grace's, a native speaker of Greek.

I have a good friend who is a doctor and I really admire her. She is very knowledgeable, very educated. We were talking and she said: "You know, your Greek is really very good." I said: "But when I speak you can tell I'm not a native speaker" and she said "You can tell that you know what you're saying and the way you express yourself and everything is just wonderful."

When you get someone you admire saying that to you I think it encourages you because there was a long time in Greece where I never spoke. I would go out with a group of people and I thought their Greek was so beautiful that I just wouldn't speak at all."

You were silent?

Yes. And they would say, "Don't you understand?" But I did understand. I was just silent.

My husband has never made references to the fact that my Greek is not as good or whatever. He likes my Greek – but other people would joke about it.

Continuing briefly on this path of positive evaluations of Grace's language skills, Grace noted that her mother, who had remained in Canada during the 20 years that Grace lived in Greece, appreciated Grace's modern vocabulary. Back when her mother lived in Greece, there were no words for washing machine and other modern technology, but Grace knew these words and her mother heard them from Grace and used them herself. So there were three (remembered) tributes to Grace's bilingual skills provided by her friend, her mother, and her husband.

Grace is a highly experienced ESL teacher in Canada. I asked her if, and how, her own struggles in both English and Greek were reflected in her professional practice. We had discussed how most of Grace's anxieties were related to vocabulary and pragmatics and that nothing about grammar had come up in our interview. Yet language teachers spend an inordinate amount of time on grammar and relatively little time on explicit pragmatic instruction. Grace revealed that she did indeed share her difficulties with her students – particularly her belief that grammar mistakes often do not impede meaning making but that pragmatics really affect how you seem to others. *"How you come across is really important to me and I stress this with my students."*

She recalled how her father had always seemed so rude to her friends when they phoned her. He did not accept the pragmatic conventions of saying 'hello' and 'goodbye' so he would say *"'not here' and then hang up"*. Grace contrasted her father, who did not care about changing his behaviour to suit the new language and culture with her mother, her brothers, and certainly Grace herself, who cared a great deal about conforming to the cultural norms.

We had a brief discussion about Greek classes which Grace attended as a child on Saturday mornings.

The teacher used to pull our ears and rap our knuckles. I hated, HATED the language.

Because you didn't like the teacher?

Yes. And he would teach us to conjugate verbs. What we needed was to be able to talk to our parents. When we got into high school we needed more vocabulary to be able to talk to them. And he wasn't giving it to us. I mean, more abstract things couldn't be explained to my parents...

When I asked Grace about whether she continued to have goals in English, she mentioned wait time, adopting new idioms, and her accent. When I asked what she meant by accent, she said: "I want to sound like *you*".

*****

In these next sections we will discuss the centrality of the social to emotion, to regulation and to identity. Although these three dimensions are difficult to tease apart, we will do so here for clarity. First we look at emotion, then regulation, and finally identity.

Emotions

Perezhivanie: [Russian] [*perezhiVAniye*] experience as lived through the emotions; affectivity.

Every idea contains some remnant of the individual's affective relationship to that aspect of reality which it represents (Vygotsky, 1934, p. 50).

Emotions are socially constructed acts of communication that can mediate one's thinking, behaviour and goals (Imai, 2010).

Emotions are attributes of the lived body in its social situatedness. So while there are physiological responses that are similar across people such as the constriction that causes blushing when one feels shame, the *stimulus* for that constriction (if and under what conditions it will happen) will be socially mediated. What has a particular society construed as shameful? Nudity? Drawing attention to oneself in public? Failing to honour an elder? A Vygotskian understanding of emotion emphasizes this social construction of emotions and their implication in cognition. Thinking and feeling are important ways of knowing as 'they may unite and enhance each other to yield an outcome greater than either of them alone' (Del Río & Álvarez, 2002, p. 65). The external-to-internal trajectory of *thought* was also true of Vygotsky's view of the trajectory of *emotion*; that is, emotions appear first on the social plane and only then on the psychological plane (DiPardo & Potter, 2003).

Vygotsky made numerous references to the interrelatedness, the inseparability of mind and body, thought and emotion. He believed that a major weakness of traditional psychology was the separation of intellect from affect – from 'the fullness of life' – and he sought to demonstrate 'the existence of a dynamic system of meaning in which the affective and the intellectual unite' (Vygotsky, 2000, p. 10). He wrote: 'thought has its origins in the motivating sphere of consciousness, a sphere that includes our inclinations and needs, our interests and impulses, and our affect and emotions. The affective and volitional tendency stands behind thought' (1987, p. 282).

Perezhivanie is a Russian term used by Vygotsky to refer to the emotional experience – experience as lived through the emotions. 'The emotional experience arising from any situation or from any aspect of his environment determines what kind of influence this situation or this environment will have on the child' (Vygotsky, 1994, p. 339). Certainly these past emotions and memories of these emotions follow an individual into their present. We will discuss how the past episodes that Grace selected to reveal seemed to inhibit her feelings of confidence for her future.

Vygotsky was certainly not the first, nor is he alone among scholars who challenge the dualism of mind and body – cognition and affect. In the field of second language acquisition, Krashen's well-known input hypothesis created the metaphor of the 'affective filter' whose position (raised in protection mode or lowered in receptive mode) determined the processing of language and the development of linguistic skills (1981). Krashen did not and does not work in the SCT paradigm, but his acknowledgment, decades ago, of the crucial role of emotion in SLA was distinct in the field at the time. Second language researcher Dewaele called for attention to affect and emotion in SLA research and reinforced the value of learner perspectives as data. 'The learner is not only an object of scientific curiosity but also a crucial witness of his or her own learning process' (Dewaele, 2006, p. 369). Pavlenko explored a range of issues that demonstrate the consequential connections between emotion and language learning and use in her comprehensive book *Emotions and Multilingualism* (2005).

People from the fields of psychology, philosophy and education have composed eloquent titles and comments that index the centrality of emotions with respect to learning and development. Piaget (1981), in the field of child psychology, entitled one of his books *Intelligence and Affectivity: Their Relationship during Child Development*. The philosopher Spinoza claimed that the mind and the body are one and Damasio emphasized that the body (emotions) happens first and then thinking follows: 'A mind is so closely shaped by the body and destined to serve it that only one mind could possibly arise in it. No body, never mind' (Damasio, 1999, p. 143). Emotions are implicated in the thinking process itself. (*Body or embodied* is often synonymous with emotion in the literature on the mind/body connection, perhaps because some emotions are signaled through bodily changes.) *Emotion: The On Off Switch for Learning* (Vail, 1994) is the title and the message of a book authored by Vail, an educator of children with disabilities. Indeed, the metaphor is powerful.

Interestingly, the experience of Grace (and some other individuals whom we will mention later) does not really support the notion that negative emotions invariably equal *no* learning. There is evidence that negative affect does not always turn the learning switch 'off'. Rather we will see that emotions (socially constructed from the SCT perspective) mediate the learning and the participation in a variety of ways. At one end, Grace is mortified and therefore learns the names of every vegetable in English. Here we see evidence of Grace's agency – (see Chapter 1). But at other times Grace's emotions *did* seem to activate the off switch for participation. Recall that Grace was concerned about not sounding as eloquent in Greek as the people with whom she was socializing, and so she became silent in those circumstances.

Those working directly in the SCT paradigm call up the connection, if not the indivisibility, of affect and development of mind in a variety of ways. In fact, the zone of proximal development (see Chapter 2) as conceived of by Vygotsky seems, by definition, to include attention to the affective/cognitive interrelationship. 'Causing fear in a student would certainly narrow a ZPD' (Mahn, 2008, p. 28). (In keeping with our understanding of a ZPD as an activity rather than a place, we would reword this as 'reduce the possibility that a ZPD would be enacted'.)

Mahn and John-Steiner (2002, p. 49) made the point that lending support to others is a form of caring (attention to emotions) and can build confidence. They noted that Moll and Whitmore (1993) preferred to call the ZPD 'the collective zone of proximal development', emphasizing the social nature of ZPD and by inclusion, the social nature of emotion. According to Moran and John-Steiner, from a Vygotskian standpoint 'how a person, emotionally, not just cognitively, perceives his or her place within the social environment has a tremendous impact on the ability to flexibly, and perhaps creatively, respond to possibilities in that environment' (2003, p. 33). If Grace's bilingualism had been admired rather than problematized back in her classroom in the small town in Canada when she was eight years old, we wonder whether she would still be so ambivalent about whether her Greek and her English are close to native ideals.

Not only language learners but also language teachers are the subject of SCT studies addressing the thought/emotion connection. Verity (2000) narrated her emotional rollercoaster during an uncomfortable teaching situation and related how she regulated herself by appealing to an earlier, more successful self (Verity's experience struck us as the creation of an auto-ZPD in which her earlier self scaffolds her subsequent self.) DiPardo and Potter (2003) also applied Vygotskian concepts of cognition/affect to the experiences of teachers. Teachers, if they are to attend to both the minds and emotions of their students, need to have these interrelated elements respected and attended by those who are responsible for teachers. That is, caring for the affective state of students is more likely to be achieved by teachers whose affective states are cared for by their professions. (See also Deters, 2009.) We wonder whether the outcome for Grace would have been different if her teachers (and the institutions in which they worked, and society in general) had been more aptly educated on how to skillfully work with linguistically and culturally diverse students.

There are various ways to access memorable events in learning. Accounts may be retrospective or in real time. They may be oral or written. They may be constructed with a listener or simply observed (or read) by another. Grace's narrative was oral and retrospective and partly co-constructed during the course of an interview. Many of the incidents she described happened years ago. Grace's perspective at the time of the events may have been different if she had been telling her story to a different person at a different time in a different place (and in a different language – Greek, for example). While it is certainly valuable to capture the socially constructed emotions in real time through observations, emotion logs and the like as did Imai (2010), there are advantages to retrospective accounts as well. We can see what was lasting in Grace's memory as a result of the passage of time and geography.

Many other individuals are identified as contributors to Grace's emotions. It is important to keep in mind that the episodes/events within this narrative were selected for telling by Grace. She made no explicit connection between the interactions she had with others concerning her language skills and her lack of confidence in her skills, but you will note that she followed each episode with a comment about how she *felt*. Many of the comments made so long ago still seemed to resonate and affect how Grace participated in the 'languaculture' (Agar, 1994) of both of her communities. In reaction to comments and behaviors of others, that is, as a result of social interactions, she described herself as *embarrassed, mortified, worried, scared, self-conscious, silent, edgy, terrible,* [language] *deteriorated, sensitive.* There were only a few positive recollections of her language crossings.

When speaking with Grace, the interviewer found it surprising that Grace had concerns about her own English pragmatics and her accent, because Grace made no more slips than the interviewer would have. Grace reported being insecure about her pragmatic competence, about her wait time, and about her gesturing (remember how her brothers implored her to sit on her hands as she embarrassed them with her expressive body language). In contrast, the interviewer (who has interacted with Grace in other contexts) would characterize her as a vivacious communicator, demonstrative and compelling in the best possible way. It is somewhat disturbing to the three authors of this textbook that Grace did not admire her English-speaking self in the way that she deserves to be admired.

Grace chose to open her language learning narrative with the story of the aggouri/cucumber which caused her to feel embarrassment and mortification. Until that time, Grace seemed not to have realized fully that she was bilingual and that words in one language sometimes slipped out when speaking the other language. What might appear to readers of this narrative as a minor classroom incident obviously had a large impression on Grace with respect to language. Grace felt humiliated with respect to English – but as a result, she pushed herself to learn the new words she missed in class. Being embarrassed does not always result in defeat – sometimes it pushes one to work harder. Experiencing negative emotions does not always switch learning off (to use Vail's metaphor). Sociocultural theorist A. N. Leont'ev (1981) distinguished stress from tension: the former is an impediment to learning while the latter acts as an impetus to learning. We also looked to some published language autobiographies and to one recent study in particular that provided other instances where negative emotions did not always impede language learning.

Two language autobiographies that demonstrate instances of 'learning for revenge' come to mind. Ariel Dorfman wrote in his 1998 autobiography that he believed his verbally abusive Spanish teacher angered him into learning Spanish. Similarly, in her 1993 autobiography, Esmeralda Santiago explained that she learned long lists of difficult vocabulary words out of spite, just because her teacher thought she could not.

Similarly, in conducting classroom research, Imai (2010) noted a positive outcome of negative emotions. His participants were working in groups to complete a class assignment.

They experienced joint frustration and boredom, which are normally anathemas to learning. Imai showed, however, that these negative emotions in fact became a joint psychological resource which resulted in a good project.

When Grace told of her pleasure and perceptions of ability when her friend praised her language skills in Greek, she demonstrated how equally powerful are those who help us to construct positive emotions. She was 'gratified' and 'encouraged'. Decades later, a professor in a graduate course Grace was taking assumed Grace could not write a good paper. It turned out Grace wrote a terrific paper which was retained by the professor as an exemplar. The professor had harbored negative expectations about Grace's English but the classroom experience turned out to be an endorsement of Grace's academic skills in English. Grace realized then that English was once again dominant – but only when the professor approved of her paper (*other-regulated*).

Grace made numerous references to interactions with and reactions of her brothers (who had never lived in Greece). They frequently made fun of her and coached her on English pragmatics and seemed still able to destabilize her confidence with respect to participating in English. Grace's husband helped her with her Greek when she felt insecure. Her husband '*has never made references to the fact that my Greek is not as good or whatever. He likes my Greek – but other people would joke about it.*' Expats in Greece would criticize one another's English, albeit while laughing. The message for Grace was clear – her English had deteriorated.

It is not evident however that the instances of encouragement, her friend's complimentary comments about Grace's skill in Greek, the lack of criticism from her husband (about her Greek) and her mother's admiration of her lexical knowledge in Greek in any way made up for the feelings of embarrassment and concern she had as a result of her brothers, her early teacher, her graduate school professor and those Greek speakers in whose presence Grace stayed silent. Although she may well be fully accepted as a native user of English, she did not identify herself as such without some reflection. Nor is she '**Greek-**Greek', and she could not bring herself to write in the 'pompous' manner that is expected when writing in Greek. 'That's not me.' (Keep this in mind when reading the section on Identity.)

Regulation

Although causality is difficult to prove, it seems reasonable to assume that if others have made us feel linguistically less than competent, we will be more likely to mistrust our own language production. Although bilingual, although a successful English teacher (and at the time of the original interview, a teacher educator as well), Grace described many instances which demonstrated that others mediated her perspective of her own language abilities in both English and Greek. In the SCT literature (e.g. Lantolf & Thorne, 2006), self-regulation refers more to the ability to determine for oneself what elements of one's language use are right or wrong, appropriate or inappropriate. The concept of regulation may be extended to include one's ability to evaluate not only discrete elements like morphology or pronunciation, but also one's general performance, one's legitimacy, as a user of a language. (Here, regulation and identity seem to meet.) Grace's evaluation of her linguistic abilities is not determined by 'self'; rather, she referred to the evaluations of her teacher(s), (*'I needed the encouragement of my profs'*) her brothers, her husband, and others. For example, Grace went to Greece thinking she was fluent, but found out she was not. She thought she had a clear idea of her fluency and had achieved self-regulation but found she had to depend on her husband to correct her (and still does today). '*I always ask my husband...*'.

Frawley and Lantolf argued for the 'principle of continuous access'; learners often re-access earlier stages of development when their regulation of mental behaviors becomes de-automatized (1985, p. 282). Grace may have returned to earlier stages of development in order to regain what she had once achieved and had since lost control of. However, it may be that some of her language problems were a result of neologisms, that is, new words that had entered the language, or other changes in pragmatic functions that had come into the Greek language while Grace was living in English in Canada.

Grace did demonstrate self-regulation, we believe, in the following statement:

> I realized that some of the things are cultural – some types of discourse – that's where I'm not coming across as a native speaker and I am very conscious of that. So I say to myself "okay count! – count to 3. And **then** say something". Or when I go to the front office and I want to ask one of the girls something, I say [to myself] "Stop, think, and **then** speak."

Counting to three regulated (or mediated) her production. Similarly, her private speech acted as regulation/mediation when she advised herself to stop, think and then speak. Grace demonstrated self-regulation in the sense that she anticipated a miscommunication and took steps to avoid it. But is Grace's insecurity a result of her brothers constantly destabilizing her sense of confidence, or is it actual lack of pragmatic weaknesses? We cannot know from the data we have.

Poehner (2008, p. 48) noted Gal'perin's division of labor into three components: orientation (attitude to the action); execution (production of the action); and control (evaluation of the action). In much SLA research, it is the execution (or production) stage of language that is most often assessed, perhaps because the other two are more difficult to measure or observe through traditional means. What people say is audible; what people write is visible. An individual's *attitude* towards the language and their assessment of their language are not as visible or audible as is the actual language they produce. Poehner allowed that through dialogue, issues in the two less obvious components may become clearer. Indeed, throughout Grace's narrative we heard her perspective about her attitude towards and her evaluation of her languages. However, we know little about her execution (performance) in Greek beyond what she says about it. We do not have evidence of her actual Greek language production. We have more evidence of her execution of English (the interview is conducted in English) and although *our* evaluation of Grace's performance is much more positive than her self-evaluation, we defer to and report the emic (lived experience) perspective that she provides.

Newman (2003) cautioned against regarding regulation as a straight and permanent progression from other- to self-regulation. There are times when self-regulation means seeking other-regulation, that is, seeking the help of others may indicate and lead to a (re)turn to self-regulation (also Poehner, 2008, p. 44). This important point is made elsewhere. Aljaafreh and Lantolf considered other-regulation to be a 'collaborative frame' (1994, p. 480) and stressed the negotiation involved. Van Lier addressed the dialectic, the balance between what he calls self-repair and other-repair (1988). Newman posited that when engaged in difficult tasks on their own, children occasionally must take the initiative to enlist the help of teachers and more knowledgeable peers (2003, p. 287). Thus, when Grace enlisted the help of her husband, she may have been demonstrating self-regulation in knowing to ask for other-regulation; this phenomenon is called 'adaptive help seeking' by Newman. The question remains, though, whether the help was really required as a matter of actual difficulty (execution) or imagined/ perceived difficulty caused by Grace's affective experiences (orientation).

Identity(ies)

Holland and Lachicotte acknowledged that while Vygotsky did not develop fully the notion of self, he did 'formulate an important nascent understanding of identity formation and its significance for processes of cultural and social change' (2007, p. 101). According to Penuel and Wertsch (1995), Vygotsky never actually used the word *identity* but they provided us with some assumptions about what Vygotsky might have contributed had identity been an issue at the forefront of development as is it today. There are multiple understandings of identity, some representing identity as stable (or at least partly stable; see Fishman, 1977), while others represent the ebb and flow, the appearance and disappearance of identities as one's contexts and circumstances change.

Two identity theorists who construed identity as being socially constructed are Erikson (1968) and Mead (1934, 1982). Penuel and Wertsch (1995) suggested that to Erikson, identity was more stable than Vygotsky would have claimed. That is, Erikson looked for a trajectory that led to a final and coherent identity. Mead, on the other hand, seemed to not have an end point in mind. That is, he understood identity as a sense of one's self in multiple social roles. Identity that is socially developed and interpreted and adjusted according to shifts in the context would be more congruent with SCT. We refer you to Holland and Lachicotte (2007) for a more detailed discussion on how Vygotsky's understanding of identity, implicit in his work, would be more aligned with Mead.

Identity comes into play each time we interact with others. We all engage in multiple identities (according to Holzman, 2009, we perform our identities). Grace named numerous roles and affiliations – those that were somewhat stable such as sister, daughter, teacher, wife, mother – and others that were more temporary, such as expat. Grace's narrative was not limited to a snapshot of a particular time in her life; rather, we are privy to part of the genesis (history) of her linguistic identities. Some identities are ascribed by others, while others are claimed by the individual him or herself. Grace referred often to her ascribed identity and her narrative illustrated confusion at times:

- *They think I am Greek-Greek; I don't sound Canadian; I want to sound like you.*
- *Maybe people thought I was Greek-Greek you know because I had been away so long.*
- *But then they* [in Greece] *hear my accent and they'll say "she's not one of us so let's not pay attention".*

Each affiliation, however, had a dimension of language: language that was expected, language that was produced (or withheld); and language that was adequate or inadequate according to perspectives and assumed judgments.

Our approach to Grace and her languages is not an approach taken by traditional SLA researchers. We have not looked at Grace's language production and we have not analyzed her discourse. Many SLA studies involving emotion and motivation examine the correlation between the affective self and language proficiency, i.e. actual linguistic outcomes are evaluated. For example, the body of work by MacIntyre (1998; MacIntyre & Gardner, 1994) demonstrated that language performance is negatively correlated with language anxiety. MacIntyre defined anxiety as 'negative emotional reaction when using a second language' (1998, p. 27.) The data we are provided with in this interview, however, are Grace's reflections on her experiences and feelings about herself as a speaker and a member of the English-speaking community in Canada and the Greek-speaking community in Greece. She lived in both worlds and seemed to feel totally at home in neither. MacIntyre, Noels and Clément (1997) found that anxiety can bias perceptions of linguistic performance. Grace's narrative reminds us how fragile one's (language) ego is and how easily destabilized one's confidence may be. Someone considered a competent user of a language may nevertheless evaluate him/herself quite harshly.

Identity is never determined by one person alone but is socially constructed. It seems that perception of linguistic performance too is socially constructed. Others evaluate our performance and how we react to those evaluations make bi- and multilingualism more or less comfortable – more or less a source of pride and strength (Kinnear, 2004). While we have just written that we are not conducting *discourse analysis* in this textbook, particularly conspicuous to us was Grace's use of the pronoun *them* to refer to native speakers of English and *them* to refer to native speakers of Greek. Positioning analysis – i.e. how one locates oneself in relation to others – would be salient here. (See Davies & Harré (1990) and Bamberg (1997) for in-depth discussions of positioning in narrative analysis work.) Where, we wonder, and with whom does Grace belong in this linguistic landscape? We noticed that the only time her pronouns included herself in a community occurred when Grace referred to the expats during her time in Greece. In this case, discourse analysis would prove an illuminating method and sociocultural theory a theoretical lens.

We are sobered to realize how even highly proficient bilinguals may still be *affect*ed by the judgments of others. Each of us, in roles as teachers, researchers, or simply members of a language community, has opportunities to scaffold or demolish depending on how we respond to language efforts of others. Grace's narrative reminds us how respectful we must be with that power.

Current controversies

What constitutes success in language learning? Traditional SLA looks at production data to determine successful learning. However, pragmatic performance, critical to Grace the learner and Grace the teacher, is not attended to very often in teaching. When pragmatics *is* looked at, the measures are not holistic; rather, studies analyze discrete elements of language, such as use or non-use of particular politeness markers. Appropriate use equals success. We have no such data in this narrative. That is, we cannot say much about the accuracy or appropriacy of Grace's linguistic performance. What we can say with certainty, though, is that how Grace feels about herself as an English speaker and as a Greek speaker was constructed *socially*. That is, exams or objective measures did not mark her feelings of success or failure; interactions with others accomplished that. Test scores, we imagine, would not override Grace's (socially constructed) feelings of her linguistic abilities. Perhaps there is no absolute measure of communicative abilities, only 'perceptions of one's competence' (Steinman, 2007).

What *is* success in learning a language? Is it only using language accurately, or does it include feeling good about oneself as a user of the language and as a member of that language community? Is it mastery or appropriation (see Chapter 1)? Do the existing models of communicative performance make room for feelings?

Key research relevant to emotion

In the Imai study, students working collaboratively kept logs and found that particular emotions mediated in interesting and unexpected ways the achievement of their goals. An examination of their collaborative dialogue in group work demonstrated the social construction of emotions.

> Imai, Y. (2010). Emotions in SLA: New insights from collaborative learning for an EFL classroom. *The Modern Language Journal*, 94(2), 278–291.

Verity, a language teacher who was struggling in an unfamiliar context, collaborated with her previous, successful teaching 'self' in order to regain her footing and her affective equilibrium. This study speaks also to identity.

> Verity, D. (2000). Side affects: The strategic development of professional satisfaction. In J. Lantolf (Ed.), *Sociocultural theory and second language learning* (pp. 179–197). New York: Oxford.

Key research relevant to regulation

ESL learners of various levels of proficiency and native English speakers were given tasks of varying complexity. Their metalanguage, externalization and the nature of their regulation are described. Task complexity determined the nature of regulatory talk more than language proficiency did.

Frawley, W. & Lantolf, J. P. (1985). Second language discourse: A Vygotskian perspective. *Applied Linguistics, 6*, 19–44.

Key research relevant to identity

Deters interviewed internationally educated teachers with respect to how their identities were assigned and (re)formed as they participated in their professional communities in Canada. Identity, agency and emotion were key aspects in her findings.

Deters, P. (2009). *Identity, agency, and the acquisition of professional language and culture: The case of internationally educated teachers and college professors in Ontario.* Unpublished PhD thesis, Ontario Institute for Studies in Education at the University of Toronto, Toronto, Ontario.

In Kinnear's study, biracial bilingual adolescents, 'hafu's', were asked to write for publication about growing up and going to school in Japan. An Activity Theory analysis shows how one participant, Sarah, used the writing and revision process to examine the complexity of the identities assigned to her by adults and peers in Japanese and American cultures in interaction with the identities she and her friends constructed for themselves. Sarah's writing and revision culminated in a redefinition of 'normal' and her own identity as a normal biracial, bilingual, bicultural teen.

Kinnear, P. (2004). *Through writing for publication, a biracial, bicultural, bilingual adolescent explores identity and normalcy: Sarah in her own words.* Unpublished PhD thesis. Ontario Institute for Studies in Education at the University of Toronto, Toronto, Ontario.

Questions to explore for research and teaching

1. Grace confirmed that her own experience of language learning had become part of her curriculum when she teaches. This speaks to the genetic method, i.e. in order to understand Grace's behaviour as a teacher, it is crucial to know her experience and development as a learner over time. Pinar (1994) suggested that most of us, on either a conscious or an unconscious level 'work from within'.

How does your own autobiography as a learner and as a student, contribute to your beliefs and practices as a teacher and/or a researcher?

2. Have negative emotions ever constrained your ability to learn? When and why? Have negative emotions ever noticeably enhanced your ability to learn? When and why? What implication do these experiences have for your teaching and/or for your research?

3. Timing matters. Context matters. Interactions matter.
Grace was bilingual/bicultural in a small town in Canada at a time when and in a place where she was an oddity. Fast forward 40 years and the world (including the small town in Canada) is a different place. We now speak of transnationals, of global citizens.

How might Grace's feelings about her linguistic repertoire been differently felt by herself and others today?

What advice would you have given Grace's Grade 4 teacher with respect to the 'aggouri' incident in light of what we now understand about language learning, identity and affect?

4. In your own practice, have you seen evidence of movement from other-regulation to self-regulation on the part of your students or your research participants? Do you, as a teacher and/or as a researcher, also move from self-regulation to other-regulation from time to time? When?

5. What other SCT concepts might be identified in Grace's story? (See the Key Terms at the beginning of each chapter for SCT concepts.)

6

Sandra's story: A teacher's dilemma

KEY SCT tenets related to activity theory

- An activity is purposeful, human social behavior

- The same action may have different goals for different people

- Material and symbolic tools mediate the interaction between the individual and the social

- People can pursue multiple goals simultaneously

- New goals will emerge during an action in an activity

- Multiple activities are linked in networks of activity systems

Setting of this narrative

Languages: French and English

Context: English in the workplace teacher and student, graduate program in Applied Linguistics in Ontario, Canada

Activity theory

Introduction

This chapter introduces the concept of <u>activity theory</u>. Vygotsky concerned himself throughout his work with the relationship between the individual's mind and socially organized ways of knowing and acting. The explanations suggested by Vygotsky's contemporaries in psychology did not satisfy him. He wanted a way to theorize *and* investigate the integration rather than the separation of mind and act, of individual and society. Vygotsky proposed in Russian *dejatel'nost'*. The English translation 'activity' is confined to things we do. We engage in physical activities or leisure activities or after-school activities or the many classroom or learning activities teachers cultivate as part of their teaching repertoires. However, the Russian term refers to something much larger and more abstract. Ryle (1999) wrote, 'The concept of *activity* is poorly rendered by the English word; in activity theory the implication is of high-level, motivated thinking, doing and being of an individual in a given social context' (p. 413). English fails to provide us with a word that encompasses all of that meaning. Education is an activity in the Russian sense. As you read this chapter remember that Vygotskian 'activity' is a much broader term than English 'doing stuff' activity.

In this chapter, you will first read a teaching and learning story. Sandra is an experienced ESL teacher who is also a graduate student in Applied Linguistics. Marc is her student. This story is woven from the following sources: a major term paper Sandra wrote for one of her graduate school courses; her teacher's reflections on Sandra's paper; excerpts from Sandra and Marc's email correspondence; and excerpts from Sandra's responses to questions posed by the authors of this textbook. Following the story, we introduce you to the terminology of activity theory. We then use activity theory to analyze and interpret Sandra and Marc's email exchange and the tension Sandra felt this represented for her. When we look at Sandra's story, we use the lens of Engeström's activity system networks. The concept of activity and activity theory provide analytical tools that can help us, Sandra and other teachers understand the tensions and paradoxes that occur in teaching and learning. Activity theory facilitates this because it does not separate the social or the individual but always looks at the interactions of the two. In David Russell's words, 'The object of the analysis is neither text nor minds nor conceptual schemes per se but what is in between – the social intercourse' (1997, p. 509). Activity theory helps us focus on the process and the product simultaneously because of its focus on the interaction. As you read Sandra's story, think about the different perspectives – social and individual – that intersect and interact with one another.

Finally, we invite you to explore some of the controversies initiated by Vygotsky's attempts to redefine the relationship between individuals and the world they inhabit. We hope that you begin to consider how this development of sociocultural theory may help you understand your own teaching and learning.

Sandra's story: A teacher's dilemma

Sandra and Marc met in an English in the Workplace (EWP) setting in which Sandra taught and Marc studied, for three years. Sponsored by a labor union of which Marc was a member, the classes were held off-site and students were paid one hour of wages for every two hours they came to class. Classes were small, populated by French-Canadians working for the same company.

Marc was doing extremely well and frequent out of class missives (via e-mail) attested to his positive response to Sandra's teaching, his growing comfort in using English, and the concrete, powerful changes he was beginning to effect at his workplace as a result of his growing competence and confidence in English. Marc was the only student who used email to extend his classes. Yet, while the student and the teacher were both pleased with the student's progress and participation, Sandra's reflection from her graduate student perspective had occasioned several concerns. In her graduate coursework Sandra had been introduced to the ideas of critical pedagogy in second language teaching. Critical pedagogy asks teachers to become aware of the traditional relationship between the teacher and her students. Critical pedagogy challenges the distribution of power and agency in this (and other) relationships and examines the possible effects of the unequal distribution. Provoked by these thoughts, Sandra began to question her own role and goals during the many interactions between herself and her student. This created a tension within herself. She questioned the way her long-practiced actions maintained or developed asymmetrical power constellations and the effect that might have on students in general and Marc in particular.

Sandra describes the context:

The level of the students in my sessions was between CLB 4 and 7' over the 4 areas (listening, speaking, reading, and writing). Not many of the guys were interested in writing – at all. They were mostly there to talk, to fill in their time, to try to understand why Quebec and Ontario were so different, to complain about the company they worked for and the union, and to laugh with each other. They included me in their jokes, and overall, it was a very warm atmosphere. They were all French-Canadian who had been transferred from a site in Quebec which had closed.

Sandra opens her term paper describing her reflections with an out-of-class incident:

...the student and his wife were driving down my street one afternoon, and having noticed me working in the garden, stopped in to say hello. As the guests chatted to my husband about how they were adjusting to life in their new city, my student mentioned that his wife, who wasn't enrolled in English classes, was having an easier time because there was no one (such as his teacher--me) to make her feel like a "dead duck." The student sent me an email later that day to inquire as to whether his use of the idiom was correct. I sent this response:

It was very nice to see you and your wife today. Thanks for dropping by. I should make one thing clear: you are correct about the idiom: "dead duck" and as you said, it means "with no hope of being successful; a failure" but I would not use it the way you did. (You are none of those things, as you must realize.) But, perhaps, that is how it feels when I correct you.

I would say you are like a "sitting duck" because I have the fire power, and you are just doing what comes naturally to you. (Floating on a sea of English...). So when I

point out a different (more Anglo) way to say something, it is too easy for me to "target" your (mis)use of words, or stress, or idioms.

I realize that I am being too hard on you, so I will try to give you more explanation, and not so much frustration!

Here is an excerpt of Marc's reply (unedited):

When I learn a new word or a new expression I just try to put it in context. I fail often. I'm not frustrated if you correct me. It's not at my company I will learn the best way to say things. You are the best reference I know and your not too hard on me. Don't feel embarrassed. It's OK that way.

Sandra continues in her paper:

In every such online conversation, complicated aspects of the interaction between student and teacher are apparent ... Consider the affirmation of the role of direct instruction in the student's sentence. "It's not at my company I will learn the best way to say things." This phrasing provides an example of a key issue. The sentence is grammatically correct English, sounds quite sophisticated, and is quite likely a direct translation from French. However, the innate reaction of a native speaker (NS) is "That's not the way we say it." Yet, how detrimental is it to deliver such correction? This is often what students ask for; why does it seem so rude and limiting to focus on such subtleties? Moreover, how can teachers navigate such complex and nuanced discourses? Apart from the interpersonal considerations, there is also the difficult question of editing. We are compelled to ask, "Whose voice is it that needs to be heard?" What would be lost if a voice like this student's, and the individual behind it, were suppressed or replaced? At the same time, the writer is reassuring me, in the role of teacher, that there is a need for corrective feedback, and that he is not offended or frustrated to receive it. What can teachers learn about student motivation, empowerment, and modes of communication that could offer insight into teaching practices?

Later in the paper, Sandra continues:

Yet in the culture of the classroom, the asymmetrical relationship of teacher/learner, even when enacted as facilitator/participant, often acts as a barrier to authentic communication and mutual respect. Meanwhile, efforts to break down this barrier may lead to difficult, even exploitative, situations and must not be underestimated.

Sandra worries about her intentions, about Marc's intentions in these spatially extra-curricular interactions and calls up the powerful voices of SLA researchers whose work prompts or at least helps her to voice her thoughts. In a conversation with her professor, Sandra agrees that critical theory, a major thread in her graduate course readings and discussions, *"put some order to my thoughts"*:

Pierce and Toohey contend that "[r]esearchers have focused, in particular, on the often unequal relations of power between language learners and target language speakers, arguing that SLA theory has not given sufficient attention to the effects of power on social interaction" (2001, p. 312). Their intention is to raise awareness as to the constraints on learners, and the huge investment of emotional energy that is required to engage in communication with NSs [native speakers]. In my case, the learner indeed had the right to speak and to write, but is it fair to say that there was no abuse of authority? It is likely that the learner and the teacher had unstated, possibly unexamined, motives when engaging in the correspondence. In the adoption of methodology intended to redress the asymmetrical relationship between teacher and learner, I may in fact have been relying on a social norm of assumed social distance while in fact gaining emotional support (through direct compliments), constructive feedback (through explicit comments offered by the student), and evidence of effectiveness (observed through the learner's improvement). While it is impossible to know the rationale of the student, it can be assumed that some benefit accrued to him through this communication. Therefore, it might be useful to consider more apparent results. As will be shown below, Marc's enthusiasm for learning and his application of his L2 in a number of domains, coincided with his apparent transformation from a quiet, self-described loner to an outgoing, interactive advocate.

When I first met Marc, he told me he preferred to spend time in the woods rather than talk to people, and that if he didn't say anything in class, it was not because he didn't want to learn; he just didn't have much to say. Within a short time, this same student could be relied on to provide practical and moral support within his workplace. In addition, he demonstrated community engagement in a number of ways, as well as becoming a resource and mentor to his classmates. Norton Peirce addresses the challenge faced by immigrant women who "felt uncomfortable talking to people in whom they had a particular symbolic or material investment" (1995, p 19). The participants of her study had to reestablish their lives from the most basic requirements of housing and employment. Her informants were starting with little material support, and were not welcomed into the sphere of their former professions or social status. Marc acknowledged his good fortune of having accepted his company's relocation incentive and retaining his job without sacrificing family unity as his wife had migrated with him. Yet, his identity as a second language learner was evident, since the axis of language was an area of contention within the plant. Vocal as well as discrete hostility toward Quebecers was constant. Most of the time, Marc could ignore or overlook such personal assaults. But at times, he found himself in 'conflictual' situations, similar to those described by Parks and Raymond (2004), who investigated Chinese MBA students in a Canadian university setting. In Parks and Raymond, a Chinese student overcomes a critical incident by asserting herself in order to "combat a Canadian student's perception of her as a poor student (Parks & Raymond, 2004, p. 384). In Marc's case, he was unable to confront his (drunk) antagonist; his strategy, one most people would rely on, was to confide in a(n Anglophone) coworker who had noticed a change in Marc's demeanor. His sense of outrage was most salient when he witnessed the mistreatment of other minorities, but he also defended his own opinions, at one point countering the opinion of an obdurate Quebecer about life in Ontario. This information was mostly provided in his emails to me and tells of the context in which this student operated, and gives some insight as to his personality, or at least how he presents himself to his correspondent.

Activity theory

Activity theory, as first proposed by Vygotsky and developed further by Leont'ev conceptualizes human cognition in relationship to human physically and socially motivated activities. What we do to satisfy our physical needs as well as what we do to satisfy our psychological needs is seen as socially mediated actions rather than individual actions in a social context. This was Vygotsky's attempt to theorize the dynamic interaction of the individual and the socially constructed practices, norms and institutions. In his attempt to make this more explicit, Leont'ev defined three layers of an activity – motive, action and conditions. We will address these in more detail later in the chapter. An activity theory approach puts the focus on the *interactions* of multiple individual and social forces rather than on an individual mind.

Activity theory provides one way of holding in simultaneous focus multiple aspects of observable human endeavors. The activity theory framework allows us to avoid many of the dichotomies – individual–society, micro–macro, present–historical, cause–effect – that plague attempts to analyze complex interactions. It assumes a more dialectical perspective. Activity theory also underscores the generative power of Vygotsky's thinking. Vygotsky only proposed the idea of activity and did not live long enough to formulate a coherent and complete theory. Some of his contemporaries, mainly A.N. Leont'ev and his students, continued to work with the ideas and develop them inside Russia. Within Europe, Yrjö Engeström, a Finnish psychologist developed and systematized the Russian model of activity theory; it is his (Engeström, 1999) model of activity theory and activity system networks that has become predominant outside of Russia.

Engeström's visual interpretation of activity theory has been known to intimidate students with its triangles divided up and labeled with double-headed arrows and confusing terminology. But activity theory (and all its triangles) can provide a way of understanding complex, dynamic situations, like a classroom and classroom conversations. It can make visible the relationship between the individual and the collective, the private and social planes.

Vygotsky began with the idea of mediation (see Chapter 1) and constructed a simple triangle (Figure 6.1) to represent his reconceptualization of stimulus and response:

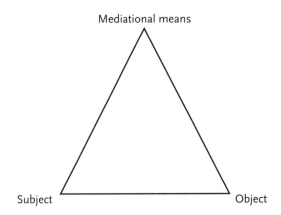

Figure 6.1 Vygotsky's first 'triangle'

An **agent** or **subject** (a person), for example, asks a question (a stimulus) that requires an answer (a response) which is the **object** or **goal** of asking the question. The action of answering the question is mediated by symbolic and possibly material means. The mediational means are used to formulate and broadcast the question. For example, Marc sends Sandra an email to ask about his use of 'dead duck' in their conversation. Marc has used English (a symbolic mediational means) and a computer (a material mediational means), both social inventions, to ask his question.

When Vygotsky added symbolic and material mediational means to such an action, he implied multiple simultaneous interactions with communities, their rules, and divisions of labor. A question is not asked separately from the context(s) that created the mediational means or the context that prompted it. The question does not simply occur *in* a social setting but everything about the question is an active part of asking. Who Marc is, who Sandra is, their relationship, and the context in which that relationship exists are all active parts of the action. To further reflect Vygotsky's assertion that learning occurs on the social plane first, his definition of symbolic mediational means includes the potential effect on the agent as well as the goal (see Chapter 1). This reverse potential is represented with the bidirectional arrows.

Leont'ev attempted to make the relationship between the individual and society more explicit when he defined activity as a socially and culturally meaningful activity that fulfills a basic biological or psychological or social need like satisfying hunger or achieving status. The **motive** is the drive to fulfill that need. Motive is both cognitive and emotional. Vygotsky did not separate emotion from cognition (see Chapter 5). Activities, driven by basic biological, psychological or socially constructed motives, are instantiated by multiple **actions** with **goals.** The actions and goals are specific to the individuals, the time and the place. So, Marc took the action of writing an email to get an answer (goal) to his question as he worked to fulfill his psychological/social needs (motives) to learn and to communicate.

Leont'ev added another layer of complexity when he considered that all actions take place in unique circumstances or **conditions.** For Marc, the conditions were asking the question in English to his English teacher by way of an email. Marc asked his question in English and not in French because he was writing to his English language teacher. Leont'ev described the automatized mental moves we use to carry out these actions as **operations.** Operations are familiar and used unconsciously. Marc did not have to figure out how to use his computer to send an email or how to compose the sentences he used to ask his question. However, the use of the idiom 'dead duck' is not yet an operation for Marc in the condition of his second language use, hence his question. The simple triangle leaves much of this process invisible. Marc's language learning history, the rules and roles of the English language learning context he and Sandra are engaged in, and the larger context in which this takes place are only implied.

Engeström expanded the triangle as he attempted to make all of these interactive elements (agents and their histories, individual and social contexts, mediational means, goals) explicit. His expanded triangle helps to keep the context visible. Engeström's expanded triangle (Engeström, 1999) is currently the most commonly used representation of the **action** in an activity system. Other times the triangle represents a group involved in multiple actions within an activity. We prefer to think of the triangle, first, as representing the **action** as that is the most concrete and visible of the three aspects of activity theory that Leont'ev developed.

Sandra's action

Sandra responded to an email from Marc after he had seen Sandra working in her garden and stopped to chat.

> It was very nice to see you and your wife today. Thanks for dropping by. I should make one thing clear: you are correct about the idiom: "dead duck" and as you said, it means "with no hope of being successful; a failure" but I would not use it the way you did. (You are none of those things, as you must realize.) But, perhaps, that is how it feels when I correct you.
>
> I would say you are like a "sitting duck" because I have the fire power, and you are just doing what comes naturally to you. (Floating on a sea of English....). So when I point out a different (more Anglo) way to say something, it is too easy for me to "target" your (mis) use of words, or stress, or idioms.
>
> I realize that I am being too hard on you, so I will try to give you more explanation, and not so much frustration!

We can build two triangles from Sandra's perspective. One can represent Sandra's action and the other can represent Marc's action (as Sandra understands it). Sandra is the **subject** or **agent** in the first triangle. Her immediate goal is to answer Marc's query about the use of 'dead duck' (Figure 6.2).

Figure 6.2 Sandra's goal

Sandra's action is mediated by the computer and her use of English. So, now we can begin to see Vygotsky's (1978, p. 40) original triangle (Figure 6.3).

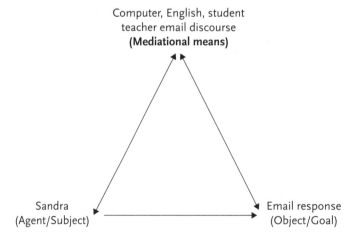

Figure 6.3 Sandra's email action triangle

Engeström's perspective picks out the **rules** of the student–teacher email discourse which Sandra and her students implicitly and perhaps explicitly agreed on at the beginning of the course. Sandra used email as a way to extend the classroom learning. She invited questions which she would answer. She also used email to notify her students of any changes to the course and they also used it to notify her if they were going to miss class or be late. Engeström added rules to the triangle along with more arrows to reflect the way that the rules were also mediated and how they shaped and were shaped by the goal and by Sandra (the agent) (Figure 6.4).

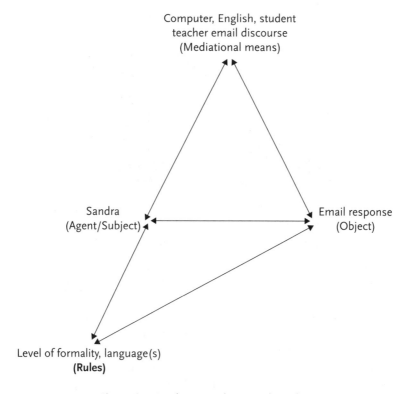

Figure 6.4 Sandra's email action plus rules

A **division of labor** exists between Sandra, the teacher and Marc, her student, in this action. The terminology and the concept of labor reflect the Marxian philosophical roots of Vygotsky's work (see Harry Daniels, 1996; Davydov, 1999; Rene van der Veer, 2007). Sandra's job as the teacher is to answer Marc's questions, to evaluate Marc's linguistic performance and to support and extend his learning of English in the workplace. Marc also has a job: to ask questions, to attend the classes and to complete the activities Sandra presents. The arrows indicate that the division of labor both shapes and is shaped by the rules of this particular action, the subject, the goals and the mediating artifacts (Figure 6.5). The process of this activity, the rules and the division of labor may both change. Part of the messiness and power of activity theory comes from this notion that none of these categories or their relationships is static.

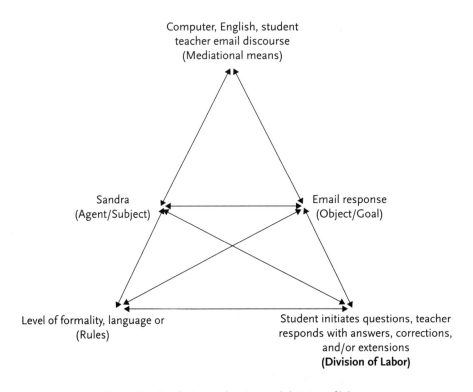

Figure 6.5 Sandra's email action and division of labor

Although this particular action, using email to clarify a point of meaning and usage, immediately involves only Marc and Sandra, they are both part of a <u>community</u> that engages in similar actions. Sandra's and Marc's <u>community</u> in this system is made up of the other English in the Workplace (EWP) students who correspond with Sandra. Each of these individuals has a unique set of *triangles*. It would be possible (but very, very messy) to diagram the email community with multiple subjects/agents, multiple actions and multiple goals. Such attempts can show some of the possible ways a group of people create a community by sharing goals, experiences and a sense of the rules that govern behavior while simultaneously pursuing a number of different goals and even outcomes (Figure 6.6).

The immediate goal of Marc's question may provide him with the information or feedback he needs to use 'dead duck' in conversation. Sandra, by answering Marc's question in a timely, supportive and knowledgeable way maintains her role in the community and also supports the community and a shared goal or <u>outcome</u> of the <u>activity</u>, of improved workplace language proficiency and workplace productivity. The outcome indexes the activity (in Vygotsky's sense) of which the action represented by the expanded triangle is a part. This reminds us that this action is not an isolated one but one of many that are part of a dynamic, socially constructed way of being and acting in the world. We can name this, 'teaching and learning English in the workplace.' This layer of activity and motive, not shown but indexed in Engeström's model, reminds us of Vygotsky's quest to understand the complex interactive relationships between the individual and the context that create the mind.

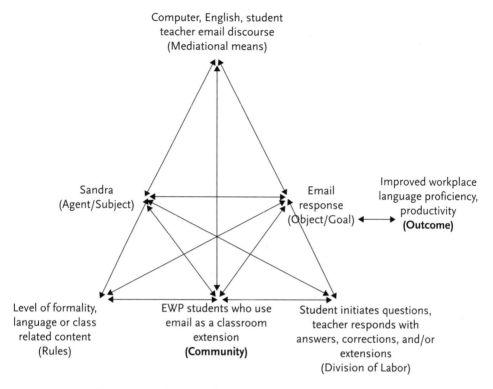

Computer, English, student
teacher email discourse
(Mediational means)

Sandra
(Agent/Subject)

Email
response
(Object/Goal)

Improved workplace
language proficiency,
productivity
(Outcome)

Level of formality,
language or class
related content
(Rules)

EWP students who use
email as a classroom
extension
(Community)

Student initiates questions,
teacher responds with
answers, corrections, and/or
extensions
(Division of Labor)

Figure 6.6 Sandra's email action and community and outcome

We can construct a similar triangle to represent Marc's action as understood by Sandra. In the triangle that Sandra might construct of Marc's action, Marc is the subject or agent. This triangle represents, as Sandra attempts to make sense of it, his perspective on the rules, the community, the division of labor and a different goal. Note that his goal is different and that he conforms to the division of labor, asking a question and expecting an answer (Figure 6.7).

These two triangles (Figures 6.6 and 6.7) represent two <u>actions</u>, **Action 1**, sending and **Action 2**, receiving an email, that are part of this **activity:** teaching English in the Workplace. Engeström sees the multiple actions in an activity as part of a more inclusive **activity system**. This is a simple activity system. Each of these 'stop-frame' representations captures only part of several dynamic interactions often occurring simultaneously. Other actions that are part of this activity system would include all of the different things Sandra and her students have done in their lessons over the course of the class. By drawing these two triangles we can focus on a particular action from a particular perspective without completely hiding or ignoring other aspects of the actions. We can observe and question what we think we see. Using the triangles that capture different actions allows us to re-examine actions in our teaching and learning and perhaps understand them differently, especially when we understand that this particular action is part of **one** activity system and each of us participates in multiple activity systems which also interact. Engeström acknowledges this and labels interacting activity systems an **activity system network**.

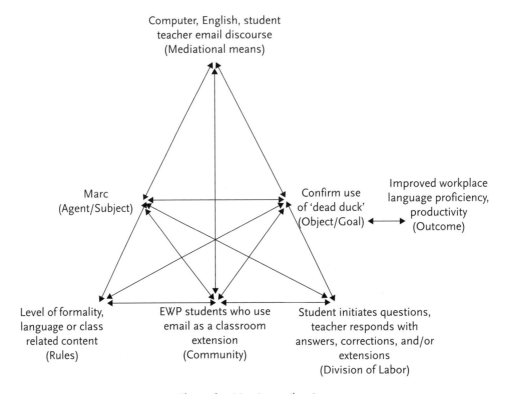

Figure 6.7 Marc's email action

What can we understand from examining Marc's and Sandra's triangles?

Sandra opened her email, found Marc's email, read it and responded. Sandra's action was mediated by both symbolic and material means. These signs/symbols and tools mediate Sandra's pursuit of her object or goals and the outcome associated with those objects or goals.

All the goals of an action are not always apparent or stated at the beginning. Many goals or objects emerge in the course of the action in addition to the ones articulated at the beginning. Sandra's first goal was probably to answer Marc's question about the appropriateness of his use of the idiom 'dead duck'.

Two areas of the triangles remind us of the background and goals of Sandra responding to a student email query. The **rules** – the promptness with which Sandra responds, the tone of her response, and the amount of information she includes in her response – emerged from the guidelines Sandra set and the way the class used email. Most teachers set classroom rules at the beginning of a class. Teachers can set the rules for how the class is conducted (one kind of action), for homework, for completing and submitting assignments and even for contesting the rules. Sandra's original rules may have included such things as reporting absence, asking questions or clarifying tasks. The community (the off-site language class) may have expanded the guidelines/rules to include the sharing of Power Point slide shows. The **division of labor** – who asks and who answers questions – was shaped by past classroom interactions of community members and Sandra's past experiences and current thinking.

Sandra introduced the rules for email at the beginning. She articulated the goal of extending the classroom. Each of the students brings his or her own experiences with classroom rules, routines, and the division of labor to the new class and in the course of the classroom interaction a new set of rules and division of labor may emerge. During the course, only Marc appeared to adhere to Sandra's particular goal of extending the classroom. As Sandra noted in her interview, the rules and the goals changed, 'Several other guys corresponded by email, but usually specific questions about things they or their families needed.... Two or three of them continue to send PowerPoint slide shows and jokes, but only Marc used email to extend his classes.' So the rules and goals had changed for most of the students through the interactions over time. However, Marc still acted on Sandra's original goal, perhaps because it supported his own goals.

Tensions and opportunities in activity and actions

We can use Leont'ev's concepts of *conditions* and *operations* to help understand how Sandra's activity as a graduate student interacts with her activity and actions as an EWP teacher. As an experienced second language teacher, much of what Sandra does in her EWP activity system, under the condition of a mandated, EWP program for a large manufacturing company, occurs as operations, i.e. actions she carries out automatically. She has developed her teaching strategies, a repertoire of operations through her participation in many different activity systems over her years as both student and teacher. But a tension in the interaction between her teaching system and her graduate student system have forced some of these teaching operations out of the automatic operations level and back into the conscious or examined level of goals.

Before considering how motive, goals and operations interact, consider some of the other activity systems Sandra participates in: the graduate class she attends; marriage; homeowner; professional ESL educator; and no doubt many others. Marc also participates in multiple activity systems, some shared with Sandra and others which are not. Each of these systems has a different degree of interaction or overlap with their shared EWP system. Engeström, as he worked more and more with activity theory, moved from his elaborated triangle to the concept of activity system *networks* in order to capture the dynamic interaction of the systems with one another. Engeström sees the tensions and contradictions that can occur within and between activity systems as possible sites for potential change or learning. Examining Sandra's experience through an activity system lens spotlights at least one of these tensions, her ambivalence about the student–teacher relationship in her classroom. We can use activity system analysis to see tensions and contradictions within and between Marc's activity systems as well, for example the tensions he experienced as a participating member of both the Anglo-dominated workforce and his French-Canadian community in Ontario.

By looking carefully at Sandra's response to Marc, we can see evidence of a tension between two of Sandra's activity systems. In her response, Sandra reassures Marc that he has understood and used the idiom correctly, but she emphatically repositions him as someone to whom the meaning of the idiom *does not* apply. We can take this as a product of the tension produced by actions in Sandra's graduate student system. We can see this in Sandra's story if we look at what happened to Sandra's teaching practice as she described it in the final paper that makes up part of the narrative that began this chapter.

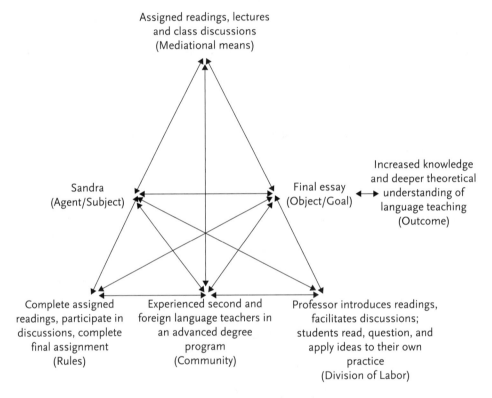

Figure 6.8 Sandra's graduate class

Sandra's graduate class is an activity system of its own (see Figure 6.8). We have used the triangle in this case to represent a summary of the many actions that occur in the course of taking a graduate class rather than the very specific action of responding to Marc's email shown in Figure 6.6. A reader of activity theory research can become confused because writers do not always clearly indicate what level of abstraction the triangle represents. One activity Sandra engaged in as part of the graduate class activity system was completing assigned readings. This is not just one action in a graduate course. Reading, questioning, discussing, making notes, thinking, making meaning through all of these actions are part of the activity of 'reading'.

Sandra acknowledged that critical pedagogy with its emphasis on and examination of power and dominance in the language classroom, became a mediational means by which Sandra examined her practice. 'It put some order to my thoughts.' So what **had been** operations, (automatic things she did) such as correcting a student's utterance, engaging in email correspondence with students and assuming the role of 'authority' were called into question. Once brought to consciousness by this questioning she could no longer act without thinking. Making teaching decisions in line with her new understanding emerged as goals in her practice. A tension existed between Sandra's learning, her object in her graduate studies and the rules and division of labor in her EWP system. Yet another system, the married homeowner, rubbed up against the two and one particular exchange crossed the boundaries of both the graduate studies system and the EWP system.

Sandra traced this phenomenon clearly when she opened her paper with the story of how Marc and his wife stopped by, they chatted and then Marc emailed her with a question about his use of the idiom 'dead duck.' Her response to this email, which she quoted, not only answered Marc's questions but referenced her own ambivalence about a practice she had earlier not given conscious thought to, when she wrote, 'but I would not use it the way you did. (You are none of those things, as you must realize.) But, perhaps, that is how it feels when I correct you.' Now, we can begin to see what Sandra may have tried to do in addition to providing Marc with an evaluation of his linguistic performance. Part of her response manifested her concern with power and how she perceived the asymmetrical student–teacher actions she participated in. From that tension or contradiction, another goal emerged and she extended her feedback and provided an additional idiom, 'sitting duck'.

Here we can see that Sandra articulated how she has come to understand her actions of giving feedback and correcting student utterances. Her choice of 'sitting duck' as an extension of the vocabulary/idiom usage lesson explicitly addressed her concern with the issue of power between student and teacher.

It is possible to see evidence in her final paragraph of yet other emergent goals, promising Marc not to be so hard on him, setting up a goal perhaps for herself, to change the tenor of her relationship with her student and provide more explanation than corrective feedback. Within this action Sandra addressed cognitive and emotional goals simultaneously.

A node of tension had grown at the interstices of Sandra's graduate student activity system and her EWP teaching system (see Figure 6.9). In her graduate student system she read, discussed and wrote of the use and abuse of power by teachers in second language classrooms. Simultaneously she continued to use the repertoire of teaching strategies and student–teacher interaction patterns she had found to be effective in her years of practice. An interaction in two other systems provoked a new or different goal in her email response: social interactions between adults and the student–teacher email system. A routine response under these conditions was no longer routine. Sandra became acutely conscious of how she responded to Marc's query. An operation, Sandra's routine response to correct and offer additional, related vocabulary to a student, generated a new object or goal – to resolve the tension between Sandra's correction practices and a new perspective; distribution of power in the student–teacher relationship. She wrote:

> Yet, how detrimental is it to deliver such correction? This is often what students ask for; why does it seem so rude and limiting to focus on such subtleties? Moreover, how can teachers navigate such complex and nuanced discourses? Apart from the interpersonal

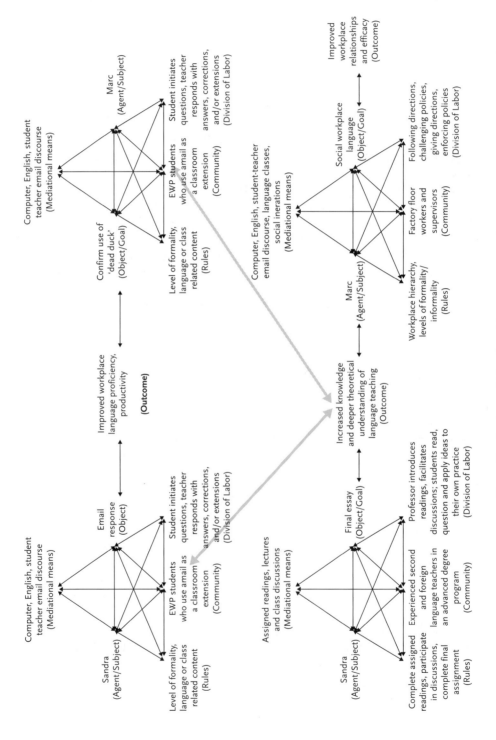

Figure 6.9 Sandra and Marc's activity system network

considerations, there is also the difficult question of editing. We are compelled to ask, "Whose voice is it that needs to be heard?" What would be lost if a voice like this student's, and the individual behind it, were suppressed or replaced?

At the end of her graduate essay Sandra has not resolved this tension. She appears to have access only to her perspective, her actions in the activity. This example, using Engeström's combination of activity system and activity system networks, could open Sandra's examination of both her response to Marc's request for evaluation and correction and Marc's response to her concern about the power distribution. It could allow Sandra to interrogate the tension that the interacting systems have created.

> **When I learn a new word or a new expression I just try to put it in context. I fail often. I'm not frustrated if you correct me. It's not at [my company] I will learn the best way to say things. You are the best reference I know and you're not too hard on me. Don't feel embarrassed. It's OK that way.**

Marc's response gives tantalizing hints of his construction of the community, the division of labor, the rules and the goals and the outcome. If Sandra could see how Marc constructs these actions she might understand that the action for Marc was different than it was for her, and accordingly the power relationship. Sandra alludes to these when she wrote, 'Yet, his identity as a second language learner was evident, since the axis of language was an area of contention within the plant. Vocal as well as discrete hostility toward Quebecers was constant.'

How triangles can explicate (interaction at the network level)

Through the lens of activity theory, it becomes possible to pick out and see the complex interactions between an individual, the symbols and tools that mediate Sandra's worlds, the tensions and contradictions that prompt further interaction, and the actions that provide evidence of internalization. Both triangles, (Sandra's and Marc's, Figures 6.6 and 6.7, respectively) represent the EWP class from Sandra's perspective. Changing the subject or agent changes the positions and relationships in each of the categories as well as the goals. If Sandra considers the relationship and the goals, from Marc's perspective, as represented in Figure 6.10, she might understand the action differently. She might be able to see another perspective of the student–teacher relationship.

If Marc's goal is to establish himself as a competent user of English in his work activity system, then the corrective feedback Sandra gives him in the EWP system can mediate that action. Marc made liberal use of the mediational means of the email extension of their EWP classroom with each question he addressed to Sandra. He also made one of his goals clear (i.e. improving his English) when he responded to her concern, related to her growing awareness of the power she held as the teacher. By asking questions and demanding feedback on his attempts to incorporate new words and expressions into his language, Marc also exercised power in the relationship. Sandra provided evidence that may be interpreted as Marc making use of Sandra in order to accomplish his emerging goal: to change his own position among his co-workers. Sandra wrote in her paper:

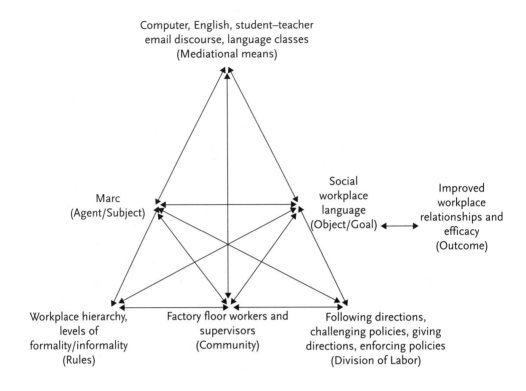

Computer, English, student–teacher
email discourse, language classes
(Mediational means)

Marc
(Agent/Subject)

Social
workplace
language
(Object/Goal)

Improved
workplace
relationships and
efficacy
(Outcome)

Workplace hierarchy,
levels of
formality/informality
(Rules)

Factory floor workers and
supervisors
(Community)

Following directions,
challenging policies, giving
directions, enforcing policies
(Division of Labor)

Figure 6.10 Marc's EWP activity system

When I first met Marc, he told me he preferred to spend time in the woods rather than talk to people, and that if he didn't say anything in class, it was not because he didn't want to learn; he just didn't have much to say. Within a short time, this same student could be relied on to provide practical and moral support within his workplace. In addition, he demonstrated community engagement in a number of ways, as well as becoming a resource and mentor to his classmates.

Yet, Sandra still worried about the abuse of power. Perhaps if she could have looked at this same action through Marc's activity system network, she could have resolved her own conflict.

Current controversies

The concept of activity and the instantiations of it have created an intricate map of related theories, concepts and research. Much of this messy landscape results from the unfinished work of Vygotsky, the politically interrupted and reinterpreted work of Vygotsky, and the quality of the translations from Russian into English and other languages. Activity theory has been interpreted and applied at different levels of abstraction. It has been applied both to individuals and to institutions. Marxist philosophy grounds much of activity theory. However, this connection has been mostly ignored in the West where activity theory has been criticized for not addressing the interactions within socially constructed institutions with a critical perspective. But what seems to be most troublesome to many is the fundamental assumption that people are social beings who embody their contexts and are not merely influenced by them. This appears to contradict the assumption, especially prevalent in North America, that although people operate in social contexts, for each individual knowledge is individually, psychologically developed and possessed.

As Vygotsky and Leont'ev's work became known outside of Russia in the early 1960s, their work began to impact European and Western psychology but in different ways. Russian psychology and Russian thinking reflected a more integrated conceptualization of the individual and society, of affect and cognition which contrasted with the West's, specifically the North American focus on individual achievement, individual cognition and an almost complete separation of affect from cognition. Daniels (1996) wrote:

> Interestingly, whilst attempts to develop Vygotsky's work in Russia have not foregrounded semiotic mediation but have foregrounded the analysis of social transmission in activity settings, much of the work in the West has tended to ignore the social beyond the interactional and to celebrate the individual and mediational processes at the expense of the consideration of socio-institutional, cultural and historical factors. (p. 9)

Politics entered the fray in North America just as it had in Russia. Although Marxian philosophy is an integral force in Vygotskian thinking, all references were cut from the first North American translations of Vygotsky. Without the Marxian philosophy, the application of the concepts of activity and activity theory have taken very different turns. In anthropology and sociology, the focus has been more on the group role and the group dynamics in the production of culture and who can belong as represented by Engeström's expanded triangle. As Daniels (1996) stated, Lave and Wenger's ideas of a community of practice and legitimate peripheral participation have had significant impact on both organizational and educational thinking – the classroom as a learning community – although the focus has often been conflated with socialization into a role or group practice and values (See Chapter 2).

North American researchers and teachers have been most comfortable asking teaching and learning questions focused on individuals and their individual cognitive changes. Researchers and teachers have concentrated on finding generalizable steps to learning for all individuals regardless of context. These questions have considered the impact of social and affective factors on individual learning. The questions have generally not considered social and affective factors, the individual, and learning in multidirectional relationships. Activity theory's reconceptualization of the relationship between learning, the individual and the context challenges that more familiar view of learning. In addition, activity theory has been applied to complex organizations as well as dialogues between two students, without clearly defining the terms. The agent may be plural or singular, the actions singular or multiple over months or minutes. Perhaps more importantly, research and analyses through an activity theory framework challenge the linear cause and effect model of learning centered inside an individual's brain with a model that positions learning in the varied interactions between individuals.

Indeed, at first glance activity theory with its multiple triangles and double-headed arrows appears to have little to do with the immediate needs of an individual trying to make herself understood in a new language and new context, or the teacher's dilemma in facilitating this development. We hope that looking at Sandra's and Marc's interaction through activity theory helps our readers to understand that activity theory provides a non-reductionist way of looking at the amazingly complex process of language learning and teaching. Larsen-Freeman (Harry Daniels, 1996; Larsen-Freeman, 1997) has advocated for the use of activity theory and increasingly for complexity theory in second language research. Complexity theory, like activity theory assumes systemic interconnectedness and dynamism of phenomena. However, unlike activity theory, complexity theory has its roots in economics and physics whereas activity theory has its roots in the social interaction of human beings.

Key research relevant to activity theory

Much of the research that used activity theory as the primary theoretical framework has focused on educational institutions rather than on second language contexts (Brostrom, 1999; Larsen-Freeman & Cameron, 2008). The following study looked at international students in a first-year writing course designed specifically for second language learners.

Charles Nelson and Mi-Kyung Kim used activity theory to examine '(1) how international students in a first-year university rhetoric and composition course appropriated concepts and tools of rhetoric and self-evaluation; (2) how these concepts and tools mediated their learning to write in English; and (3) how tensions and contradictions in the class led to changes in the composition activity system' (p. 1). Their activity theory analysis, informed by Engeström's (1987) concept of expansive learning and Wells' (2002) ideas about dialogue as a mediational means, made use of the interactive relationships among the elements in activity theory to understand what 'worked' and what 'didn't work' for students over the term, e.g. inclusion of non-native speaker writing models. The analysis made starkly clear that although all of the students were involved in the same activity system, they were not all involved in the same actions with the same goals, e.g. getting high marks, making lifelong connections. The activity theory analysis showed that students from different schooling experiences brought different rules and even different divisions of labor to their current classroom, and how these created tensions and contradictions for the students and the teacher. This analysis demonstrated that both the teachers and the students create learning activity settings. It also revealed the possible sites of tensions and contradictions at the social and individual level.

Nelson, C. P. & Kim, M-K. (2001). Contradictions, appropriation, and transformation: An activity theory approach to L2 writing and classroom practices. *Texas Papers in Foreign Language Education*, 6(1), 37–62.

Wells explored the role of dialogue and the role of the socially constructed symbolic artifact of language in a classroom to mediate the learning–teaching activity in an elementary classroom science activity. The article also shows his own attempts to 'represent the simultaneous and complementary contribution of both modes of action to an outcome that is both material and "ideal [symbolic]"' (1999, p. 59).

He focused on dialogue not just as a mediational means but also as the object of actions by the participants in the dialogue to produce meaning.

Wells, G. (2002). The role of dialogue in activity theory. *Mind, Culture, and Activity*, 9(1), 43–66.

Although this study is not a second language study, it highlights how the use of an activity theory analytical framework can facilitate different understandings of an issue. Roth and Tobin (2002) examined the experiences of teacher candidates in their practicum experiences through an activity framework in order to improve the effectiveness of the program. Their analysis showed how they reached different conclusions through the use of activity theory rather than through the use of other analytical tools that focused on more linear models (e.g. factor analysis).

Roth, W. M. & Tobin, K. (2002). Redesigning an "urban" teacher education program: An activity theory perspective. [research]. *Mind, Culture, and Activity*, 9(2), 108–131.

Haneda reconceptualized writing as a social activity in a foreign language classroom. She used activity theory to understand the differing uses of mediational means or linguistic resources of both readers and writers and the differing goals of students engaged in the same writing tasks. Based on her analysis, she suggested several implications for teachers and curriculum planners. For example, the activity theory analysis highlighted the needs and goals of heritage language learners, a group that has received little attention in second language research. Her analysis also suggested that more deliberate attention be paid to understanding the rhetorical norms of the target language genres in second language writing instruction.

Haneda, M. (2007). Modes of engagement in foreign language writing: An activity theoretical perspective. *The Canadian Modern Language Review*, 64(2), 301–332.

Lei used activity theory to analyze Chinese university students' English writing strategies in an elite university in southern China. She focused on rule-mediated, artifact-mediated, community-mediated and role-mediated strategies and the contradictions students experienced as they engaged with these. The activity theory analysis highlighted the interaction of diverse mediating strategies the students used. Lei suggests that if writing instructors helped students become conscious of the nature of these mediating strategies they would also be helping students to develop their own ability to mediate their writing from diverse resources.

Lei, X. (2008). Exploring a sociocultural approach to writing strategy research: Mediated actions in writing activities. *Journal of Second Language Writing*, 17, 217–236. doi:10.1016/j.jslw.2008.04.00.

Questions to explore for research and pedagogy

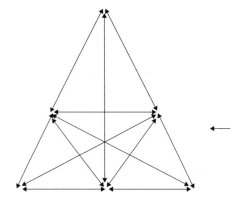

Figure 6.11 Blank Triangle

Activity theory can help us see both the immediate interaction and the larger context which is part of that interaction. Using activity theory allows us to reframe the tensions and contradictions we experience.

Use the following questions to help you understand how activity theory can be used in second language teaching and learning.

1. Given the information in the story, use Figure 6.11 to analyze the email action from **Marc's** perspective. From his perspective describe the power relationships in the classroom and in the email. Think about how Marc's goals may be different from those of his classmates. How might these differences have shaped Marc's use of the email action within the EWP activity system? How might Marc understand what Sandra called 'student voices'?

2. Consider a tension in your own teaching. What is the action? Who is (are) the subject(s)? What is the goal, the outcome? What are the rules? What is the division of labor? Who

makes up the community? What are the mediational means? Where are the tensions or contradictions in the system? What possible changes could you make?

3. Consider a tension in your own learning, including language learning. What is the action? Who is (are) the subject(s)? What is the goal, the outcome? What are the rules? What is the division of labor? Who makes up the community? What are the mediational means? Where are the tensions or contradictions in the system? What possible changes could you make?

4. What other SCT concepts might be identified in *Sandra's Story*? (See the Key Terms at the beginning of each chapter for SCT concepts.)

Notes

1. Canadian Language Benchmarks see http://www.language.ca/display_page.asp?page_id=206 This range describes students who listen and understand simple conversations with considerable effort, participate in short, routine conversations, write simple narratives about familiar topics and read simple short texts to students who comfortably follow formal/informal conversations on familiar topics at normal rates, participate in problem-solving and decision-making conversations, write coherent paragraphs on concrete, familiar topics and understand the main ideas, key words and most important details in moderately complex texts.

7

Yang: Being assessed

SCT tenets related to second/foreign language assessment

- Assessment is a social and cultural activity

- Language performance is co-constructed

- Language instruction and language assessment form a dialectical unity of language development

- Fairness and equity in language assessment occur during a ZPD

Setting of this narrative

Languages: English, Chinese (Yang), Korean (Eun-mi)

Context: Speaking English for academic purposes course, Canada

Key terms in this chapter

(see glossary at the back of this textbook)

Assessment

Tests (psychometric, traditional)

Dynamic assessment

Assessment from an SCT perspective

Introduction

In this chapter we ask the question 'what does an SCT perspective contribute to a consideration of second/foreign language assessment?' By assessment, we are referring to the process of documenting students' language learning. This process might include, for example, **tests**, portfolios and **dynamic assessment** procedures. In our classes, depending on our goals, we use a variety of assessment procedures ranging from informal to formal, and formative to summative. The use of tests is particularly pervasive.

We tend to take the use of tests for granted. However, underlying their use is a set of assumptions about the knowledge and abilities being tested that are different from those of SCT. For example, in general, we think of tests as something that must be done *alone*. It is considered *cheating* to ask a peer for help, to use a dictionary, or to search the internet. Why? This is just one of the assumptions to be addressed in this chapter.

We begin with Yang's story. At the time when Yang told the story, he had completed an Academic Preparation Program at a Canadian university, and was about to take a relatively high-stakes exit test. It was high stakes in the sense that if Yang passed it, he would fulfill the language entrance requirements of the university he hoped to attend. The particular year that Yang took this test, two different forms of the speaking part of the test were administered on an experimental basis (Brooks, 2009; in preparation). Thus, Yang's speaking abilities were assessed in two different ways: in interaction with an examiner (a teacher in the program, but not his own teacher), and in interaction with a peer (from another English for Academic Purposes (EAP) course). As it turned out, Yang and his peer Eun-mi obtained higher scores when interacting with each other than when each interacted with the examiner. Moreover, qualitative analyses of their spoken English during the two test formats indicated that Yang and Eun-mi co-constructed a more linguistically and socially complex interaction than each did when interacting with an examiner.

We make use of Yang's story to mediate an understanding of what an SCT perspective contributes to a consideration of second language assessment. The discussion focuses attention on second and foreign language testing as a mediated, goal-driven *activity* (see Chapters 1 and 6) with social and educational consequences.

The discussion further focuses attention on *what* is being tested: an individual's knowledge and abilities versus distributed (co-constructed) knowledge and abilities. Within an SCT perspective, individuals are understood as co-constructing abilities and knowledge with the people and artifacts integral to their contexts (see Chapters 1 and 3) rather than as individuals who 'possess' abilities and knowledge. From an SCT perspective, performance does not 'belong' to an individual, but is distributed across people and artifacts. Thus who and what mediates performance is important. As McNamara stated, 'the issue of interlocutor support (or the lack of it), its nature, distribution, and effects assume importance from a Vygotskyan perspective' (1997, p. 455) (see Chapters 2 and 5).

To date, the consideration of second language assessment from an SCT perspective has been dominated by a discussion of **dynamic assessment**. Dynamic assessment, developed within the domain of educational psychology, owes its origins to Vygotsky. The application of its theory and practices to second language teaching and learning is recent (Lantolf & Poehner, 2004), and studies investigating the use of dynamic assessment for second language assessment are few in number (e.g. Erben *et al.*, 2008; Poehner, 2008, 2009). We are keen to follow developments in this new area as we recognize the potential of dynamic assessment to facilitate the instruction/assessment interface in second language development. In this chapter, our intention is to discuss dynamic assessment, and to broaden the ways we think about assessment in general when we take an SCT perspective.

In this chapter, we rely on the reader already having internalized from previous chapters some of the important concepts of SCT: mediation and mediational means; ZPD; interrelatedness of cognition and emotion; collaborative dialogue; and activity theory.

Yang: Being assessed

I'm from China and my name is Yang. I'm 25 years old. I'm here because I need to make my English better. I want to go to university in Canada. But if they say my English isn't good enough for university, I still need to learn English to get a better job back in China. I've been studying English here every day for a few months now. Tomorrow we get tested. I hope I do well, but I'm a bit nervous. The teacher told us we're going to get tested two different ways. One way is that one of the teachers that teaches the other classes will have a conversation with me, and the other way is that me and another student I don't know from another class will have a conversation. So I guess the big difference is that in one case I talk with a teacher, and in the other, I talk with another student. I wonder which test will be easier?

******

So I took those tests yesterday and because one of the teachers asked me to tell her what I thought of them, I'll tell you too. First of all I feel a bit tired. It's my first time to take tests for the whole day! In my opinion, the two kinds of speaking tests is good...I mean, are good. But they need different strategies. And they also need different abilities. Interacting with a partner is quite different from interacting with a teacher. For example, the time is different. I mean with the teacher, it's like an interview and I talk much more than the teacher. But in my opinion, with the other student, I have to control the time. I cannot talk too much because if I am a very strong speaker whereas if the other student is not, I have to encourage her to speak a lot. I have to make it 50%, 50% each. I have to make it equal like real conversation. If you always talk, it's not a conversation; it's not real.

Some of my friends in my ESL class think that when we're paired with another student, it's not fair. What if they match you with someone who is not talkative or maybe with someone who is very talkative? My friends think that neither is fair, but in my opinion I think it's okay because it's just like real life. We will meet different people and we have to share the conversation and keep it going, so I think it's okay whoever we're matched with. Besides, it's more real because it's not very often that I talk that long (10-15 minutes) alone with a teacher.

My partner was from Korea. In the test with her, we have to cooperate. I listen carefully to her and catch her points so I can make interesting points too, in response to her. We really communicated. With my partner, I try to encourage her because she's not talk too much, so I ask some questions so she can give her own example or experience about this topic (Netspeak) *[see excerpts 1 and 2 below]*. But the teacher just asked some questions about what I thought about how we don't watch TV as much as we used to, and I just find some idea to put in there and go blah blah blah. But I have to make it sound well-organized *[see excerpt 3 below]*. I think both tests show my real speaking ability because to do both, I have to use different strategies. In my future life, I need both.

Anyhow, the teacher asked me this morning which I liked better, the test with the teacher or with the other student. After I thought about it, I still like better the test with my peer because we keep each other going. We each have ideas. With the teacher, I feel a little bit tired. Another type of test that might be good is when the teacher gives you some situation and you role-play with your partner. Maybe that could be more interesting.

******

Excerpts 1 and 2 are taken from the transcript[1] of Yang and Eun-mi on the topic of "netspeak".

EXCERPT 1

111. Y: [laughs] I, I'm not young generation
112. E: I remembered when I, when I, when I join the one chatting site?
113. Y: Yeah
114. E: But you know after five minutes later
115. Y: Yeah
116. E: I just got out because I [laughs]
117. Y: [laughs] Okay
118. E: I couldn't understand
119. Y: Yeah
120. E: What they said
121. Y: Although they speak Korean
122. E: Yeah, yeah right [Y laughs], very short form
123. Y: Yeah?
124. E: And I **never** heard this kind of language before
125. Y: Yeah, yeah
126. E: So I was shocked, 'Ah oh, I'm very out of date person' [laughs]
127. Y: Maybe they kind of a- a- abridge the language
128. E: Yeah
129. Y: Abridge and then just to cut it
130. E: Yeah right
131. Y: To abridge it, yeah I think maybe same thing happened in China

132. E: Uh huh
133. Y: because uh when I, I talking with my **cousin**, then
134. E: Yeah
135. Y: those teenagers
136. E: Ah
137. Y: They usually like uh, uh chatting in the Internet room
138. E: Yeah

EXCERPT 2

195. Y: Because my cousin is in uh British now
196. E: Yeah
197. Y: He's in Man- Manchester
198. E: Uh huh
199. Y: Man-ches-ter?
200. E: Manchester?
201. Y: Or yeah, that city, and uh for learning uh English so uh, if I chat with her, I think we use a little bit sh- uh short-cut?
202. E: Mm
203. Y: Those things, those uh language or vocabulary
204. E: Yeah
205. Y: But sometimes I don't know that. I just ask her and she explained it to me.
206. E: Mm
207. Y: So yeah, I want to keep close relation with teenagers [laughs].
208. E: Yeah, I also, I
209. Y: Yeah
210. E: I won-, I won't be, how can I, out of date person?
211. Y: Mm hm
212. E: Yeah I want to [laughs]
213. Y: [laughs] You're young yet
214. E: Yeah, in the near future if I have a child [Y laughs] maybe I want to communicate well with them
215. Y: Okay
216. E: Because yeah [laughs] and
217. Y: Just 'mm hm' [E laughs] special baby language [laughs]
218. E: Yeah and um, if I, if I avoid this kind of maybe current, maybe I can't, uh I can't work anywhere, you know
219. Y: Mm hm
220. E: Nowadays I think about I have, I'm addictive to use computer
221. Y: Uh huh?
222. E: you know, yeah, without computer I can't live one day, [laughs, Y laughs] just only one day, yeah, yeah
223. Y: Yes
224. E: When I went travel I all the time go to somewhere and to check my e-mail and
225. Y: Yeah sure

226. E: what happened to me
227. Y: Yeah, yeah
228. E: And yeah, if somebody sent e-mail I ch-, I want to check
229. Y: Mm hm
230. E: Yeah
231. Y: Sure, so in this case we have to know those language of
232. E: Yeah
233. Y: computer or the commun- communication wi- wi- by using computer
234. E: Right
235. Y: That's really important. Maybe uh, in, in the future m- uh the people should learn some more about computer language
236. E: Yeah right

*****

Excerpt 3 is taken from the transcript of Yang and the examiner on the topic of advantages and disadvantages of decreasing TV viewing.

EXCERPT 3 (Yang)

3. Y: I believe it's uh, uh there's more advantage uh than uh disadvantage of uh decreasing of the television viewing
4. T: Mm hm
5. Y: I mean um because uh if the, first, um there's a lot of people uh watching the television before
6. T: Mm hm
7. Y: And uh so they have to spend a lot of time to uh watching television
8. T: Mm hm
9. Y: And maybe mm they had no enough, uh they, they did, did-, didn't have enough time to uh practice
10. T: Mm hm
11. Y: Or I mean the physical practice
12. T: Mm hm
13. Y: to go to swim
14. T: Mm hm
15. Y: or something so it's not good fe- for health
16. T: Mm hm
17. Y: Maybe uh it cause some, maybe we call p- couch potato? [laughs]
18. T: Yeah [laughs] yeah yeah
19. Y: That's funny but I heard,
20. T: Yeah
21. Y: Yeah so, so I think uh it's not good fel- [slip of tongue] for health so, so in this case if the people uh mm will go for another activities
22. T: Mm hm
23. Y: Um I think it's go- uh in this case
24. T: Mm hm, yeah

25. Y: it's good for people's health. And secondly I think um, it's uh for the television I
          mean we usually uh ha- uh watching television uh in uh, dinner time
26. T: Mm hm
27. Y: With the family
28. T: Mm hm
29. Y: And so maybe uh we, everybody just uh watching the television, so uh
30. T: Mm hm
31. Y: we lack of time
32. T: Mm hm
33. Y: For uh communication with the family members.
34. T: Mm hm, mm hm.
35. Y: And uh so uh it's not good for uh family relationships.
36. T: Mm hm

******

What does an SCT perspective contribute to a consideration of second/foreign language assessment?

Yang's story illustrates two fundamental points we wish to make in this chapter that follow from considering second and foreign language assessment from an SCT perspective. The first point is that assessment is a social and cultural activity (see Chapter 6). The second point is that second language performance is jointly constructed (see Chapters 2 and 3).

Assessment as a social and cultural activity

We encourage you to review Chapter 6 and consider Yang's story making use of Engeström's triangles with Yang as the subject and Eun-mi as one of the mediational means. Consider what the rules, community and division of labor were for each of the assessment formats. It would be interesting, too, for you to compare your discoveries with another set of triangles you create for other assessment procedures, for example, portfolios. Furthermore, we hope you might have the opportunity to undertake such a project with at least one other person who has had different experiences than you have had with assessment and assessing.

We would expect that you will have much to discuss and perhaps even have difficulty reaching consensus as to what to include. More important, however, is that you will come to see clearly that what Yang engaged in was a social activity, and that the different formats involved different rules, communities and divisions of labor. Furthermore, the particular formats of the test that Yang took (e.g. dialogic rather than monologic; speaking rather than writing; spontaneous rather than memorized) and what they intended to measure (e.g. overall proficiency versus vocabulary knowledge versus grammar; oracy versus literacy) were culturally determined.

Assessment tools and procedures are not created in a vacuum. They reflect the values and beliefs of the broader society in which they are developed and used. For example, *what* is assessed when assessing reading? This is, in fact, a culturally loaded question, and the answer(s) reflects to a large extent what the dominant society values, what counts as being able to read. Is it important to be able to read comic books? religious texts? newspapers? novels? historical documents? netspeak? ancient texts? classical literature? textbooks? music? We can ask similar questions with respect to writing. In some indigenous cultures, for example, the form writing takes is pictorial and artistic. However, mainstream Western culture has only begun to consider developing literacy tests which are multimodal in nature.

Similarly, assessment procedures reflect the historical context of their development. Why did large-scale tests of English proficiency initially focus on reading, vocabulary knowledge and grammar? The answer is not simple, but certainly the theories of language and measurement dominant at that time played, and still play, fundamental roles. Today's current emphasis on testing speaking and writing in the assessment of second/foreign language proficiency in North America is strongly associated with the 'communicative competence' movement which emerged from the UK in the 1970s. Communicative language teaching which resulted from this communicative competence movement has had little impact in many countries, while in others such as China and Japan, it has created much controversy as it runs counter to historical traditions such as the scholarly importance of the written word.

Tests that measure individual characteristics (traits) have, not surprisingly, been developed within the discipline of psychology. The theory of measurement that has developed from the process of measuring characteristics of individuals is known as the subdiscipline of **psychometrics**. Psychometrics is based on a number of assumptions, principles and procedures, some of which we will discuss in the section about controversial issues. Here, it is important to recognize that like all theories, it is a product of its cultural and historical roots. Psychometrics carries with it a deeply embedded bias to the effect that human beings possess a number of stable characteristics that can be measured (e.g. intelligence, language ability). The focus is on the individual. In order to measure accurately an individual's knowledge or ability, it is important to 'neutralize' the impact of anything (variables, factors) which might distort it. This process of neutralization is known as standardization. Thus, within a psychometric framework, when testing an individual, it is important to make use of procedures to standardize these variables so that the context can be considered the same for all test-takers. These procedures include scripting what examiners (interviewers) say and training raters to use a set of predetermined criteria, scales and/or descriptors (rubrics) when scoring performance-based assessments of the writing or speaking of an individual.

Traditional (psychometrically-based) tests are construed as a way of finding out what an individual knows or can do. Through the use of a particular instrument or procedure, a score (or scores) is provided from which we are to infer the ability or knowledge 'held' by that individual in a particular domain (e.g. calculus, foreign language). In this sense, tests are static instruments from which inferences are drawn about what a person knows, or is capable of doing, at a particular point in time and across contexts.

As we will see, an SCT perspective suggests that some of these culturally bound assumptions can be questioned by reminding us that performance is social in origin, and is mediated by people and artifacts in our present and past contexts. Second/foreign language performance is co-constructed. In the next section, we will look at what it means for assessment to think about second/foreign language performance as a social, co-constructed activity rather than a solitary one.

Assessment as a jointly constructed performance

In a brief section in her book on speaking assessment, Luoma (2004) discussed activity theory and sociocultural approaches. She pointed out that 'it is important to consider their implications for assessment, not least because they challenge some current orthodoxies of assessment ... the main challenge is directed at the emphasis in current assessment practices on the individual speaker' (p. 103).

> Whereas sociocultural theory considers any interactions as joint action governed by cultural norms, the logic that underlies most modern assessments of speaking is that the examinee's performance can be evaluated in isolation. The tester is responsible for the discourse environment, which should be held as constant as possible for all examinees, and the examinee provides a sample of language that gets rated.[2] (Luoma, 2004, p. 103)

An important aspect of Vygotsky's sociocultural theory of mind is that performance is jointly constructed. We do not act alone, ever. Our behavior is always mediated by others and/or by cultural artifacts, whether present in the immediate environment, or internalized as cognitive/affective symbols that mediate our activity (see Chapter 1). Our cognitive functioning is not a characteristic of an isolated individual; rather, it is part of the activity occurring between individuals as they act with mediational means (Wertsch, 1998). Yang's experience of being tested highlights the distribution of cognitive and affective functioning among individuals.

In this section, consisting of four subsections, we consider joint performance as it is co-constructed (a) between peers (Yang and Eun-mi); (b) between student and examiner (Yang and his examiner); (c) between student and rater (Yang and an observer. Yang did not talk about this aspect of being tested, but it constitutes an important part of the story); and (d) between expert (often the teacher) and student. In Subsection d, we will discuss a special case of joint performance known as **dynamic assessment**.

(a) Joint performance co-constructed between peers Yang and Eun-mi

Yang's reflections on the differences between interacting with a peer and interacting with the examiner are interesting. He was inclined to think that interacting with a partner was 'more real', although he recognized that in his future life, he would have to do both. Yang felt that he and his partner 'really communicated'. They 'kept each other going', each contributing ideas and asking questions of each other. As the transcripts of Yang and Eun-mi show (Excerpts 1 and 2), the pair were engaged (affectively and cognitively involved) in their conversation, and they seemed to move seamlessly across turns: asking, responding, paraphrasing, reformulating, contributing new ideas, offering opinions, joking, and so forth.

For example, in turns 118 and 120 of Excerpt 1, Eun-mi pointed out that when she tried to join a chat site, she 'couldn't understand what they said' and Yang completed her sentence in turn 121 'although they speak Korean'. He then built on what Eun-mi said about the 'very short form' of Korean used, by offering an explanation (turn 127), 'Maybe they kind of a- a-abridge the language', introducing a new sophisticated lexical item in doing so. In this exchange, Yang supported and added to Eun-mi's contribution.

In Excerpt 2, it is Eun-mi who expanded Yang's story about his teenage cousin's knowledge of netspeak by providing reasons why she, like Yang, did not want to be an 'out of date person' (turn 210). Her reasons included wanting to be able to communicate well with her future children (turn 214), for future work possibilities (turn 218) and for email (multiple turns). Yang provided a summary of their discussion 'That's really important...people should learn some more about computer language' (turn 235).

Overall then, in Excerpts 1 and 2, we observed Yang and Eun-mi building on what the conversational partner said, co-constructing an emerging and engaging conversation that demonstrated their ability to use language for a variety of communicative and pragmatic functions. In this peer–peer context, Yang and Eun-mi contributed equally. Brooks' (2009) analysis of Yang and Eun-mi's transcript indicated that each contributed 50% of the observed features of interaction (e.g. asking a question, requesting elaboration, paraphrasing, incorporating peer's words, finishing sentences), and that each talked about the same amount in terms of number of turns. This calculation corresponds with Yang's view that 'with the other student, I have to control the time. I cannot talk too much because if I am a very strong speaker whereas if the other student is not, I have to encourage her to speak a lot. I have to make it 50%, 50% each. I have to make it equal like real conversation. If you always talk, it's not a conversation; it's not real.' Yang was right on target of his goal of speaking '50/50', and also on target about the authenticity of his conversation with Eun-mi. In the next subsection, the contrast between peer–peer co-construction of speaking performance and examiner–student co-construction becomes apparent.

(b) Joint performance co-constructed between the examiner and Yang

Yang summarized his experience of being tested by the examiner as 'With the teacher, I feel a bit tired.' He was tired because he felt he had to talk more, and instead of the lively discussion Yang had with Eun-mi, he just found 'some ideas to put in there and go blah, blah, blah', albeit in an organized fashion (see Excerpt 3). He did not have to listen carefully to the examiner 'so that I can make interesting point too, in response to her' as he did with Eun-mi. Compared with being tested with Eun-mi where he used 21 different interactional features, Yang used 16 interactional features with the examiner. More striking is the contrast between Eun-mi's use of 21 interactional features with Yang and only four with the examiner (Brooks, in preparation). Overall, for the 16 students analyzed in Brooks (2009), students contributed only 27% of the interactional features when interacting with an examiner.[3] These figures indicate the importance of person and context in the co-creation of speaking performance. They also may reflect the rules and division of labor that traditionally guide assessment activity.

Overall, the research in testing has supported what we have learned from Yang and Eun-mi. In both peer–peer and examiner–student contexts, the co-constructed nature of the interaction has been documented. However, in the examiner–student context, the behavior of the examiner often led to an asymmetry in the discourse structure (e.g. van Lier, 1989) and differentially supported or handicapped the performance of the student (e.g. Brown, 2003, 2005). Research on peer–peer interaction in test situations (e.g. Taylor, 2000, 2001) has suggested it may be a 'potentially viable and effective alternative which addresses some of the concerns surrounding the more traditional approach' (Taylor & Wigglesworth, 2009, p. 328). The research leaves no doubt that speaking performance is not solo performance, but is jointly constructed by participating individuals.

> The individual and the environment form an inseparable dialectical unity that cannot be understood if the unity is broken. As Vygotsky often said, if we want to understand the property of water that allows it to extinguish fire, we cannot reduce it to its component elements – oxygen and hydrogen. (Poehner & Lantolf, 2005, p. 239)

(c) Joint performance co-constructed between the raters and Yang and Eun-mi

Yang did not talk about raters in his story. However, raters are an important aspect of the process and context of being tested. For speaking tests, sometimes the examiner is also the rater; sometimes the rater is an observer present at the time of testing; and sometimes the rater is a person external to the test session but who later listens to a tape-recording or views a video of the session.[4] In the study in which Yang participated, two individuals rated the students' speaking performance. As it turns out, these two raters rated Eun-mi and Yang similarly when they were conversing together; that is, they awarded them each the same score suggesting the raters might be awarding them one score for their co-constructed performance. However, in the larger data set of 37 pairs, this happened only eight times suggesting that it is much more likely that the raters did not conceive the performance as co-constructed but as two individual performances (Brooks, 2009, p. 351). An SCT perspective argues that such a finding occurs because the raters' judgments are mediated by a belief that performance is a characteristic of an individual, not of a pair or group. In other words, the supposedly 'objective' judgment made by raters is mediated by socially constructed beliefs, as well as by the criteria, scales and descriptors raters have been trained to use.

Another way to consider the issue of rater impact on scores is to try to disentangle why a rater makes a particular judgment. Brown (2003) found that examiners' behavior varied across examiners and across test-takers. Sometimes an examiner provided prompts, supportive comments, and so forth which, not surprisingly, helped test-takers to improve their performance; in these cases, the raters provided a more positive rating. From an SCT perspective, it is clear that the speaking performances of the test-takers were co-constructed with the examiner.[5] From a traditional testing perspective, the performance of the test-takers would be interpreted as their independent, autonomous, speaking abilities.

In traditional testing, raters are trained. Training aims to standardize or 'calibrate' raters so that each rater becomes a replication of each other. They are usually trained by being provided with the rubrics of the rating scales and by being provided with a number of performances to rate. The procedure involves continuous rating of samples until the raters are able to provide ratings similar to the norm. It is argued that training raters so that they all rate similarly enhances the fairness of the procedures. While it is indisputable that fairness is enhanced, from an SCT perspective training raters creates an artificial, non-agentive consensus that cannot be maintained because each rater's behavior is mediated by their beliefs about second language learning and testing (e.g. Erdosy, 2004). This is evidenced in the need to constantly retrain raters, who, as they are distanced from their training, return to their default beliefs.

(d) Joint performance co-constructed between an expert (often the teacher) and student: Dynamic assessment

In this subsection, we consider **dynamic assessment.** Yang and Eun-mi guided each other towards better performance, creating a ZPD (see Chapter 2). However, their trajectory was not planned or intentional. In dynamic assessment, the co-construction of performance is mediated by an expert who deliberately guides the student towards development. Dynamic assessment is a form of assessment in which the goal is to modify learner performance during the testing process itself. Dynamic assessment has its roots in Vygotsky's concept of the ZPD (see Chapter 2).

> The goal of working in the ZPD is not simply to help learners to master a specific task but to help them to develop a principled understanding of the object of study that will enable them to transfer from the given activity to other activities. (Poehner & Lantolf, 2005, p. 257)

It was Vygotsky's colleague Luria (1961) who provided the label 'dynamic'. Luria did so to contrast static with dynamic approaches to testing. A static approach measures an individual's knowledge and abilities, alone, at one point in time. A dynamic approach, however, is one in which an expert interacting with a student, mediates the student towards a performance that he or she will be able to carry out on his or her own in the future. Dynamic assessment is future oriented; it allows us to glimpse the future by seeing what students do not yet know how to do on their own (the 'becoming' of the 'becoming/being' dialectic in Holzman (2009)) in contrast to measuring outcomes of their past learning. In essence, the expert co-creates a ZPD with the novice through a form of collaborative dialogue.

In Chapter 3, we discussed collaborative dialogue as a form of interaction between peers, where expertise shifts between them. In dynamic assessment, however, there is only one expert, the teacher/examiner, who guides the student contingently towards an appropriate response. The expert knows the goal and attempts to push the student to rely on his/her own agency to achieve it. For example, in dynamic assessment, the expert does not immediately provide students with a correct response, but may offer suggestions, ask questions and help them to language (see Chapter 3) their decision-making processes about how to linguistically perform their intended meaning. The researcher in the Aljaafreh and Lantolf (1994) study (see Chapter 2) provided mediation that moved along a dimension of implicit to explicit support. The quality and quantity of mediation was controlled by the learners' responsiveness. It is in this sense that dynamic assessment is a process of co-regulation. It is a means of transforming not knowing into knowing.

Whereas the focus of most assessment is on product (outcome), the focus of dynamic assessment is on process. The intent is not to provide the learner with a correct response, but to assist the learner to get there. Through interaction with the mediator/expert, a student's understanding of, and control over, a particular aspect of language is revealed. In this way the expert is able to discover the *source* of the problem, information that can then be used to provide appropriate instruction/mediation. This inseparable link between assessment and instruction is a key feature of dynamic assessment. As Lantolf (2009) stated, assessment and instruction are 'both moments of a single process' (p. 356); 'inseparable components of the same dialectical activity...as tightly conjoined as two sides of the same coin' (Lantolf & Poehner, 2008a, p. 274).[6]

Dynamic assessment takes place during interactions in which interventions are provided. Finer grain distinctions relate to how intervention is conceived and delivered during dynamic assessment (Donato, personal communication, 2010). In some cases the intervention is pre-established (often referred to as an interventionist approach), and in other cases, the intervention is emergent (often referred to as an interactionist approach). In both approaches, assessment and instruction are inextricably linked: assessment uncovers what and how much mediation a learner needs and in so doing, provides guidance as to the nature of the instruction needed to further development. The goal of dynamic assessment is to mediate development; the assumption is that change will occur during the process. That is, *development should occur during the process designed to assess it.* This goal is contrary to the goal of traditional testing wherein no opportunity for change is provided (an issue of construct validity); furthermore, test developers would not be pleased if change occurred between two administrations of the same test[7] (an issue of reliability). We will return to these points below in the section on current controversies.

During an interventionist approach, a set of prefabricated clues and hints related to the test item or task is given to students. If students are unable to do the item or task, they are given the clues in a fixed order beginning with the most implicit and proceeding to the most explicit which is the correct response, sometimes accompanied by an explanation. Although the hints and prompts are responsive to whether learners are succeeding in the task, they are, in fact, not responsive to an individual's particular problem because both their wording and order of presentation are fixed. Examples include computer learning programs that direct a student to the next question or to a series of remedial steps depending on the answers a student provides. This 'fixed' feature of an interventionist dynamic approach is different from an interactionist approach to dynamic assessment.

During an interactionist dynamic assessment, the expert and novice are responsive to each other, thus constructing both the process and product of the performance together. 'Mediation in interactionist DA [dynamic assessment] is not predetermined but is instead negotiated with the individual, which means that it is continually adjusted according to the learner's responsivity' (Lantolf, 2009, p. 360). In theory, this characterization suggests that interactionist dynamic assessment provides the conditions for perhaps the most fair and equitable testing process possible because it is adjusted to each specific learner's development. In practice, we must ask how able is each expert to co-construct each learner's best performance?

Lantolf and Poehner (2007) provided examples of interactionist dynamic assessment in the DVD that accompanies their manual on dynamic assessment. Antón (2009) wrote of an example in which Learner A, in recounting a narrative during a placement test situation, was reminded that the past should be used. Once reminded, the learner used the past tense with little difficulty. Learner B, once reminded to use the past, was unable to consistently use that verb form. Without the assessment through mediation from the tester, the two learners might have been placed at the same level in the program. Examples of dynamic assessment being used in a classroom context can be found in Poehner (2009).

Considerable research and theorizing about dynamic assessment have occurred in the fields of psychology, education and special education (e.g. Feuerstein *et al.*, 2003; Haywood & Lidz, 2007; Lidz, 1987; Lidz & Elliott, 2000; Sternberg & Grigorenko, 2002), but only recently has attention been paid to it in the second language learning and testing literature (e.g. Lantolf & Poehner, 2004; Poehner & Lantolf, 2005). We will discuss the research of Ableeva (2008), Erben *et al.* (2008), and Poehner (2009) in the section on key research.

Current controversies

By asking ourselves what an SCT perspective contributes to a consideration of second and foreign language assessment, a clash of paradigms between traditional psychometric testing and socioculturally oriented assessment becomes apparent. The greatest clash concerns the goals of assessment. As we have seen, SCT approaches have the learners' development at heart so that change that occurs during the assessment process is seen as positive and valid (Swain, 2001). Traditional approaches, driven as they are by psychometric considerations, aim to measure learners' second language ability at one point in time, and neither expect nor want change to occur during the assessment process itself.

Let us consider this fundamental difference in more depth by examining what this clash of goals implies with respect to four aspects of assessment: validity, reliability, scoring and fairness.

Validity

Validity is a complicated construct in itself (e.g. Fulcher & Davidson, 2007), and includes construct validity, predictive validity and consequential validity. Here we will consider only the most fundamental meaning of validity: construct validity. The question that is asked concerning construct validity is: 'does the test accurately reflect what one claims to be measuring?'. For example, if we intend to measure a learner's speaking ability, does the assessment procedure we use accurately do that? Of course, to answer that, one has to have a definition of 'speaking ability'. Traditional (psychometric) testing is based on the assumption that speaking ability is a stable trait of the individual, and as such, remains the same independent of the context. This is contrary to an SCT perspective, in which context/ environment is considered to be the *source* of development.

Psychometric testing assumes neutrality of, for example, tester, rater and testing situation. It assumes that language ability is the result of a language user's fixed, internal, cognitive abilities. An SCT perspective recognizes that speaking performance is the outcome of the reciprocal influences of the speaker, tester, rater, and other elements on each other. As we indicated earlier in this chapter, Vygotsky pointed out that one cannot understand how water extinguishes fire by deconstructing it into its elements of hydrogen and oxygen. Oxygen, after all, supports fire rather than destroys it. It is the unity of oxygen and hydrogen that must be examined in order to understand its ability to extinguish a fire. It is in this sense that SCT compels us to look at speaking performance as an inseparable unity of performer *and* context, as being a co-constructed 'joint performance'.

We saw Yang's performance change depending on whether he was interacting with the examiner or his peer. He made use of different language functions and strategies in the two testing formats. And, in fact, the score Yang obtained (based on a rating scale) when interacting with his peer was higher than the score he obtained when he interacted with the examiner. From a traditional psychometric perspective, this is an unwanted result because it means that performance varied with context rather than being a stable trait of an individual. From an SCT perspective, this result is not at all surprising, and is, indeed, what one would expect. Together Yang and Eun-mi accomplished something different than Yang and the examiner (see point 3 below re Scoring).

Some psychometrically oriented researchers in the field of language testing have accepted that context must be taken into account in test performance (e.g. Bachman, 2002a, 2002b). However, as Chalhoub-Deville (2003) pointed out, researchers maintain a theoretical distinction that performance-in-context is different from the abilities underlying performance (competence). This distinction allows for the maintenance of the assumption that language abilities are a characteristic of an individual which are transferable to other contexts. If this distinction is not maintained, then there is no basis on which psychometric generalizations about language abilities across contexts can be made.[8]

In sum, the very construct of *what* is being measured differs between traditional and SCT perspectives. SCT considers language performance as a mediated, co-constructed activity; traditional approaches consider language performance as a manifestation of an underlying stable set of abilities which may be differentially drawn upon depending on contextual variables.

Reliability

Psychometrically, a reliable test is one in which performance is the same across different learners of the same ability level, or across different administrations of the same test with the same individuals. However, as we have seen, the goal of the procedures used in dynamic assessment is to support learners' development through the use of guided prompts, cues and questions. Change is expected and viewed positively. How learners respond to the mediation provided is more important than is the final score. The intent is not to discover what learners know at a moment in time, but rather to move them forward using appropriate mediation so that in the future they will be able to generalize their knowledge to new contexts. In other words, the concept of reliability as used in traditional testing is simply not applicable to dynamic assessment. Because dynamic assessment integrates instruction and assessment, change (development) is necessarily an artifact of the process (Lantolf & Poehner, 2008a).[9]

Scoring

The controversy concerning scoring has barely been broached in assessment circles. In 1997, McNamara bravely asked the question 'whose performance?'. But to date, all indications are that the testing profession is still determined that scores will be assigned to individuals, even when students are tested in pairs or groups. Taylor and Wigglesworth (2009) pointed to this issue, asking 'whether individual or shared scores ... should be awarded to test-takers in order to acknowledge the inherently co-constructed nature of paired interaction; and if so how such an approach might be operationalized alongside, or instead of, the traditional practice of raters assigning each individual test-taker their own individual score' (p. 334). From an SCT perspective, we must ask how scores based on interaction among participants can be interpreted as an indication of individual performance. Can they be interpreted as individual performance at all? If the answer is no, then it is time to make testing more compatible with the 'inherently co-constructed nature of paired interaction' and less with the demands of psychometric theory.[10]

Fairness

It is the intention of assessors that their practices of assessment be fair. Gipps (1999) provided a historical overview of the relationship between a society's desire to be fair and the development of assessment tools and procedures. She argued that major developments in assessment have been driven by attempts to achieve fairness. In the past, it was thought fairer to have tests than to have decisions made based on an individual's background (meritocracy). Standardization of procedures was the next step in the quest for fairness. Standardization, it was thought, would create a similar context for all test-takers so that differences in performance across test-takers would not be related to differences in instruments or procedures followed. But, as we have seen, an SCT perspective argues that the source of language performance is 'person + context', or, as Wertsch *et al.* (1993) stated it: 'agent-operating-with-mediational-means'. Homogenization (a leveling of the playing field) of context, or separation of context, does not make sense within the theory. Within SCT, fairness means treating people differently to create, teach and learn during their emerging ZPDs.

This chapter is not a statement against psychometric approaches. Rather it has been written to posit that an SCT approach to assessment broadens and enriches the interpretation of second language performance as a social, mediated and co-constructed activity compared to other approaches to assessment which focus on the individual. We think it is fruitful to think of second language performance in this way. For example, portfolios, usually thought of as the work of an individual, are much more richly seen as artifacts creating, and created by, the process of development. This process of development has also been mediated by others, the self and existing artifacts. Furthermore, portfolios can then be understood as not just the work of an individual, but related to the affordances and constraints offered by the contexts in which that individual works. Thinking about second language performance in these ways should advance the assessment–instruction dialectic of language development.

Key research relevant to an SCT perspective on testing

Ableeva's (2008) study is unique in researching listening comprehension from a dynamic assessment perspective. She compared dynamic versus non-dynamic procedures for assessing the listening comprehension of university students of French as a foreign language. She demonstrated that students whose individual performances were similar had different ZPDs. Learners' difficulties in comprehending French were related in some cases to lexical comprehension and in others to cultural knowledge, aspects which non-dynamic assessment could not uncover. Ableeva concluded that dynamic assessment was useful for both the diagnosis of problem sources and the development of appropriate instructional mediation.

> Ableeva, R. (2008). The effects of dynamic assessment on L2 listening comprehension. In J. P. Lantolf & M. E. Poehner (Eds), *Sociocultural theory and the teaching of second languages* (pp. 57–86). London: Equinox.

Erben *et al.*'s (2008) study is unique in examining the process of diffusion and adoption of dynamic assessment by students and faculty at a program level. They described their attempts at changing the examination procedures in pre-service ESOL courses to emphasize dialogic interaction and mediation. The authors stated an intention to further investigate the ongoing process of resistance and acceptance to changing the examination procedures through the lens of activity theory.

> Erben, T., Ban, R. & Summers, R. (2008). Changing examination structures within a college of education: The application of dynamic assessment in pre-service ESOL endorsement courses in Florida. In J.P. Lantolf & M. E. Poehner (Eds), *Sociocultural theory and the teaching of second languages* (pp. 87–114). London: Equinox.

Poehner's (2009) article is one of very few research-based papers exploring the use of interactional dynamic assessment with an entire classroom of students. The students were in Grade 4 and were learning Spanish for 15 minutes a day. The teacher made use of an inventory of prompts (symbolic artifacts), sequenced from implicit to explicit, to mediate her students' linguistic development. She tracked her students' responses on a mediational chart while teaching, thus helping her to monitor individual and class development in the emerging class ZPD. In order to create a class ZPD, one must consider the class as more than just a context for individual development, but as a 'psychological entity composed of individuals with differential forms of expertise working cooperatively to carry out activities that no single group member could do independently' (p. 475).

Poehner, M.E. (2009). Group dynamic assessment: Mediation for the L2 classroom. *TESOL Quarterly, 43*, 471–491.

See also, Lantolf, J.P. & Poehner, M.E. (in press). Dynamic assessment in the classroom: Vygotskian praxis for L2 development. *Language Teaching Research.*

Questions to explore for research and pedagogy

The reader will recognize that in many of these questions we have drawn upon the SCT concepts presented in previous chapters.

1. There are three transcripts provided in this chapter. What inferences about the participants' performance specifically and generally do you draw from the dialogues observed in these transcripts?

2. How would you 'score' the performance of Yang and Eun-mi? What ways might you assess the quality of their performance? Do you think each student should receive a separate score? Why or why not? Can pairs be assessed in ways that are equally fair to both participants?

3. Look back at Excerpt 3. If you had been the examiner, what kinds of mediation (assistance) might you have provided Yang?

4. Consider a testing event that you are familiar with and analyze it from the perspective of activity theory. Drawing Engeström's triangles may mediate this process.

5. What assessment activity do you consider to be fair and equitable? Why? What could be done to make it more fair and equitable?

6. What assessment activity do you consider to be problematic? Why? What could be done to make it more fair and equitable?

7. How would you interpret the meaning of 'group dynamic assessment'?

8. What is the role of languaging in dynamic assessment?

9. With the exception of research on the effect of anxiety on test performance, the literature in second language testing is complacent about the cognitive/emotive interface. Using your own experiences, or that of your students or research participants, describe your understanding of the cognitive/emotive interface in assessment.

10. What might the reactions of your colleagues/program be to implementing dynamic assessment? How might it be incorporated into the overall assessment process?

11. When is a psychometric approach to assessment necessary? Why?

12. What other SCT concepts might be identified in Yang's story? (See the Key Terms at the beginning of each chapter for SCT concepts.)

Notes

1. Transcript conventions used: [ ] = transcriber's commentary; - = incomplete utterance; ? = rising intonation; **bold** = emphasis; underlining = overlapped speech

2. This quote is also relevant to the assessment of writing, and written and spoken comprehension.

3. Note that in the Brooks study, the examiners were *not* given a script to follow. In other words, their interaction was not standardized, and the examiners were free to interact as they wished.

4. Or who reads what the student has written in the assessment of writing.

5. This is one of the main reasons for standardization: to control for and therefore eliminate examiner and rater effects in order to get a 'pure' picture of the test-taker's ability. From an SCT perspective, this does not make sense: why would one want to obtain a score independent of mediation and context? Is that even possible?

6. There is a tendency to think that dynamic assessment is just one way of doing formative assessment because of the close link between assessment-instruction-learning in both. However, in the case of formative assessment, learning is expected to happen *after* the assessment as a result of the assessment outcomes, not as a result of the assessment process itself. Furthermore, as with most other assessment practices, the focus is on individual, not co-constructed, performance.

7. Assuming, of course, that no learning took place between the two administrations.

8. Chalhoub-Deville argued that 'individual ability and contextual facets interact in ways that change them both' (p. 369). The reciprocal interaction represented in her arguments (e.g. Chalhoub-Deville, 2003) is a grand step forward from assuming one-way, linear, causal models.

9. The issue of measuring change/development over time is one that is being addressed by psychometricians, but the literature is sparse because most assessment research and practice focuses on snapshot assessment at one point in time, and measuring change over time is challenging (Barkaoui, personal communication, December 11, 2009).

10. Psychometricians have developed some statistical procedures that do take into account dyads and assume non-independence of the data (e.g. multilevel modeling). Statistical and measurement models (e.g. Rasch modeling, generalizability theory) have been developed that claim to be able to remove context (i.e. examiner/rater effects and task effects) statistically to obtain a 'true' estimate of ability. But an SCT perspective, as we have already noted, sees person and context as part of an inseparable unity. The psychometric goal is incompatible with an SCT perspective.

8

Maria and the Beatles; Jean-Paul and Second Life

The floor is yours

In each of the first seven chapters of this textbook we focused on one or several specific SCT concepts in order to facilitate your understanding of each concept. It is important to realize, however, that the concepts work in dynamic interaction with one another to form the coherent and rich sociocultural theory of mind. We now ask you to think across *all* the concepts as doing so deepens the understanding of learning–teaching phenomena. Please refer back to the Contents to review the concepts before you begin the challenge that we offer you in this chapter.

Over the period of writing this textbook, we have taught several intensive courses, making use of the stories. To obtain a grade, students were required to complete a two-part written assignment following these instructions:

> The assignment for this course is to write a narrative that has to do with second/foreign language learning or teaching. As the narrative is to be based on your own experiences, it should be written in the first person. Concentrate on the details rather than generalizations about the experience. The narrative should be between 3-5 pages in length.
>
> After you have written your narrative, analyze it, making use of one or two of the SCT concepts you have learned about in this course. In your analysis, it is important to show how the SCT concept(s) mediates a deeper understanding of your own narrative, and allows you to transfer your understanding to other contexts.

The stated goal of the assignment was to continue the process of internalization of SCT concepts mediated by the students' own narrative.

Two of these assignments appear in this chapter. We asked two students, Maria and Jean-Paul (their real names), if we could use the narratives they wrote as a basis for this final chapter of our textbook: *The Floor is Yours.* We chose these two stories because they delighted us, and because we thought they held great potential for SCT analyses. The first narrative consists of a conversation between two teachers who look to the Beatles for inspiration. The other takes us outside the walls of the traditional classroom and into cyberspace – specifically, Second Life.

Here is your challenge

We have not analyzed or interpreted these last two stories for you. Neither have we provided you with the excellent analyses Maria and Jean-Paul carried out. Rather we are presenting these narratives stripped of their analyses in order to afford you the opportunity to make use of the SCT concepts you have been reading and languaging about in the seven preceding chapters. You might wish to connect quotes from Vygotsky, or other authors you have been reading, with one or other of the stories. Certainly, you will want to consider how the various SCT concepts you have been learning about inform your understanding of Maria and Jean-Paul's experiences. Look carefully for interactions that illustrate concepts.

We ask you not to think about what the *correct* answers might be. There are no correct or perfect answers. Rather, engaging you in the *process* of trying to understand the situations through SCT eyes is the goal of this final chapter. We hope that you have the opportunity to collaborate with another individual and see how your analyses differ! However, even if you work on this alone, you have all the preceding chapters to refer to for help as you engage in your analysis.

Essentially we ask you to attempt to make sense of these narratives in SCT terms, and to consider what might be universal in the specifics of each story. The floor is now yours!

Maria and the Beatles
by Maria Trovela

"We prefer to speak to you directly in class and we want to hear your beautiful native accent more. We learn more from hearing you speak. We do not need to speak with each other so much," Sungjoo wrote in her email to me on behalf of the class. I had been teaching to this group of adults all over the age of 45 in a community English class for about a month. They were accustomed to a more traditional teacher-fronted language class and were not convinced about the effectiveness of learning from interaction. Although I had been scaffolding them into collaborative group work and explained how interaction was a vital part to learning a language, I still received email asking for lessons to be more teacher-fronted. I decided to try a different approach to ease their apprehension. I decided to tell a story that used deep metaphor.

I wanted to adapt a story about the beginning of the Beatles from a book called, *Outliers: Stories of Success* by Malcom Gladwell. I believed it would work well with my group. Tom, my good friend and colleague, had already told a version of this story to one of his classes. One day, over coffee, we talked about it.

"So, you know Gladwell's story about the Beatles?" I said to Tom. "I'm going to use it with my adult class."

"Oh, yeah, that's a good one," he replied.

"Ok, so I'm going to start off with, 'The Beatles were just a normal high school band when they were invited to play in uh, strip clubs in Hamburg...' Oh, wait. I can't say that! Excuse me...off the top of my head... Anyway, so, 'The Beatles were a normal high school band and they weren't anything special, but they were invited to play in clubs in Hamburg. They played for hours and hours each night, which made them great...' Ugh!" I stopped in disgust. "This is sounding so bad. How did you tell this story, Tom?"

"Well, I actually began with a question. I asked, 'Do you know the Beatles?' And of course, almost everyone in the class did. Then, I said something like, 'Well, in 1957, seven years before they became famous, the Beatles were a struggling high school band. They weren't particularly talented or amazing. As a matter of fact, they could only play a few original songs and a few cover songs. All that changed when they were invited to play in clubs in Hamburg, Germany in 1960. Clubs in Hamburg would hire young bands because they didn't have to pay them a lot of money. And uh...so the Beatles played for up to four months out of a year, up to seven days a week, and almost eight hours a night. Can you imagine that? They had to be entertaining for eight hours straight! In the beginning, they didn't know a lot of songs and they certainly didn't know any German songs, but they learned the more they played. Now, by 1964, the Beatles played live almost 1,200 times! If you total up all those hours the Beatles spent playing their instruments since they got together in 1957, they played about 10,000 hours. 10,000 hours!' And then I finished with something like, 'And all those hours of practice is really what made them great.'"

"Okay, let me give it another go. 'In 1957, the Beatles were just an ordinary high school band. Then in 1960, they had a chance to go to Hamburg, Germany to play in the clubs there because the club owners could pay them less money. And the Beatles at that time weren't very good. In the beginning they could only play a few songs...' Oh, I could say something more here... 'So when the audience requested songs that they didn't know, they would try it anyway...um, I'd imagine that they probably asked the person in the audience to sing a few bars until they figured out the chords...' yeah, that's a good one to put in... 'and uh, and so eventually they learned new songs this way--by interacting with the audience like that. So, they played in Hamburg for...' what was it again? Oh yeah... 'four months out of the year, um...seven days each week, and uh, eight hours a night. And they did this for about two years! That gave them over 10,000 hours of practice by the time they became famous in 1964. It's what made them great.'" As I finished, I was still unsatisfied with my attempt.

Sensing this, Tom replied, "Pretty good, I like how you added that bit in, but you can flesh out even more of the story to make it relate to your class more," he said to me. "So for example, you can emphasize that they didn't have a teacher in the club teaching them new songs. They played to learn, and they learned as they played. As a matter of fact, they weren't very confident in the beginning. They made lots of mistakes, but because they were hired to play for eight hours a night, they had to keep going. You know, things like that. You can make the scene more vivid and bring your students into it."

Then I asked, "Cool ideas. I'm going to say those things. Hmmm, but ending on 10,000 hours? I don't know about that. What's your punch line, anyway?"

"Punch line? This isn't a joke," he replied.

"I mean, punch line, like, the central message that you want to communicate. I just call it a punch line. And if we end it on '10,000 hours of practice', I'm afraid the students will feel overwhelmed by that. They might think that learning English is a huge, impossible undertaking. 10,000 hours! To tell you the truth, 10,000 hours of anything doesn't sound like fun."

Tom thought for a minute. "Anytime you tell a story, the students are going to pull their own meanings from it anyway, but you do have a good point there. We want to turn them on to English, not off. Hmm, let's see..."

"Well," I interrupted, "How about saying they spent those hours interacting with the audience and each other, playing their instruments in new ways, learning to cover other songs, writing new songs, and most importantly...They spent 10,000 hours of having fun doing all that..."

"Yeah, yeah, that's it," Tom enthused. "You could connect the hours with the strategies they used and with having fun. And maybe end the story by bringing it full circle to the fact that in the beginning they were just an ordinary high school band." He stopped talking out loud and began to mouth words to himself as his hands moved invisible blocks on the table. After a moment of this, he continued, "Maybe say something like, 'Most people think the Beatles' success came from Paul or John's musical genius, but it is really because they had that opportunity to play so much early on in Hamburg. They made so much progress every time they picked up their instruments to play. So in the beginning, the Beatles weren't amazingly talented, or geniuses, right? Each night they played was another opportunity to get even better at what they did.'" He looked down on the table, his hands moving one imagined block next to another block as he said, "Hey, that's also a nice way to work in incremental versus entity theory. Nice. I think telling the story with that kind of an ending would work on even more levels. Thanks for challenging that ending."

"Oh no...thank YOU! Can I try the whole thing from beginning to end?"

"Sure, go ahead," he obliged.

I was able to tell the story from beginning to end including the new insights and nuances to the story that emerged from our discussion. I felt pleased that with Tom's help, I was able to not only fill in the gaps of the story, but I was also able to incorporate the new dimensions of the story. My punch line solidified as I practiced the story with Tom for the last time.

My gaze lowered to my hands, which swirled in the space before me and occasionally touched down on the table signaling that an idea was just completed. I said, "Performing in Hamburg at first must have been really exciting, and at the same time, really strange to the Beatles. In Liverpool...they were only playing short one-hour gigs, but in Hamburg...they had to play for several hours. You can imagine how uncomfortable and difficult that was, can't you? However, it forced them to play in new ways...which built up their strength and confidence. Um...Each time they picked up their instruments and interacted with the audience and each other...they made progress. And...that's what we're doing here in our class. Each time you interact with each other, it is an opportunity to use your English...uh, which is like an instrument, in different ways. Each time we interact...uh, we can discover how our classmates use their English, their instruments. And...most of all, like the Beatles, the more you interact, the more you are getting closer and closer to 10,000 hours of practice."

"It needs just a little more polishing up, but it sounds great!" Tom's voice broke the spell I was in. "I think you've got it!" We lifted our coffee mugs, which by now held ice-cold coffee and made a toast to the Beatles, to Gladwell and to telling a good story.

During the next few days, I practiced telling the story to myself several times throughout the day. I even practiced it silently when in public places. On the other hand, if I happened to be in a place where I had privacy, I practiced it out loud until I could tell the whole story automatically and naturally from memory. All of that rehearsing paid off. At the next class meeting, I told the story to my class smoothly and from the heart.

Gladwell, M. (2008). *Outliers: Stories of Success.* New York: Little, Brown and Company.

Lag, Bling, and Prim Hair
Adventures in Second Life Netspeak
by Jean-Paul Duquette

the dictionary meaning of a word is no more than a stone in the edifice of sense, no more than a potentiality that finds diversified realization in speech (Vygotsky, 1986, p. 245)

"Before we begin the show, can everyone take off any AOs and HUDs. Also, any particle effects or bling is going to contribute to lag, so please be considerate." It was the summer of 2008, and I was attending my first fashion show ever. In some ways, it conformed exactly to my preconceived notions regarding such events. A catwalk jutted perpendicularly from the hardwood floor of a stage. A crowd of about forty onlookers surrounded the catwalk on both sides, dressed to the nines themselves. As the models strode onstage and down toward the audience, the room suddenly hummed with the sound of campy house music, appreciative applause, and the click-clack-clicking of camera shutters. So just what was the MC going on about?

Well, there was one major difference between this particular fashion show, and the ones I had seen on television: this one was being conducted in the online virtual world known as Second Life. Second Life was created by Linden Labs in 2002 as an open-ended "creationist capitalist" software platform (Boellstorff, 2008, p. 206). Unlike most goal oriented Massively Multi-Player Role-Playing Games (MMRPGS) like Everquest, World of Warcraft or EVE Online, the "residents" of Second Life, as they are referred to, were left to their own devices regarding what they would do given only a nondescript "avatar", an, at least initially, anthropomorphic digital representation of themselves; some free design tools and an empty world (Terdiman, 2008). Six years later, and Second Life is a thriving community with an estimated 400,000-600,000 users online at any one time, and millions of registered accounts, with its own unique economy, sub-cultures and linguistic conventions (McKeown, 2008).

I had become interested in using Second Life as a learning tool because of my interest in developing my students' learner independence and through a basic appreciation of Engestrom's view of activity theory. As I saw it, looking at the sides and points of his triangle (Betts, 2006, p.4), the use of virtual worlds seemed a perfectly logical path to take when developing an independent learning schema; if the goal is a continued increase of language proficiency even after formal classes have ended, it made little sense to use artifacts, rules and a division of labor based on traditional in-class group work. As Second Life can be accessed by anyone owning a computer and having an Internet connection (the software is free), it seemed an ideal tool for my students.

But back to the fashion show and the MCs rather cryptic pronouncement about "AOs and HUDs." I wasn't a complete "newbie" (newcomer) myself; I had spent free time in virtual chatrooms, played online shooting games and had even once ventured into the text-based virtual fantasy worlds of MUDs (Multi-User Domains/Dungeons), so I was familiar with much of the acronym and emoticon filled slang of Netspeak

(Crystal, 2006, p. 27-65). However, I did not have a clue as to what an "AO" or "HUD" was. I did have some idea what "lag" was, though, from recent experience.

My second week in Second Life, I had visited a night club. Not just any night club, either; this place impressed. A huge warehouse held multiple dance floors with lighting effects and an elevated DJ booth. If one looked down as one's avatar danced, one would notice that the entire dance floor was actually a giant video screen playing a video file in accompaniment to the music. But walking in with some "real life" acquaintances, my avatars movements became jerky, and the animations around me jumpy and indistinct. "What the hell is this? I'm all slowed down."

"The lag here's pretty bad tonight," my friend said. "Lots of people tonight and the prim count must be ridiculous." Well, I had no idea what "prims" were, but "lag" seemed related to the standard English dictionary definition, "to stay or fall behind" (Merriam-Webster). Clearly something was "falling behind" and my best guess was that it was in direct relation to the number of avatars a Second Life location could contain at any one time. It turns out I was only partly right.

Though not perhaps yet a separate dialect, Netspeak in Second Life was the language of an unfamiliar speech community, and I had not yet participated fully enough in the culture to be privy to nuances. At the club, I could drop the issue without revealing my ignorance to those around me. Although my interlocutor would have certainly assisted, there was simply no social imperative to push him further.

Back at the fashion show, the situation was somewhat different. If I failed to comply with the MC's request, there was a chance that my ignorance could affect the dozens of people involved with the event. This was a language problem I couldn't afford to ignore. Luckily, Second Life allows direct person-to-person instant messaging (*IMing*), pragmatically similar to whispering (Boellstorff, 2008, p. 13). I turned to the faerie (!) sitting beside me, and asked, "I'm sorry, I'm really new. How do I know if my AOs and HUDs are off?"

The elfish woman responded, "AOs are animation overrides. HUDs are Heads Up Displays. If you've picked up any walking or gesturing animation sets, just turn them off. ;)". As a matter of fact, I had recently picked up a free walking animation (the default one given is considered a bit of a duck waddle (Mansfield, 2008, p. 8)), so I clicked on my screen to turn it off.

"And "bling" is like shiny jewelry, right?" I made the connection with the now commonly used "bling-bling."

"Right," came the response. "You're not wearing any so that's fine. If you wear too much flash or too many prims, you'll slow the whole sim down."

Well, I had come this far, I might as well ask the question most on my mind. "And prims are like clothes and stuff with a lot of detail?"

"Well, yes," she said. "But a prim is any object. The hair I'm wearing is high prim because it's made of many small strands. Yours is less, because it's got less. Though it still looks good," she added quickly.

So, as it turned out, the key to my understanding of all the unfamiliar vocabulary presented here was the concept of a "prim." However, it was not until a social situation presented itself that required my complete understanding of its significance that I was able to learn it directly. One could argue that a simple browsing through the Second

Life forums could have easily dispelled my confusion. Also, as a teacher looking to use Second Life in the classroom, this is probably something I would teach my students explicitly, as I would worry that the circuitous nature of natural 'fact-finding' might demotivate students to the point of frustration. However, by learning through social interaction as I did, a web of interlocking implications was already under construction when the impetus for learning "prim" became unavoidable, and both the specific meaning and the cultural significance of "lag," "bling" and "particles" became instantly comprehensible once that keystone was in place.

A few weeks later, I was talking with the sexiest avatar that I'd seen in awhile, a Ms. Aeon. She was tall, long-legged and had skin as photo-realistic as a Vogue cover model (in fact, she may have actually been *less* airbrushed). An obvious newbie had just walked by, her default hair and skin an indicator of her unfamiliarity with Second Life. We sent her off with some advice on where to get some 'decent' clothes for free, and after the newcomer had gone, we had a little chuckle at her expense. But then Ms. Aeon turned to me and said, "You know maybe we should go shopping sometime. I know a decent place or two."

I turned to her suspiciously. I had done a lot of work on designing my avatar in recent weeks. Was she implying I still looked like a newbie? "What, you don't like my clothes?"

"No, no, you're fine. Though maybe your hair. It's pretty low-prim..."

I was embarrassed. "Ah, I like it this way," I lied. "Low-prim count makes it easier for everyone, right?"

"Yes, that's true," she laughed. "It is sort of selfish for me to wear an *avi* (avatar) like this one all the time ;)". I had dodged a bullet, and my reputation as a (somewhat) experienced user was secure.

The next day, however, I went out and bought some really good hair. Ethical concerns are one thing in Second Life, but appearance and a sense of in-group camaraderie trump all, and that, like language, was something I had learned more effectively through social interaction than through traditional instruction.

Betts, J.D. (2006). Multimedia arts learning in an activity system: New literacies for at-risk children. *International Journal of Education & the Arts*, 7(7), 1–43.

Boellstorff, T. (2008). *Coming of age in Second Life*. Princeton: Princeton University Press.

Crystal, D. (2006). *Language and the internet*. (2nd edition). Cambridge, UK: Cambridge University Press.

Mansfield, R. (2008). *How to do everything with Second Life*. New York: McGraw-Hill.

McKeown, L. (2008, November 8). Project for language learning at Virtual Campus in Second Life. In L. McKeown (Chair), *Language Education and Immersive Learning*. Kyoto: Symposium conducted at Ritsumeikan University, Graduate School of Language Education and Information Science.

Merriam-Webster. (n.d.). *http://www.merriam-webster.com*. Retrieved November 7, 2008, from http://www.merriam-webster.com

Terdiman, D. (2008). *The entrepreneur's guide to Second Life: Making money in the metaverse*. Indianapolis: Wiley Publishing Inc.

Vygotsky, L. (1986). *Thought and language*. Cambridge: The Massachusetts Institute of Technology.

Discussion

What did we learn?

We intended to write an accessible textbook introducing sociocultural theory to second language teachers, researchers and students. We began the book because we used sociocultural theory in our research and teaching. Each of us had come to SCT via different routes, having immersed ourselves in Vygotsky's writings and the writing of diverse researchers and practioners who claim Vygotskian or sociocultural foundations. As we wrote, we became even more committed to a central position for SCT in second language teaching, learning and research. As Vygotsky would have predicted, we found our experiences transformative.

What did we learn through an activity theory lens?

We (the **agents**) engaged in the activity of reading, writing, speaking and listening as academics. Our **goal** was to produce a textbook that would make sociocultural theory accessible to newcomers to the theory. The **outcome** was to contribute to the educational literature of second language learning and teaching, specifically to the **mediational means** that would develop theoretical understandings. Our immediate **community** was small, just the three of us, although we were simultaneously part of a larger sociocultural theory community, sometimes in face-to-face encounters and other times through the books, chapters, and articles we read and films we watched. The encounters, the readings and our discussions continued to mediate our understanding of sociocultural theoretical concepts.

At the beginning, each of us had brought to the writing activity our own set of **rules** and **practices**. In order to collaborate we had to make the rules and practices evident. We engaged in dialogue and negotiated our collective writing rules. Each of us adapted to new ways of writing. Simultaneously, we experienced a **division of labor** for this endeavor. We observed a fluidity in the division of labor. We each at some point took a 'first go' at a chapter and at another time took on the initial interpretation of a narrative. That particular **activity system** was part of a larger **network of activity systems** that included Linda's work at York University, Merrill's at the Ontario Institute of Studies in Education, and Penny's at University of Toronto Mississauga. Each of those networks connected with our individual personal, academic, linguistic and work histories.

What did we learn through a zone of proximal development lens?

We found we created our own **ZPD** activity as we worked with our diverse teaching and learning experiences, our **everyday concepts** of SCT and the **scientific concepts** we found in Vygotsky's and other scholarly writings about SCT. Definitions and explanations each of us had read many times over, had introduced to students, and had used in our own research became **artifacts** that we examined and re-examined. In the process we strengthened, expanded and deepened our understanding .

We found ourselves comfortably using words that had previously sat somewhat uncomfortably on our tongues (e.g dialectic). The ZPD had to be syntaxed as a verb and not a noun, so we no longer talked about being *in* a ZPD but what we did *during* a ZPD. Part of what we did during a ZPD was to language. We found ourselves laughing when we caught ourselves using **private speech** with ourselves. We also realized that we were using private speech with each other to **mediate** our own understanding of a concept, a word or a challenging paragraph in a reading. After a particularly long and intense session in the early stages of *Madame Tremblay*, when we had even considered discarding the story as a mediating artifact for the concept of a ZPD, we sat back and realized we had created our own ZPD for understanding the ZPD. The story, Linda's first drafts at analyzing the story, our own definitions and experiences of what we thought were ZPDs in our teaching experience and the reading we did all mediated our co-created ZPD. We had answered many of our questions about the nature of ZPDs, and about who and what can mediate a ZPD. We also noticed that what had been constant, conscious attention to the prepositions we used had given way to a much more consistent, unconscious use of *during* when we talked about the ZPD.

What did we learn about dialectic and dialectial unities?

We checked the definitions of **dialectic** as we worked. We could recite thesis–antithesis–synthesis but when it came time to use the word dialectic or dialectical with confidence and authority in relation to the narratives, we hesitated. As we challenged one another, we began to realize we were engaging in dialogues that were dialectic. We also experienced the dialectical tensions as we worked through our understanding of symbolic and material mediational means. Our intense languaging often achieved what we think was a dialectical unity. We understand languaging (in the form of collaborative dialogue and private speech) as an important mediational means in our process of internalization.

What did we learn by using narrative?

We used narrative to explore SCT concepts for a number of reasons. Bruner influenced us with his eloquent writing on narrative as a sense-making activity. Bamberg fascinated us with his 'small' stories. Together we attended their talks at the Georgetown University Roundtable conference in April 2008. What we heard reinforced our decision to use narratives to mediate our explanations and analysis of the SCT concepts and your understanding of them. We consider narrative, as used in this textbook, to be the bridge between everyday and scientific concepts of SCT. Our own languaging about them integrated stories we told one another, conceptual analyses and the narratives we used in this textbook.

One of the most powerful functions of the narratives for us and many of the generous people who responded to our early drafts was the way it instantiated the affective–cognitive dialectic as opposed to an affective–cognitive duality. We and our readers responded to the characters on an affective level as well as a cognitive level. Readers had likes and dislikes and they were not always the same. Mme Tremblay catalyzed both negative and positive memories and evaluations. Some saw her as a not-so-good teacher and M. Dominique as an outstanding principal. Others loved Mme Tremblay and the classroom drama. For some, the story took them immediately back into their own French immersion experiences. But the important thing was the emotional connection the characters evoked and how that mediated the readers' cognitive engagement with the SCT concepts. It appeared that this engagement encouraged discussions of teaching and learning beyond the immediate narrative.

Our engagement in this textbook has become part of our own narrative. Each of us sees our teaching, learning and writing lives in SCT terms more consistently. We have gone back to earlier research and reinterpreted the data from an SCT perspective. We will continue to research and write course outlines from an SCT base. We will continue to think about implications of SCT for research, for teaching, for teacher education and for researcher education for many years to come.

More importantly, what is your narrative as you engaged with the textbook? How have you made sense of sociocultural concepts and your teaching and learning experiences? How will you continue to think and apply these concepts in your teaching, learning and research?

Glossary

Action
The physical and cognitive manifestations of the things a person does to satisfy psychological and physical needs. Different actions may be directed toward the same goal or the same action may be directed toward different goals, depending on the individual's context and history.

Activity
Sets of various actions (see above) motivated by socially or culturally constructed goals.

Activity theory
Developed first by Leont'ev in an attempt to articulate and make operational Vygotsky's conceptualization of the generative, mediated interaction of individuals and their multiple goal-oriented contexts. Leont'ev proposed three parts, activity/motive, action/goal and conditions/operations, in order to better investigate and connect individual and social interactions.

Affect/Cognition
Affect: emotions and feelings. Cognition: thought and knowledge. Often considered separately, Vygotsky insisted they be treated as a unity.

Affordance
An opportunity; a property of the environment which offers the possibility of action to an individual. A person's environment offers many affordances for language learning, but which ones are taken up and used will depend on the person's goals and what is seen as useful to attain them.

Agency
All individuals are agentive, that is, they behave in certain ways according to their motives and goals. What people are able to do depends on the particular constraints and affordances that are present in the situation. These affordances and constraints vary across cultures and may be material or symbolic.

Agent/Subject
The individual who carries out an action. Agent and subject are synonymous.

Artifact
Material or symbolic object produced by people, e.g. pencils, books, graphs, or language. Any artifact may become a mediational means or tool.

Assessment
The process of evaluating. Usually the focus is on measuring the knowledge and skills of an individual, but assessment can also be of a group, institution or educational system.

Assessment can be formative or summative, quantitative or qualitative, process or product oriented, or a combination of these.

Collaborative dialogue
Dialogue that is knowledge-building. Collaborative dialogue involves at least two persons who co-construct knowledge that may be new for one or both of them.

Community of practice (COP)
COP is a social theory according to which individuals gain access to a group through participation. They gradually take on (or not) the practices, behaviors and beliefs of the central members. Language is, of course, a key entry point or barrier.

Complexes
Vygotsky organized the development of concepts across a continuum. Complexes are more stable than earlier generalizations (heaps) but not as stable as scientific concepts. The generalizations or categories represented by complexes are related by concrete, physical experiences.

Conditions – *see also Operations*
The setting (physical or mental) in which actions take place. Under certain conditions the actions are carried out unconsciously – they are routines (operations). However, the same unconscious operations may become conscious actions if the conditions change.

Dialectic
Exists when there is a tension between two or more phenomena e.g. social and individual. A dialectic does not always get resolved (and if it did, the dialectical relationship would cease). Often, a continuing dialectic creates an environment for creativity and fruitful debate. Lois Holzman (2009) explains in a comprehensive manner why SCT is a dialectic theory.

Dynamic assessment
A process-oriented form of assessment during which an expert provides cues and questions to mediate the learner towards an independent performance in the future. This future orientation allows the assessor to project development by seeing what the learner can do with help. In contrast, most other assessment procedures measure outcomes of past learning.

Everyday or spontaneous concepts – *see also Scientific concepts*
Understandings individuals develop from their experiences to solve various cognitive/emotional problems. Everyday concepts are not systematic or have a very limited 'system'. They are not applicable across all contexts and are often applied unconsciously.

French immersion
In Canada, officially an English/French bilingual country, there are various modes of delivering French instruction to non-Francophone students from kindergarten through high school. The default system of French instruction in Canadian schools is known as Core French. Some schools provide a more intensive program – French Immersion – which teaches the language through curricular content for part or all of the school day. Please see the many websites detailing the various programs, for example http://www.statcan.gc.ca/pub/81-004-x/200406/6923-eng.htm

Genesis
The process of becoming and changing. Genesis refers to the history of an individual or a phenomenon.

Goal
Sometimes used interchangeably with 'object'. Goal usually refers to the desired result an individual consciously tries to achieve.

Higher mental processes
Consciousness. Higher mental (cognitive and emotional) processes are those under the control of the individual. These processes include intentional memory, attention and planning. The origin of all higher mental processes is social.

Imitation
Conscious, reflective, goal-oriented repetition of observed behaviors (including language). These deliberate performances are one of the mechanisms learners use to internalize learning and development.

Intermental (interpsychological) processes
Processes that occur between individuals.

Internalization
A social process transformed into a psychological process. In other words, internalization refers to the process by which the intermental becomes intramental. It is the process through which individuals appropriate mediational means and use them to regulate their own behavior. It is a process of learning and development.

Intersubjectivity
Assumes that people are 'on the same page'; that is, they are connected in some way. These people are thinking or talking or writing about a particular subject. Although they do not necessarily agree with one another, they are experiencing joint attention.

Intramental (intrapsychological) processes
Processes that occur within one individual.

Language play
Unrehearsed, deliberate manipulation of language forms and or meanings, e.g. puns, rhymes, jokes.

Languaging
The process of making meaning and shaping knowledge and experience through language. Languaging organizes and controls (mediates) mental processes during the performance of cognitively complex tasks.

Mediation (material and symbolic)
All human behavior is organized and controlled by material (i.e. concrete) and symbolic (i.e. semiotic) artifacts. Mediation is the process which connects the social and individual.

Mediational means (tools, signs/symbols, artifacts)
The material and symbolic tools that organize or regulate our behavior. Generally speaking, material tools (e.g. hammer) are directed towards changing the environment whereas symbolic tools (e.g. language) are directed towards changing our psychological selves, as well as others. Mediational means are human made, and therefore are considered as culturally constructed.

Microgenesis – *see also Genesis*
The processes involved in the formation and unfolding of a psychological process, for example, the internalization of the meaning of a word in a specific context.

Object
Sometimes used interchangeably with 'goal'. Object usually refers to the problem or purpose toward which activities are directed.

Ontogenesis – *see also Genesis*
The development of an individual over his/her lifespan, in particular the internalization of mediational means over a lifetime.

Operations – *see also Conditions*
The automatized or unconscious routines of an individual as they are being carried out.

Perezhivanie
This Russian term used by Vygotsky refers to experience as lived through the emotions.

Private speech (self-directed speech; speech for the self; self-talk; intrapersonal communication)
Speech that is social (intermental) in origin and form but psychological (intramental) in function. It is used by individuals to mediate their own behavior.

Regulation (object; other; self)
Human behavior is controlled (mediated) by objects, people and the self. Developmentally, object regulation precedes other regulation which precedes self-regulation. However, when the environment becomes complex, individuals may revert to other or object regulation.

Rules
The socially agreed upon set of behavioral guidelines in an action or activity. They may be implicit or explicit in any given action.

Scaffolding
This metaphor from engineering/construction refers to the provision of support to learners. The support is dismantled when the learners are able to manage without it. Although Vygotsky did not use this term, scaffolding is often linked to the emergence of the zone of proximal development. This concept is aligned with SCT if the scaffold is removed gradually and is contingent upon the responsiveness of the learner to it.

Scientific concepts – *see also Everyday concepts*
Systematic principles consciously applied to understanding diverse phenomena.

Tests (psychometric, traditional)
Those instruments which have been developed to measure language skills and knowledge using psychometric principles, for example, multiple choice tests.

Zone of proximal development (ZPD)
An interaction during which, through mediation, an individual achieves more than she could have achieved if she had been working alone. During the ZPD, learning leads development.

Bibliography

Ableeva, R. (2008). The effects of dynamic assessment on L2 listening comprehension. In J. P. Lantolf & M. E. Poehner (Eds), *Sociocultural theory and the teaching of second languages* (pp. 57–86). London: Equinox Publishing.

Agar, M. (1994). *Language shock: Understanding the culture of conversation.* New York: William Morrow & Co.

Aljaafreh, A. & Lantolf, J. P. (1994). Negative feedback as regulation and second language learning in the zone of proximal development. *The Modern Language Journal, 78,* 465–483.

Antón, M. (2009). Dynamic assessment of advanced second language learners. *Foreign Language Annals, 42*(3), 576–598.

Bachman, L. F. (2002a). Alternative interpretations of alternative assessments. Some validity issues in educational performance assessments. *Educational Measurement: Issues and Practice, 21*(1), 5–18.

Bachman, L. F. (2002b). Some reflections on task-based language performance assessment. *Language Testing, 19*(4), 453–476.

Bailey, K. & Nunan, D. (1996). *Voices from the language classroom.* Cambridge: Cambridge University Press.

Bailey, K. M. (1991). Diary studies of classroom language learning: The doubting game and the believing game. In E. Sadtono (Ed.), *Language acquisition and the second/foreign language classroom* (pp. 60–102). Singapore: SEAMEO Regional Language Center.

Baker, M. (2006). *Translation and conflict: A narrative account.* London: Routledge.

Bakhtin, M. M. (1981). *The dialogic imagination* (C. Emerson & M. Holquist, Trans. Vol. 1). Austin: University of Texas Press.

Bamberg, M. (1997). Positioning between structure and performance. *Journal of Narrative and Life History, 7,* 335–342.

Barton, D. & Tusting, K. (Eds), (2005). *Beyond communities of practice: Language, power, and social context.* Cambridge: Cambridge University Press.

Behan, L., Turnbull, M. & Spek, J. (1997). The proficiency gap in late immersion (extended French): Language use in collaborative tasks. *Le journal d'immersion, 20,* 41–42.

Bell, J. (2002). Narrative inquiry: More than just telling stories. *TESOL Quarterly, 36*(2), 207–213.

Belmont, J. (1995). A view from the empiricist's window. *Educational Psychologist, 30,* 99–102.

Benson, P. & Nunan, D. (2004). *Learner stories: Difference and diversity in language learning.* Cambridge: Cambridge University Press.

Bernstein, B. (1999). Vertical and horizontal discourse: An essay. *British Journal of Sociology of Education, 20*(2), 157–173.

Besemeres, M. (2006). Language and emotional experience: The voice of translingual memoir. In A. Pavlenko (Ed.), *Bilingual minds: Emotional experience, expression and representation* (pp. 34–58). Clevedon, UK: Multilingual Matters Ltd.

Block, D. (2003). *The social turn in second language acquisition*. Washington, DC: Georgetown University Press.

Borer, L. (2005). Speaking to the self and to others: The role of private and social speech in the retention of second language vocabulary by adult academic learners. Unpublished Doctoral, OISE/University of Toronto, Toronto, Ontario.

Brooks, L. (2009). Interacting in pairs in a test of oral proficiency: Co-constructing a better performance. *Language Testing, 26*(3), 341–366.

Brooks, L. (in preparation). Oral proficiency testing: To interact in pairs or not? PhD dissertation. Ontario Institute for Studies in Education University of Toronto, Toronto, Ontario.

Brooks, L., Swain, M., Lapkin, S. & Knouzi, I. (2010). Mediating between scientific and spontaneous concepts through languaging. *Language Awareness, 19*(2), 89–110.

Brostrom, S. (1999). Drama games with 6-year-old children: Possibilities and limitations. In Y. Engeström, R. Miettinen & R.-L. Punamaki (Eds), *Perspectives on activity theory* (pp. 250–263). Cambridge: Cambridge University Press.

Brown, A. (2003). Interviewer variation and the co-construction of speaking proficiency. *Language Testing, 20*(1), 1–25.

Brown, A. (2005). *Interviewer variability in language proficiency interviews*. Frankfurt, Germany: Peter Lang.

Bruner, J. (1990). *Acts of meaning*. Cambridge, MA: Harvard University Press.

Bujarski, M., Hildebrand-Nilshon, M. & Kordt, J. (1999). Psychomotor and socioemotional processes in literacy acquisition: Results of an ongoing case study involving a nonvocal cerebral palsic young man. In Y. Engeström, R. Miettinen & R.-L. Punamaki (Eds), *Perspectives on activity theory* (pp. 206–227). Cambridge: Cambridge University Press.

Carter, K. (1993). The place of story in the study of teaching and teacher education. *Educational Researcher, 22*(1), 5–12+18.

Casey, K. (1996). The new narrative research in education. *Review of Research in Education, 21*, 211–253.

Chaiklin, S. (2003). The zone of proximal development in Vygotsky's analysis of learning and instruction. In A. Kozulin, B. Gindis, V. S. Ageyev & S. M. Miller (Eds), *Vygotsky's education theory in cultural context* (pp. 39–64). Cambridge: Cambridge University Press.

Chalhoub-Deville, M. (2003). Second language interaction: Current perspectives and future trends. *Language Testing, 20*(4), 369–383.

Cole, M. (1995). Sociocultural historical psychology: Some general remarks and a proposal for a new kind of cultural-genetic methodology. In J. Wertsch, P. del Rio & A. Álvarez (Eds), *Sociocultural studies of mind* (pp. 187–215). Cambridge: Cambridge University Press.

Cole, M. (1996). Cultural psychology. Available from: http://greenlightwiki.com/heuristic/search_space

Cole, M. (2009). The perils of translation: A first step in reconsidering Vygotsky's theory of development in relation to formal education. *Mind, Culture, and Activity, 16*(4), 291–295.

Cook, G. (2000). *Language play, language learning*. Oxford: Oxford University Press.

Cummins, J. (2000). *Language, power and pedagogy: Bilingual children in the crossfire* (Vol. 23). Clevedon: Multilingual Matters.

Cummins, J. (2001). Instructional conditions for trilingual development. *International Journal of Bilingual Education and Bilingualism, 4*(1), 61–75.

Cummins, J. (2006). Identity texts: The imaginative construction of self through multiliteracies pedagogy. In O. Garcia, T. Skutnabb-Kangas & M. E. Torres-Guzmán (Eds), *Imagining multilingual schools: Languages in education and glocalization* (pp. 51-68). Clevedon, UK: Multilingual Matters.

Daiute, C. & Lightfoot, C. (Eds), (2004). *Narrative analysis: Studying the development of individuals in society.* Thousand Oaks, CA: Sage Publications.

Damasio, A. (1999). *The feeling of what happens: Body and emotion in the making of consciousness.* New York: Harcourt Inc.

Daniels, H. (Ed.). (1996). *An introduction to Vygtosky.* London: Routledge.

Daniels, H. (2001). *Vygotsky and pedagogy.* London: Routledge.

Daniels, H., Cole, M. & Wertsch, J. V. (Eds), (2007). *The Cambridge companion to Vygotsky.* Cambridge: Cambridge University Press.

Davies, B. & Harré, R. (1990). Positioning: The discursive production of selves. *Journal for the Theory of Social Behaviour, 20*(1), 43–63.

Davydov, V. V. (1999). The content and unsolved problems of activity theory. In Y. Engeström, R. Miettinen & R.-L. Punamaki (Eds), *Perspectives on activity theory* (pp. 39–53). Cambridge: Cambridge University Press.

Del Río, P. & Álvarez, A. (2007). Inside and outside the *zone of proximal development*: An ecofunctional reading of Vygotsky. In H. Daniels, M. Cole & J. V. Wertsch (Eds), *The Cambridge companion to Vygotsky* (pp. 276–306). Cambridge: Cambridge University Press.

Deters, P. (2009). Identity, agency, and the acquisition of professional language and culture: The case of internationally educated teachers and college professors in Ontario. Unpublished Doctoral, OISE/University of Toronto, Toronto, Ontario.

Dewaele, J. M. (2006). Investigating the psychological and emotional dimensions in instructed language learning: Obstacles and possibilities. *The Modern Language Journal, 89*(3), 376–380.

DiPardo, A. & Potter, C. (2003). Beyond cognition: Vygotskian perspective on emotionality and teachers' professional lives. In A. Kozulin, B. Gindis, V. Ageyev & S. Miller (Eds), *Vygotsky's educational theory in cultural context* (pp. 317–345). New York: Cambridge University Press.

Donato, R. (1994). Collective scaffolding in second language learning. In J. P. Lantolf & G. Appel (Eds), *Vygotskian approaches to second language research* (pp. 33–56). Norwood, NJ: Ablex.

Donato, R. & Lantolf, J. P. (1990). The dialogic origins of L2 monitoring. In L. F. Bouton & Y. Kachru (Eds), *Pragmatics and language learning* (Vol. 1, pp. 83–97). Urbana-Champaign IL: University of Illinois.

Dorfman, A. (1998). *Heading south, looking north.* New York: Penguin.

Dorfman, A. (2004). Footnotes to a double life. In W. Lesser (Ed.), *The genius of language: Fifteen writers reflect on their mother tongues* (pp. 206–214). New York: Pantheon.

Dunn, W. E. & Lantolf, J. P. (1998). Vygotsky's zone of proximal development and Krashen's *i* + 1: Incommensurable constructs; incommensurable theories. *Language Learning, 48*(3 September), 411–442.

Engström, Y. (1987). *Learning by expanding. An activity-theoretical approach to developmental research.* Helsinki: Orienta-Konsultit.

Engeström, Y. (1999). Activity theory and individual and social transformation. In Y. Engeström, R. Miettinen & R-L. Punamäki (Eds), *Perspectives on activity theory* (pp. 19–38). Cambridge: Cambridge University Press.

Erben, T., Ban, R. & Summers, R. (2008). Changing examination structures within a college of education: The application of dynamic assessment in pre-service ESOL endorsement courses in Florida. In J. P. Lantolf & M. E. Poehner (Eds), *Sociocultural theory and the teaching of second languages*. London: Equinox.

Erdosy, M. U. (2004). *Exploring variability in judging writing ability in a second language: A study of four experienced raters of ESL compositions* (No. RR-03-17). Princeton, NJ: ETS.

Erikson, E. H. (1968). *Identity: Youth and crisis*. New York: Norton.

Fernandez, M., Wegerif, R., Mercer, N. & Rojas-Drummond, S. M. (2001). Re-conceptualising scaffolding and the Zone of Proximal Development in the context of symmetrical collaborative learning. *Journal of Classroom Interaction, 36*(2), 40–54.

Feuerstein, R., Falik, L., Rand, Y. & Feurstein, R. S. (2003). *Dynamic assessment of cognitive modifiability*. Jerusalem: ICELP Press.

Fishman, J. (1977). What is ethnicity? In H. Giles (Ed.), *Language, ethnicity and intergroup relations* (pp. 15–52). London: Academic Press.

Flavell, J. H. (1966). Le langage privé. *Bulletin de psychologie, 19*, 698–701.

Fleer, M. (2009). Understanding the dialectical relations between everyday concept and scientific concepts within play-based programs. *Research in Science Education, 39*, 281–306.

Frawley, W. & Lantolf, J. P. (1985). Second language discourse: A Vygotskyan perspective. *Applied Linguistics, 6*(1), 19–44.

Fulcher, G. & Davidson, F. (2007). *Language testing and assessment: An advanced resource book*. London: Routledge.

Georgakopoulou, A. (2008). Thinking big with small stories in narrative and identity analysis. Retrieved from http://www.clarku.edu/~mbamberg/Papers/Alex%20 Georgakopoulou.doc.

Gibbons, P. (1991). *Learning to learn in a second language*. Newtown, NSW: Primary English Teaching Association.

Gibbons, P. (2003). Teacher interactions with ESL students in a content-based classroom. *TESOL Quarterly, 37*(2), 247–273.

Gipps, C. (1999). Socio-cultural aspects of assessment. *Review of Research in Education, 24*, 355–392.

Grevisse, M. (1980). *Le bon usage* (onzième edition). Brussels: Ducolot.

Guerrero, M. C. M. de (2005). *Inner speech--L2: Thinking words in a second language*. New York: Springer.

Guk, I. & Kellogg, D. (2007). The ZPD and whole class teaching: Teacher-led and student-led interactional mediation of tasks. *Language Teaching Research, 11*(3), 281–299.

Gullberg, M. (2006). Some reasons for studying gesture and second language acquisition (Hommage à Adam Kendon). *IRAL, 44*(2), 103–124.

Gullberg, M. & McCafferty, S. G. (2008). Introduction to gesture and SLA: Toward an integrated approach. *Studies in Second Language Acquisition, 30*(2), 133–146.

Gutiérrez, A. G. (2008). Microgenesis, *method* and *object*: A study of collaborative activity in a Spanish as a foreign language classroom. *Applied Linguistics, 29*(1), 120–148.

Haenen, J., Schrijnemakers, H. & Stufkens, J. (2003). Sociocultural theory and the practice of teaching historical concepts. In A. Kozulin, B. Gindis, V. S. Ageyev & S. M. Miller (Eds), *Vygotsky's education theory in cultural context* (pp. 246–266). Cambridge: Cambridge University Press.

Hall, J. K. & Verplaetse, L. S. (Eds), (2000). *Second and foreign language through classroom interaction*. Mahwah, NJ: Lawrence Erlbaum Associates.

Halliday, M. A. K. (2002a). Language structure and language function. In J. J. Webster (Ed.), *On grammar* (Vol. 1, pp. 173–195). London: Continuum.

Halliday, M. A. K. (2002b). Modes of meaning and modes of expression: Types of grammatical structure and their determination by different semantic functions. In J. J. Webster (Ed.), *On grammar* (Vol. 1, pp. 196–218). London: Continuum.

Haneda, M. (2007). Modes of engagement in foreign language writing: An activity theoretical perspective. *The Canadian Modern Language Review, 64*(2), 301–332.

Harris, T. (2003). Listening with your eyes: The importance of speech-related gestures in the language classroom. *Foreign Language Annals, 36*, 180–187.

Haywood, H. C. & Lidz, C. S. (2007). *Dynamic assessment in practice: Clinical and educational applications*. Cambridge: Cambridge University Press.

Heath, C. & Heath, D. (2007). *Made to stick: Why some ideas survive and others die*. New York: Random House.

Holland, D. & Lachicotte, W. Jr. (2007). Vygotsky, Mead, and the the new sociocultural studies of identity. In H. Daniels, M. Cole & J. Wertsch (Eds), *The Cambridge companion to Vygotsky* (pp. 101–135). Cambridge: Cambridge University Press.

Holland, D., Lachicotte, W. J., Skinner, D. & Cain, C. (1998). *Identity and agency in cultural worlds*. Cambridge, MA: Harvard University Press.

Holzman, L. H. (1996). Pragmatism and dialectical materialism in language development. In H. Daniels (Ed.), *An introduction to Vygotsky* (pp. 75–98). London: Routledge.

Holzman, L. (2002). Vygotsky's zone of proximal development: The human activity zone Retrieved July 26, 2008, from: http://www.eastsideinstitute.org/vygotskyzone.html.

Holzman, L. (2009). *Vygotsky at work and play*. London: Routledge.

Hymes, D. (1972). On communicative competence. In J. B. Price & J. Holmes (Eds), *Sociolinguistics*. London: Penguin.

Imai, Y. (2010). Emotions in SLA: New insights from collaborative learning for an EFL classroom. *The Modern Language Journal, 94*(2), 278–292.

Johnson, K. E. (2009). *Second language teacher education: A sociocultural perspective*. New York: Routledge.

John-Steiner, V. (1985). *Notebooks of the mind*. Albuquerque, NM: University of New Mexico Press.

John-Steiner, V. & Mahn, H. (1996). Sociocultural approaches to learning and development: A Vygotskian framework. *Educational Psychologist, 31*(3–4), 191–206.

John-Steiner, V., Meehan, T. M. & Mahn, H. (1998). A functional systems approach to concept development. [Research]. *Mind, Culture, and Activity, 5*(2), 127–134.

Karpov, Y. V. (2003). Vygotsky's doctrine of scientific concepts: Its role for contemporary education. In A. Kozulin, B. Gindis, V. S. Ageyev & S. M. Miller (Eds), *Vygotsky's educational theory in cultural context* (pp. 65–82). Cambridge: Cambridge University Press.

Kinginger, C. (2002). Defining the zone of proximal development in US foreign language education. *Applied Linguistics, 23*(2), 240–261.

Kinnear, P. (2004). *Through writing for publication, a biracial, bicultural, bilingual adolescent explores identity and normalcy: Sarah in her own words.* Unpublished Doctoral, OISE/University of Toronto, Toronto, ON.

Knouzi, I., Swain, M., Lapkin, S. & Brooks, L. (2010). Self-scaffolding mediated by languaging: Microgenetic analysis of high and low performers. *International Journal of Applied Linguistics, 20*(1), 23–49.

Kowal, U. M. (1997). French immersion students' language growth in French: Perceptions, patterns and programming. Unpublished Doctoral, OISE/University of Toronto, Toronto, Ontario.

Kowal, U. M. & Swain, M. (1997). From semantic to syntactic processing: How can we promote it in the immersion classroom? In R. K. Johnson & M. Swain (Eds), *Immersion education: International perspectives* (pp. 284–309). Cambridge: Cambridge University Press.

Kozulin, A. (1986). Vygotsky in context (A. Kozulin, Trans.). In A. Kozulin (Ed.), *L. S. Vygotsky: Thought and language* (revised edition). Cambridge, MA: Cambridge University Press.

Krashen, S. (1981). *Second language acquisition and second language learning.* Oxford: Pergamon.

Krashen, S. (1985). *The input hypothesis: Issues and implications.* New York: Longman.

Lantolf, J. P. (1997). The function of language play in the acquisition of L2 Spanish. In W. R. Glass & A. T. Perex-Leroux (Eds), *Contemporary perspectives on the acquisition of Spanish. Vol 2: Production, processing and comprehension* (pp. 3–24). Somerville, MA: Cascadilla Press.

Lantolf, J. P. (2000). Introducing sociocultural theory. In J. P. Lantolf (Ed.), *Sociocultural theory and second language learning* (pp. 1–26). Oxford: Oxford University Press.

Lantolf, J. P. (2009). Dynamic assessment: the dialectic integration of instruction and assessment. *Language Teaching, 42*(3), 355–368.

Lantolf, J. P. & Appel, G. (1998). Theoretical framework: An introduction to Vygotskian approaches to second language research. In J. P. Lantolf & G. Appel (Eds), *Vygotskian approaches to second language research* (pp. 1–32). Norwood, NJ: Ablex Publishing Company.

Lantolf, J. P. & Poehner, M. E. (2004). Dynamic assessment of L2 development: Bringing the past into the future. *Journal of Applied Linguistics, 1*(1), 49–72.

Lantolf, J. P. & Poehner, M. E. (2007). *Dynamic assessment in the foreign language classroom. A teacher's guide.* University Park, PA: CALPER.

Lantolf, J. P. & Poehner, M. E. (2008a). Dynamic assessment. In G. E. Nancy Hornberger (Ed.), *Encyclopedia of language and education: Language testing and assessment* (Vol. 7, pp. 273–285). Berlin: Springer Publishing.

Lantolf, J. P. & Poehner, M. E. (Eds). (2008b). *Sociocultural theory and the teaching of second languages.* London: Equinox.

Lantolf, J. P. & Poehner, M. E. (in press). Dynamic assessment in the classroom: Vygotskian praxis for L2 development. *Language Teaching Research.*

Lantolf, J. P. & Thorne, S. L. (2006). *Sociocultural theory and the genesis of second language development.* Oxford: Oxford University Press.

Larsen-Freeman, D. (1997). Chaos/complexity science and second language acquisition. *Applied Linguistics, 18*(2), pp. 141–165.

Larsen-Freeman, D & Cameron, L. (2008). *Complex systems and applied linguistics.* Oxford: Oxford University Press.

Lave, J. & Wenger, E. (1991). *Situated learning: Legitimate peripheral participation.* Cambridge: Cambridge University Press.

Lee, J. (2008). Gesture and private speech in second language learning. *Studies in Second Language Acquisition, 30*(2), 169–190.

Lei, X. (2008). Exploring a sociocultural approach to writing strategy research: Mediated actions in writing activities. [Research]. *Journal of Second Language Writing, 17,* 217–236.

Leont'ev, A. N. (1981). The problem of activity in psychology. *The Concept of Activity in Soviet Psychology,* 37–71.

Lesser, W. (Ed.). (2004). *The genius of language.* New York: Anchor Books.

Lidz, C. S. (Ed.). (1987). *Dynamic assessment: an interactional approach to evaluating learning potential.* New York: Guilford Press.

Lidz, C. S. & Elliott, J. G. (Eds), (2000). *Dynamic assessment: Prevailing models and applications* (Vol. 6). New York: Elsevier Science.

Long, M. (1985). Input and second language acquisition theory. In S. Gass & C. G. Madden (Eds), *Input in second language acquisition.* Rowley, MA: Newbury House.

Lowe, V. (Writer) (2008). Lev Vygotsky [DVD]. In V. Lowe (Producer). At http://vygotskydocumentary.com.

Luoma, S. (2004). *Assessing speaking.* Cambridge: Cambridge University Press.

Luria, A. R. (1961). Study of the abnormal child. *American Journal of Orthopsychiatry, 31,* 1–16.

Lyotard, J. F. (1984). *The postmodern condition: A report on knowledge* (G. Bennington & B. Massumi, Trans.). Manchester: Manchester University Press.

MacIntyre, P. D. (1998). Language anxiety: A review of the research for language teachers. In D. J. Young (Ed.), *Affect in foreign language and second language learning* (pp. 24–45). Boston, MA: McGraw Hill.

MacIntyre, P. D. & Gardner, R. C. (1994). The subtle effects of language anxiety on cognitive processing in the second language. *Language Learning, 44*(2), 283–305.

MacIntyre, P. D., Noels, K. A. & Clément, R. (1997). Biases in self-ratings of second language proficiency: The role of language anxiety. *Language Learning, 47*(2), 265–287.

Magnan, S. S. (2008). The unfulfilled promise of teaching for communicative competence: Insights from sociocultural theory. In J. P. Lantolf & M. E. Poehner (Eds), *Sociocultural theory and the teaching of second languages* (pp. 351–381). London: Equinox.

Mahn, H. (2008). A dialogic approach to teaching L2 writing. In J. P. Lantolf & M. Poehner (Eds), *Sociocultural theory and the teaching of second languages* (pp. 115–137). London: Equinox.

Mahn, H. & John-Steiner, V. (2000). Developing the affective zpd. Retrieved July 23, 2008, from: http://www.aare.edu.au/03pap/ver03682.pdf understanding scaffolding and the ZPD in educational research.

Mahn, H. & John-Steiner, V. (2002). The gift of confidence: A Vygotskian view of emotions. In G. Wells & G. Claxton (Eds), *Learning for life in the 21st century* (pp. 46–58). Oxford: Blackwell.

Matusov, E. (2007). Applying Bakhtin scholarship on discourse in education: A critical review essay. *Educational Theory, 57*(2), 215–237.

McCafferty, S. & Stam, G. (Eds), (2008). *Gesture: Second language acquisition and classroom research*. London: Routledge.

McNamara, T. F. (1997). 'Interaction' in second language performance assessment: Whose performance? *Applied Linguistics, 18*(4), 446–466.

Mead, G. H. (1962). *Mind, self and society*. C. W. Morris (Ed.), Chicago: Chicago University Press (Original published in 1934.)

Miller, D. L. (1982). *The individual and the social self: Unpublished essays by G. H. Mead*. Chicago: University of Chicago Press.

Mercer, N. (2000). *Words and minds: How we use language to think together*. London: Routledge.

Mercer, N. (2002). Developing dialogues. In G. Wells & G. Claxton (Eds), *Learning for life in the 21st century* (pp. 141–153). Oxford: Blackwell Publishing.

Minick, N. (1996). The development of Vygotsky's thought: An introduction to thinking and speech. In H. Daniels (Ed.), *An introduction to Vygotsky* (pp. 28–52). London: Routledge.

Moll, L. C. & Whitmore, K. F. (1993). Vygotsky in classroom practice: Moving from individual transmission to social transaction. In E. A. Forman, N. Minick & C. A. Stone (Eds), *Contexts for learning: Sociocultural dynamics in children's development* (pp. 19–42). Oxford: Oxford University Press.

Moran, S. & John-Steiner, V. (2003). *Creativity in the making: Vygotsky's contemporary contribution to the dialectic of creativity and development*. Oxford: Oxford University Press.

Negueruela, E. (2008). Revolutionary pedagogies: Learning that leads (to) second language development. In J. P. Lantolf & M. E. Poehner (Eds), *Sociocultural theory and the teaching of second languages* (pp. 189–227). London: Equinox.

Negueruela, E. & Lantolf, J. P. (2005). Concept-based instruction: Teaching grammar in an intermediate-advanced Spanish L2 university classroom. Retrieved from http://calper.la.psu.edu/publication.php?page=wps3.

Nelson, C. P. & Kim, M.-K. (2001). Contradictions, appropriation, and transformation: An activity theory approach to L2 writing and classroom practices. [Research]. *Texas Papers in Foreign Language Education, 6*(1), 37–62.

Newman, F. & Holzman, L. (1993). *Lev Vygotsky: Revolutionary scientist*. London: Routledge.

Newman, R. (2003). What do I need to do to succeed when I don't know what I'm doing? In A. Wigfield & J. Eccles (Eds), *Development of achievement motivation* (pp. 285–303). San Diego: Academic Press.

Northedge, A. (2002). Organizing excursions into specialist discourse communities: A sociocultural account of university teaching. In G. Wells & G. Claxton (Eds), *Learning for life in the 21st century* (pp. 252–264). Oxford: Blackwell Publishing.

Nunan, D. & Choi, J. (Eds), (2010). *Language and culture: Reflective narratives and the emergence of identity*. New York: Routledge.

Ohta, A. S. (2001). *Second language acquisition processes in the classroom: Learning Japanese*. Mahwah, NJ: Lawrence Erlbaum Associates, Inc.

Olson, D. R. (1995). Writing and the mind. In J. V. Wertsch, P. D. Rio & A. Álvarez (Eds), *Sociocultural studies of mind* (pp. 95–123). Cambridge: Cambridge University Press.

Palincsar, A. S. (1999). Keeping the metaphor of scaffolding fresh--A response to C. Addison Stone's "The metaphor of scaffolding: It's utility for the field of learning". *Journal of Learning Disabilities, 31*(4), 370–373.

Pavlenko, A. (1998). Second language learning by adults: Testimonies of bilingual writers. *Issues in Applied Linguistics, 9*(1), 3–19.

Pavlenko, A. (2005). *Emotions and multilingualism.* Cambridge: Cambridge University Press.

Pavlenko, A. (2006). Bilingual Selves. In A. Pavlenko (Ed.), *Bilingual minds: Emotional experience, expression and representation* (pp. 1–33). Clevedon: Multilingual Matters.

Penuel, W. & Wertsch, J. (1995). Vygotsky and identity formation: A sociocultural approach. *Educational Psychologist, 30,* 83–92.

Piaget, J. (1981). *Intelligence and affectivity: Their relationship during child development* (T. A. Brown & C. E. Kaegi, Trans.). Palo Alto, CA: Annual Reviews Inc.

Pica, T. (1994). Research on negotiation: What does it reveal about second-language learning conditions, processes and outcomes? *Language Learning, 44,* 493–527.

Pinar, W. (1994). *Autobiography politics and sexuality: Essays in curriculum theory 1972–1992.* New York: Peter Lang.

Poehner, M. (2008). Both sides of the conversation. In J. P. Lantolf & M. Poehner (Eds), *Sociocultural theory and the teaching of second languages* (pp. 33–56). London: Equinox.

Poehner, M. E. (2008). *Dynamic assessment: A Vygotskian approach to understanding and promoting second language development.* Berlin: Springer Publishing.

Poehner, M. E. (2009). Group dynamic assessment: Mediation for the L2 classroom. *TESOL Quarterly, 43*(3), 471–491.

Poehner, M. E. & Lantolf, J. P. (2005). Dynamic assessment in the language classroom. [Research]. *Language Teaching Research, 9*(3), 233–265.

Roth, W.-M. & Tobin, K. (2002). Redesigning an "urban" teacher education program: An activity theory perspective. [research]. *Mind, Culture, and Activity, 9*(2), 108–131.

Russell, D. R. (1997). Rethinking genre in school and society. *Written Communication, 14*(4), 504–554.

Ryle, A. (1999). Object relations theory and activity theory: A proposed link by way of the procedural sequence model. In Y. Engeström, R. Miettinen & R-L. Punamäki (Eds), *Perspectives on activity theory* (pp. 407–418). Cambridge: Cambridge University Press.

Santiago, E. (1993). *When I was Puerto Rican.* Toronto: Random House.

Saville-Troike, M. (1988). Private speech: Evidence for second language learning strategies during the silent period. *Child Language, 15,* 567–590.

Schalm, S. (2009, Sept 19). Who's reading what? *The Globe and Mail,* p. 13.

Schneider, C. & Elliott, J. G. (2000). *Dynamic assessment: prevailing models and applications.* Amsterdam: Elsevier.

Schumann, J. H. (1998). The neurobiology of affect in language learning. *Language Learning, 48 (Supplement 1).*

Shepardson, D. P. (1999). Learning science in a first grade science activity: A Vygotskian perspective. *Science Education, 83,* 621–638.

Somers, M. (1992). Narrativity, narrative identity, and social action: Rethinking English working-class formation. *Social Science History, 16*(4), 591–630.

Somers, M. (1997). Deconstructing and reconstructing class formation theory: Narrativity, relational analysis, and social theory. In J. R. Hall (Ed.), *Reworking class* (pp. 73–105). Ithaca, NY and London: Cornell University Press.

Somers, M. & Gibson, G. D. (1994). Reclaiming the epistemological "other": Narrative and the social constitution of identity. In C. Calhoun (Ed.), *Social theory and the politics of identity* (pp. 37–99). Cambridge MA and Oxford: Blackwell.

Steinman, L. (2004). Language learner narratives: Bridge to SLA literature and SLA pedagogy. Unpublished Doctoral, University of Toronto Ontario Institutute for Studies in Education, Toronto, Ontario.

Steinman, L. (2007). Personal points of communicative practice. Paper presented at the Canadian Association of Applied Linguistics (ACLA/CAAL).

Sternberg, R. J. & Grigorenko, E. L. (2002). *Dynamic testing: The nature and measurement of learning potential.* Cambridge: Cambridge University Press.

Stetsenko, A. & Arievitch, I. (2002). Teaching, learning, and development: A post-Vygotskian perspective. In G. Wells & G. Claxton (Eds), *Learning for life in the 21st century: Sociocultural perspective on the future of education* (pp. 84–96). Oxford: Blackwell Publishing.

Storch, N. (2002). Patterns of interaction in ESL pair work. *Language Learning, 52*(1), 119–158.

Swain, M. (1995). Three functions of output in second language learning. In G. Cool & B. Seidlhofer (Eds), *Principle and practice in applied linguistics: Studies in honour of H. G. Widdowson* (pp. 125–144). Cambridge: Cambridge University Press.

Swain, M. (2000). The output hypothesis and beyond: Mediating acquisition through collaborative dialogue. In J. P. Lantolf (Ed.), *Sociocultural theory and second language learning* (pp. 97–114). Oxford: Oxford University Press.

Swain, M. (2001). Examining dialogue: another approach to content specification and to drawing inferences from test scores. *Language Testing, 18*(3), 275–302.

Swain, M. & Lapkin, S. (1998). Interaction and second language learning: two adolescent French immersion students working together. *The Modern Language Journal, 82*(3), 320–337.

Swain, M. & Lapkin, S. (2002). Talking it through: Two French immersion learners response to reformulation. *International Journal of Educational Research (Special issue on the role of interaction in instructed language learning), 37,* 285–304.

Swain, M., Lapkin, S., Knouzi, I., Suzuki, W. & Brooks, L. (2009). Languaging: University students learn the grammatical concept of voice in French. *The Modern Language Journal, 93*(1), 5–29.

Taniguchi, S. (2009). Becoming bilingual: Exploring language and literacy learning through the lens of narrative. Unpublished Research, University of Technology, Sydney, Australia.

Taylor, L. (2000). Investigating the paired speaking test format. *Cambridge ESOL Research Notes, 2,* 14–15.

Taylor, L. (2001). The paired speaking test format: Recent studies. *Cambridge ESOL Research Notes, 6,* 15–17.

Taylor, L. & Wigglesworth, G. (2009). Are two heads better than one? Pair work in L2 assessment contexts. *Language Testing, 26*(3), 325–339.

Thiong'o, N. w. (2004). Recovering the original. In W. Lesser (Ed.), *The genius of language: Fifteen writers reflect on their mother tongues* (pp. 102–110). New York: Pantheon Books.

Thorne, S. L. (2000). Second language acquisition theory and the truth(s) about relativity. In J. P. Lantolf (Ed.), *Sociocultural theory and second language learning* (pp. 219–243). Oxford: Oxford University Press.

Tocalli-Beller, A. & Swain, M. (2007). Riddles and puns in the ESL classroom: Adults talk to learn. In A. Mackey (Ed.), *Conversational interaction in second language acquisition* (pp. 143–167). Oxford: Oxford University Press.

Toth, P. D. (2004). When grammar instruction undermines cohesion in L2 Spanish classroom discourse. *The Modern Language Journal, 88*(1), 14–30.

Towsey, P. M. & MacDonald, C. A. (2009). Wolves in sheep's clothing and other Vygotskian constructs. *Mind, Culture, and Activity, 16*, 234–262.

Trivedi, H. (2004). Ngugi wa Thiong'o with Harish Trivedi (2003). In S. Nasta (Ed.), *Writing across worlds: Contemporary writers talk* (pp. 327–339). London: Routledge.

Turnbull, M. & Dailey-O'Cain, J. (Eds) (2009) *First language use in second and foreign language learning*. Bristol: Multilingual Matters.

Tusting, K. (2005). Language and power in communities of practice. In D. Barton & K. Tusting (Eds), *Beyond communities of practice: Language, power and social context* (pp. 36–54). Cambridge: Cambridge University Press.

Vail, P. L. (1994). *Emotion: The on off switch for learning*. Rosemont, NJ: Modern Learning Press.

Valsiner, J. & Veer, R. v. d. (2000). *The social mind: Construction of the idea*. Cambridge: Cambridge University Press.

van der Veer, R. (2007). Vygotsky in context: 1900–1935. In H. Daniels, M. Cole & J. V. Wertsch (Eds), *The Cambridge companion to Vygotsky* (pp. 21–49). Cambridge: Cambridge University Press.

van der Veer, R. & Valsiner, J. (2003). *Understanding Vygotsky: A quest for synthesis*. Oxford: Blackwell.

van Lier, L. (1988). *The classroom and the language learner*. London: Longman.

van Lier, L. (1989). Reeling, writhing, drawling, stretching and fainting in coils: Oral proficiency interviews as conversations. *TESOL Quarterly, 23*, 489–508.

van Lier, L. (2000). From input to affordance: Social-interactive learning from an ecological perspective. In J. P. Lantolf (Ed.), *Sociocultural theory and second language learning* (pp. pp. 245–259). Oxford: Oxford University Press.

Verenikina, I. (2003). Understanding scaffolding and the ZPD in educational research. (July 23, 2008), Conference paper. Retrieved from: http://www.aare.edu.au/03pap/

Verity, D. P. (2000). Side affects: The strategic development of professional satisfaction. In J. P. Lantolf (Ed.), *Sociocultural theory and second language learning* (pp. 179–198). Oxford: Oxford University Press.

Vocate, D. R. (1994). Self-talk and inner speech: Understanding the uniquely human aspects of intrapersonal communication. In D. R. Vocate (Ed.), *Intrapersonal communication, different voices, different minds*. Hillsdale, NJ: Lawrence Erlbaum.

Vygotsky, L. S. (1978). *Mind in society: The development of higher psychological processes* (M. Cole, V. John-Steiner, S. Scribner & E. Souberman, Trans.). Cambridge, MA: Harvard University Press.

Vygotsky, L. S. (1986). *Thought and language* (A. Kozulin, Trans.). Cambridge, MA: The MIT Press.

Vygotsky, L. S. (1987). Thinking and speech (N. Minick, Trans.). In R. W. Reiber (Ed.), *The collected works of L. S. Vygotsky* (Vol. 3, pp. 37–285). New York: Plenum.

Vygotsky, L. S. (1987). *The collected works of L. S. Vygotsky, Volume 1: The Problems of general psychology, including the volume thinking and speech.* New York: Plenum Press.

Vygotsky, L. S. (1994). The problem of the environment. In R. v. d. Veer & J. Valsiner (Eds), *The Vygotsky reader* (pp. 338–354). Cambridge, MA: Blackwell.

Vygotsky, L. S. (1997). *The collected works of L. S. Vygotsky: Volume 3: Problems of the theory and history of psychology.* New York: Plenum Press.

Vygotsky, L. S. (2000). *Thought and language* (A. Kozulin, Trans.). Cambridge, MA: MIT Press.

Vygotsky, L. S. & Luria, A. (1994). Tool and symbol in child development. In R. v. d. Veer & J. Valsiner (Eds), *The Vygotsky reader* (pp. 99–174). Oxford: Blackwell.

Wajnryb, R. (1990). *Grammar dictation.* Oxford: Oxford University Press.

Wardekker, W. L. (1998). Scientific concepts and reflection. *Mind, Culture, and Activity, 5*(2), 143–153.

Watanabe, Y. & Swain, M. (2007). Effects of proficiency differences and patterns of pair interaction on second language learning: Collaborative dialogue between adult ESL learners. *Language Teaching Research, 11*(2), 121–142.

Wells, G. (1999a). Using L1 to master L2: A response to Anton and DiCamillas's "Socio-cognitive functions of L1 collaborative interaction in the L2 classroom". *The Modern Language Journal, 83*(2), 248–254.

Wells, G. (1999b). *Dialogic inquiry: Towards a sociocultural practice and theory of education.* Cambridge: Cambridge University Press.

Wells, G. (2002). The role of dialogue in activity theory. *Mind, Culture, and Activity, 9*(1), 43–66.

Wenger, E. (1998). *Communities of practice: Learning, meaning and identity.* Cambridge: Cambridge University Press.

Wertsch, J. V. (1980). The significance of dialogue in Vygotsky's account of social, egocentric, and inner speech. *Contemporary Educational Psychology, 5*, 150–162.

Wertsch, J. V. (1985). *Vygotsky and the social formation of mind.* Cambridge, MA: Harvard University Press.

Wertsch, J. V. (1991). *Voices of the mind: A sociocultural approach to mediated action.* Cambridge, MA: Harvard University Press.

Wertsch, J. V. (1998). *Mind as action.* New York: Oxford University Press.

Wertsch, J. V., Rio, P. D. & Álvarez, A. (Eds), (1995). *Sociocultural studies of mind.* Cambridge: Cambridge University Press.

Wertsch, J. V., Tulviste, P. & Hagstrom, F. (1993). A sociocultural approach to agency. In E. A. Forman, N. Minnick & C. A. Stone (Eds), *Context for learning: Sociocultural dynamics in children's development* (pp. 336–356). New York: Oxford University Press.

Wood, D., Bruner, J. S. & Ross, G. (1976). The role of tutoring in problem solving. *Journal of Child Psychology and Psychiatry, 17*, 89–100.

Index

Following the text, headings in **bold** show a term which appears in the glossary on pages 149-153. 'ZPD' is used as an abbreviation for 'Zone of Proximal Development' and 'SCT' stands for Sociocultural Theory.

Haneda, M. 113
Harré, R. 88
Harris, T. 22
Heath, C. xi, 27
Heath, D. xi, 27
heritage language learners 113
heuristics xiii, 20
higher mental processes 37
Holland, D. xv, 87
Holzman, L. 20, 23, 41, 59, 128, 150
humor, study on 12
Hymes, D. 24

i+1 theory 21, 28
identity 10, 76, 87–8, 90
Imai, Y. 81, 84, 89
imitation 14 n6, 58–9
immersion program 16, 39–40, 45–6
individuality
    individualization and ZPD 29
    testing individual traits (psychometrics) 124, 130–3
    Western focus on 111
inner speech 39, 45
input hypothesis 82
'input-interaction-output' metaphor 34, 41
intellectual function of language 43
interactionist approach 129–30
intermental development zone (IDZ) 21
intermental processes 10, 27 *see also* collaborative dialogue
internalization
    definition 8
    controversy over 11–12
    and emotion 24
    languaging as mechanism 43
    as mastery 11–12, 89
    by private speech 34
    and ZPD 29
intersubjectivity 24–5
interventionist approach 129
intramental processes 10 *see also* private speech
intrapersonal communication *see* private speech

Jiménez-Jiménez, A. 46
Johnson, K.E. xv
John-Steiner, V. 16, 20, 23, 67, 83
joint/ co-constructed performance, assessment as 118, 125–30, 132
jokes, riddles and puns, research on 12
just-in-time ZPD 24

Karpov, Y.V. 69
Kellogg, D. 20, 21
Kim, M.-K. 112
Kinginger, C. 16, 28, 29
Kinnear, P. 88, 90
Knouzi, I. 26, 48, 71
Kowal, M. 39, 41
Kozulin, A. xiii
Krashen, S. 21, 41, 69, 82

L1s
    contribution to L2 learning 68–9
    languaging 45–7
    as mediational means 10
    writing in L1 first 54
labor, division of 101–2
Lachicotte, W. 87
'landings' (moments of feeling competence) 3, 4–5, 77
'languagculture' 84
language, as crucial mediating artifact in higher mental processes xiii, 37–9, 43
language play 14 n6, 44
languaging 33–50
Lantolf, J.P. xv, 2, 8, 14 n6, 20, 21, 22, 29, 30, 36, 41, 44, 68, 76, 85, 86, 90, 119, 127, 128, 129, 130, 132, 133, 134
Lapkin, S. 20, 25, 26, 48, 49, 71
Larsen-Freeman, D. 112
Lave, J. xv, 16, 27, 111
Lee, J.S. 12, 36
Lei, X. 113–14
Leont'ev, A.N. 84, 97, 99, 105
Lesser, W. 53
life histories (ontogenesis)
    generally 9, 11, 38
    Grace 77